INDIA AND FARAWAY LANDS

INDIA AND FARAWAY LANDS

5,000 Years of Connected History

ASHUTOSH MEHNDIRATTA

AMARYLLIS

AMARYLLIS

An imprint of Manjul Publishing House Pvt. Ltd.
• C-16, Sector 3, Noida, Uttar Pradesh 201301, India
Website: www.manjulindia.com
Registered Office:
• 10, Nishat Colony, Bhopal 462 003 – India
Distribution Centres
Ahmedabad, Bengaluru, Bhopal, Kolkata, Chennai,
Hyderabad, Mumbai, New Delhi, Pune

India and Faraway Lands by Ashutosh Mehndiratta

This edition first published in India in 2023

ISBN 978-93-5543-184-4

Cover design by PealiDezine

Printed and bound in India by Manipal Technologies Limited

History is far more than a series of events and the biographies of big names; it is the subtle interweaving of human actions spread over vast landscapes and through deep time, creating a dense fabric, every thread of which has significance. The wonder of it all lies in how interconnected everything is.

—Sir Barry Cunliffe, archaeologist and professor at the University of Oxford

CONTENTS

INTRODUCTION

A great way to learn about your country is to leave it.

—Henry Rollins, American singer

India and Faraway Lands is about the momentous events that took place around the globe in the past 5,000 years, how they shaped the Indian subcontinent and vice versa. In other words, this book presents a short history of the world from India's vantage point.

The idea behind this book did not emerge overnight; rather, it simmered in my mind for over two decades. The seeds of curiosity were sown in the 1990s, when I arrived in the United States as a university student. I met hundreds of students on the campus from a multitude of nations across every continent. The stimulating exchange of perspectives sparked a lifelong interest in me to understand how our world came to be.

Over the following years, marvelling at the world-class infrastructure and the abundant material wealth of North America, as well as of Europe during brief stopovers on trips to India, I wondered how, when, and why the West became more developed and wealthier than India. I had an inkling that it hadn't always been like that, which led me to revisit history books, something I had never imagined doing after tenth grade in school. Wading through bookstores and museums, I stumbled upon intriguing, lesser-known historical connections between India and other parts of the world. At some point, I started to connect the dots between these historical narratives of the world.

My parents and grandparents would often recount harrowing tales of how they lost their homes in what became West Pakistan after Partition in 1947 and their dreadful journeys across the border in overloaded 'refugee special' trains. The experiences of my family members were tied to the stories of their towns, and these stories were further linked to a wider web of the histories of the nation, and ultimately the world.

Histories of India have been mostly confined to India's boundaries, thereby missing a vital component: the story of the 'other side' or the 'outside', leaving the overall picture somewhat truncated and incomplete. The history of the British in India, for instance, began with their merchant ships landing in Gujarat in 1608. But it was around the same time that they had also landed in North America and established their first colony in Jamestown, Virginia (1607). What was going on in Britain in those days? What did the British merchants and colonists know about India and the Americas before they set sail from the shores of their tiny island nation? Who were the people who made these bold ventures possible? And why did they wait for more than a hundred years to sail out to these lands when Italian explorer Christopher Columbus had landed in the Americas in 1492 and Portuguese voyager Vasco da Gama had reached India in 1498?

Unlike India's commonly perceived image among Western historians as a static civilisation—shielded from the rest of the Eurasian continent by an arc of enormous mountain ranges in the north and surrounded by water in the south—India was an active player in world history. Steep mountain passes in the north-west, like the legendary Khyber Pass, allowed invading armies and trading caravans to pass through; the Indian Ocean was the hub of maritime trade and migration for thousands of years before humans were able to cross the Atlantic and the Pacific.[1] There must be a reason why the who's who of world history—Alexander the Great, Genghis Khan, Tamerlane, Marco Polo, Ibn Battuta,

Ferdinand Magellan, Vasco da Gama, the Duke of Wellington—set foot in India. Napoleon would have indeed sailed to India and met 'Tippoo Sahib', the ruler of Mysore, and Hitler would have marched over the 'corpse of Russia' into India had their bold and ambitious plans not been derailed.

It is surprising, however, that though India was always connected globally, Indians have historically been reluctant to explore and write about life in the outside world. In ancient texts as well as in modern usage, foreigners have been addressed with blanket terms such as *mleccha* (meaning impure foreign people), *Yavanas* (meaning, specifically, those belonging to the Greek Ionian tribe, until later usage expanded to include Romans and even Muslims), and *firangis* (meaning Portuguese or other people of European descent, though the word itself comes from the Arabic word *firanj*, meaning Franks). What prevented Indians from going beyond the horizon and studying foreign peoples, cultures, and regions? It's probable that the self-sufficiency that was an outcome of India's bountiful river systems and fertile lands did not leave much incentive to look abroad. The holiest Hindu pilgrimages located within the subcontinent further contributed to the inward orientation. Moreover, the Hindu Brahmanical order imposed restrictions on sea travel and mingling with the mleccha.[2]

In comparison, countries that were predominantly Christian or Islamic had an inherent global outlook as the followers of those faiths looked to pilgrimage sites and religious authority figures in distant lands; they could also correlate familiar traditions and a shared history across many parts of the world. For example, Ibn Battuta's travels in the fourteenth century across Africa, the Middle East, India, and Southeast Asia, covering some 1,20,000 kilometres, bear witness to the ease of mobility and the cosmopolitan nature of the vast Muslim world at the time.

Nonetheless, there were exceptions to the taboo in India against long-distance travel. Indian Buddhist monks travelled to China and Japan; diplomatic missions were sent to Rome and China; the presence of Indian merchant communities has been recorded in places like Turkey, Azerbaijan, and Vietnam; many *lascars* (Indian sailors or army servants employed on European ships) reached southern and western Europe. What remains missing, though, are the accounts of these Indian travellers or any noteworthy maps made by Indian cartographers. Taking a note of this tendency, historian Romila Thapar writes: '(to the Indian travellers) it was almost as if the exterior landscape was irrelevant'.

At the same time, travellers and adventurers from faraway lands—Greece, China, Italy, Morocco, Russia, Portugal, Holland, Britain, Ireland, France, the United States, Australia—many of whom we shall get to know in this book, wrote fascinating accounts about life in India. Their travelogues were read widely and expanded the world view of their countrymen and of many others around the world.

A new trend then emerged in eighteenth-century India. In the 1760s appeared one of the earliest 'reverse travelogues', accounts written by Indians who journeyed to the West, called *Shigurf Nama-e-Vilayet* (*Wonderful Tales about Europe*). It was a uniquely insightful work by Mirza Sheikh I'tesamuddin, a Bengali munshi who travelled to Britain from 1766 to 1769. More such travelogues followed, but regrettably they remain unknown in India to date. Continuing the trend into the nineteenth and the twentieth centuries, figures like Raja Rammohan Roy, Syed Ahmed Khan, Mahatma Gandhi, Jawaharlal Nehru, and Rabindranath Tagore wrote extensively about their travels and experiences abroad. It was their observations, ideas, and writings that ultimately shaped modern India.

After winning a hard-fought independence from the British in 1947, as India embarked upon a journey of self-reliance and restoration of national pride, along came an inward-looking mindset. The rivalry with Pakistan kept the nation occupied for decades, making it harder to look further west beyond Pakistan. At the other end, Burma (now Myanmar) locked itself in a time capsule after its independence from the British in 1948, thereby blocking India's view of further east. The armed conflict with China in 1962 led to the severing of Sino-Indian ties for at least two decades. In post-independence India, majority of the people thus grew up in an environment that was, to an extent, cocooned from the outside world.

When I returned to India in 2006, after being away for eleven years, I was keen to rediscover the homeland and travelled from the Himalayan town of Leh up north to the historic city of Madurai down south. Ancient sites like Sanchi and Ajanta Caves (both UNESCO World Heritage Sites) were breathtaking and bound to make even an uninterested visitor pause and imagine life in India over 2,000 years ago. And yet, they drew only a few Indian visitors. Likewise, history museums all over India were consistently empty and listless, as if the past did not matter.

The common folk's understanding of foreign lands, peoples, and cultures seemed rather superficial while age-old stereotypes continued to flourish despite all the buzz around globalisation, and the fact that nearly 30 million people of Indian origin lived scattered around the world. In academic circles, the focus of history writing continued to be local rather than global. Sanjay Subrahmanyam, professor of history at the University of California, Los Angeles (UCLA), known for his approach of 'connected history', quoted a profound statement made by historian Ashin Das Gupta that influenced his outlook: 'In order to understand India, you have to go out of India'.[3] An interest in India's interconnected history motivated me to build upon what I had learnt thus far and write a story of our global past for the lay reader.

To gain first-hand experience of the places that I wrote about, I interspersed my research with travels around the world—from the United Kingdom and Ireland to Portugal and Spain, Germany and Italy to Turkey and Ukraine, Indonesia and China to Australia and Fiji—exploring museums, local libraries, and landmarks, listening to tour guides, or simply watching daily life go by, and comparing my observations with old travel accounts of the same places.

Rather than being a definitive history, *India and Faraway Lands* aims to stoke the readers' curiosity about our intertwined past. With that in mind, unlike the standard 'past to present' chronological order, this book starts with the relatable modern times and moves backwards, following a 'what happened before that, and then before that' approach. To condense global history spanning thousands of years into a few hundred pages, I have had to choose breadth over depth. Any such attempt is fraught with the risk of glossing over key events or even glaring omissions and misinterpretations. I humbly assure the readers that any such occurrences are inadvertent and purely due to my ignorance.

1

THE WORLD IN TURMOIL

1930s–1990s

Only the dead have seen the end of war.

—Plato

On a February morning in 1931, Lord Irwin, the British Viceroy of India, and Lady Irwin left the Viceroy House in a carriage pulled by six horses, under a thunderous thirty-one-gun salute. They were headed to the inauguration ceremony of New Delhi, the new capital of British India, and the eighth reincarnation of the historic city of Delhi to be built in the last millennium. Week-long celebrations were planned for the grand event that included banquets, receptions, and a polo tournament.

Completed over twenty years, New Delhi, with its grand tree-lined boulevards and imposing buildings, was meant to be a symbol of the majesty and power of the British Empire. Sitting atop the Raisina Hill, at the end of the principal street called Kingsway (now Rajpath), the opulent 340-room Viceroy House (now Rashtrapati Bhawan) was the centrepiece of New Delhi.

It is indeed baffling how a mere 64,000 Britons could control the lives of over 350 million Indians.[1] Calls for independence or greater autonomy by the Indian political leaders had been getting louder since the beginning of the twentieth century. The saintly

Mahatma Gandhi had emerged as the tallest national leader, inspiring millions across the nation with his appeal for non-violent protest. The British authorities were no doubt perturbed by the growing agitation, yet they held a commanding position. 'Inwardly precarious but outwardly splendid' is how the acclaimed English author H.G. Wells characterised the British rule in India.

Meanwhile, a storm was brewing thousands of kilometres to the west of India, and it would lead to violence, death, and destruction around the globe at a scale without any parallel in human history. The then prevailing world order would be disrupted, ending centuries of European domination over Asia and Africa. Britain's crown jewel, India, would slip out of its hands, and its vast and sprawling empire—on which 'the sun never set'—would crumble and vanish.

It is to those years of turmoil that we must turn now.

THE GREATEST WAR

Britain, France, and the United States (the Allied forces) were the victorious powers of World War I, which ended in 1918 with humiliating terms imposed on a defeated Germany. Loss of territory and the astronomical amount of war reparations crippled the German economy, causing widespread unemployment and hyperinflation—in late 1923, the exchange rate for one US dollar skyrocketed to a mind-boggling 4.2 trillion German marks. In the following years, Germany had barely started to stabilise when the American stock market crashed in 1929, and the resultant Great Depression brought forth bankruptcies and unemployment at an unprecedented magnitude.

Germany turned into a disgruntled nation, and the Germans strongly felt that they had been treated unfairly. Against the backdrop of this anguish, the National Socialist German Workers' Party (popularly referred to as the Nazi Party), headed by Adolf Hitler, an Austrian by birth, came to power in 1933. Hitler's rousing speeches, in which he expressed his ideas of extreme nationalism, left the audiences spellbound. His autobiography, *Mein Kampf* (*My Struggle*), details his racist ideology, identifying the Aryan race as the 'genius' and the Jewish race as the 'parasite', and the idea of bringing *Lebensraum*, or living space, for Germans in the east at the expense of the 'inferior' Slavic people. He called the signatories of the Treaty of Versailles 'traitors' who must be removed from power, although he also expressed admiration for Britain's exploitation of the 350 million 'Indian slaves'. Surprisingly, in spite of this, many Indians have a naïve fascination with *Mein Kampf*, which continues to be a bestseller in India to date.

As a hesitant Britain watched, Germany was transformed into a totalitarian state. In blatant disregard of the Treaty of Versailles, Hitler started building an air force, the Luftwaffe, and expanding the army. To boost the economy, he beefed up the war industry, revived the automobile sector, and promoted several public works projects, like the completion of the Autobahn network. Unemployment started to fall drastically.

With Germany's confidence and self-esteem soaring, Hitler was ready to put his economic and military might to test. In March 1938, he annexed Austria, followed by Czechoslovakia in March the following year, while none of the major powers retaliated. Hitler then launched an invasion of Poland with over a million German troops on 1 September 1939, which is considered to be the beginning of World War II. Two days later, Britain and France declared that they were at war with Germany, although before they could take any military action, Hitler's invasion was complete. Poland was partitioned between Germany and the Soviet Union, with whom he had already signed a non-aggression pact.

An emboldened Hitler unleashed blitzkrieg, lightning campaigns on land and in air, and invaded Denmark, Norway, Holland, and Belgium in quick succession. Next was France, which, despite having a large and powerful army, fell with ridiculous ease owing to its abysmal military leadership and divided political elite. On the morning of 14 June 1940, German tanks rumbled down the Champs-Élysées in Paris. Italy, under the Fascist dictator Benito

Mussolini, joined Germany in the hope of a share in the war spoils.

With resistance melting away, Hitler seemed unstoppable, and there were predictions that by the end of summer, he would run over Britain. In anticipation of the impending collapse of the British Empire, his diplomats had already begun planning the future course of action. In discussions with the Afghan government, the Germans prompted them to abandon their neutral stance and join the war in return for territory in north-western India and the port of Karachi that Germany would have acquired after taking over British India.[2]

Before long, the German Luftwaffe was bombing the southern coast of Britain to pave the way for an amphibious invasion, code-named Operation Sea Lion. But they soon found out that Britain's Royal Air Force (RAF) was a formidable opponent, and switched to bombing the city of London, which the RAF was able to fend off as well. The Germans had to put a hold on their invasion plans.

To be able to continue its blistering war efforts, Germany had to secure vital supplies—oil, coal, steel, wheat, and grains—for which they were dependent on the Soviet Union, an unusual ally. Aiming to secure these resources, besides his long-term vision of *Lebensraum*, Hitler shocked the Soviet Union in June 1941 when he sent a 3-million-strong invasion force to its territory, in what was the largest military operation in history. He envisioned the annexed Soviet territory, including the highly productive lands of Ukraine and southern Russia and the oilfields of Baku, would become Germany's prized possession and a captive market for German goods, just like Britain's India.

The Nazi invasion left the poorly prepared Soviets startled, pushing them into another unnatural alliance with Britain, their old rival, and the United States, which had reverted to isolationism after World War I. Britain had viewed the USSR with deep suspicion while the United States held a general disdain for European imperialism and militaristic alliances. Britain and the United States are often seen as natural allies, but their special relationship wasn't always as steadfast either. After World War I, the United States had emerged as the foremost financial power and had witnessed an unprecedented economic boom during the 'Roaring Twenties', triggering a quiet erosion of Britain's global hegemony.[3] American military strategists had even considered the possibility of a war with Britain and had devised a plan named *War Plan Red* in the late 1920s, its classified blueprint regarded then as 'the most sensitive in the world'.

The three leaders of the alliance—the Soviet dictator Joseph Stalin, the British prime minister Winston Churchill, and the US president Franklin D. Roosevelt—could not have been more different from each other. Stalin was known for ruthlessly murdering millions of his citizens; Churchill was a flamboyant, cigar-loving aristocrat and a staunch upholder of the British Empire; and Roosevelt was known for his antagonism towards European imperialism.

While the western corner of the Eurasian continent was facing upheaval, Japan, at the opposite end, had also been battered by the Great Depression. During the economic turmoil, the idea that Japan could solve its problems by conquering others' lands and creating more living space, akin to Hitler's *Lebensraum*, had gained currency. It had actually begun much earlier with Japan's intimidation and annexation of Korea in 1910. Next came the invasion of Manchuria (north-eastern China) in 1931, and then a brutal assault on China in 1937. In Nanjing, then the capital of China, as many as 3,00,000 people were murdered and tens of thousands of women raped. After the fall of France in 1940, Japan occupied the French colony of Indo-China (Laos, Cambodia, and Vietnam), and joined a three-way military alliance with Germany and Italy known as the Axis.

When the United States imposed an oil and steel embargo on Japan to curb its aggression, the Japanese launched a shocking attack with 353 planes striking the US naval fleet at Hawaii's Pearl Harbour on 7 December 1941, killing more than 2,400 Americans. Up until this point, the American public had been inclined towards staying out of the conflict, but that changed overnight. Roosevelt called the attack 'a date which will live in infamy' in his famous address and declared war on Japan. Churchill, desperate to see America join the war, was elated as he knew this was a game changer.

From here on, the war became a 'world war' in the real sense. Intense battles raged in all corners of the globe—from the beaches of Europe to the deserts of North Africa and the Middle East, and from the jungles of Burma and Malaya to the remote Pacific islands.

India and the War

The day Britain declared war on Germany, Lord Linlithgow, the British viceroy of India, announced over a radio broadcast that India had also joined the war. He made this decision without consulting any Indian leader. Pandit Jawaharlal Nehru, the leader of the Indian National Congress, was infuriated at the unilateral decision. Mahatma Gandhi was inclined towards providing only non-violent support to the British. The rulers of several Indian princely states saw the announcement as a chance to demonstrate their loyalty to the British Crown and offered generous funding and support. Mohammad Ali Jinnah, the leader of the Muslim League, saw it as an opportunity to cooperate with the British and further his cause of creating the separate state of Pakistan.

At that point, the British India Army comprised 43,000 British and 1,30,000 Indian troops, and further recruitment for the war had started. The British authorities had been through the drill previously during World War I when over a million Indians were enlisted, though this time around the mood in India was volatile.

While the recruitment of Indian soldiers was underway, a Sikh revolutionary named Udham Singh shot dead Michael O'Dwyer in the heart of London in March 1940. O'Dwyer was the former lieutenant governor of Punjab who had endorsed the 1919 Jallianwala Bagh massacre in the city of Amritsar. The assassination brought back memories of the tragedy at a crucial time, especially when a disproportionate share of enlisted men in the British Indian Army came from Punjab. Nevertheless, the British authorities managed to paint Udham Singh as a lunatic and prevent the news from amplifying in India. The recruitment efforts continued cautiously, and the British Indian army would eventually reach 2.5 million men, with nearly a million Punjabis. It was recognised as the largest volunteer army in history.

The fall of France to German forces in 1940 sent out ripples of uncertainty as far as India, where people reckoned that Britain would go down the same path, leading to anarchy and riots in India. Mahatma Gandhi had to issue a statement to calm down the public's nerves.

The fiery leader Subhash Chandra Bose, who had resigned from the president's post of the Indian National Congress as he opposed Mahatma Gandhi's approach of non-violence, was awed by Germany's military capabilities. Bose slipped out of British imprisonment and crossed the Indian border into Kabul and from there to Moscow before finally entering Germany. He met with several Nazi leaders and argued that freeing India from British power was vital for them to win the war. Bose, who was popularly known as *Netaji* (respected leader) started delivering his nationalist speeches over radio broadcasts that created a sensation in India. After a long wait, Bose met Hitler, who felt his ideas needed more planning. Hitler feared that if the British were overthrown, India might fall into Russian hands. He told Bose that India would have to wait until the Nazis could overpower Russia. In the meantime, the British were using *Mein Kampf* to highlight Hitler's racist remarks about Indians and his disdain for the Indian independence movement in order to incite the Indian people against Germany.

In the decades leading up to the war, the United States had shown no strategic interest in India, and the American relations with India had been mostly missionary or philanthropic. To most Americans, India was nothing but a land of mysticism and extreme poverty. In the wake of growing xenophobia, not to mention the popularity of the eugenics movement that proposed selective human breeding for 'racial improvement', the United States had passed an immigration act in 1924 that effectively cut off all immigration from Asia.[4] A year later, American writer and racial supremacist Katherine Mayo travelled to India on a tour said to be organised by British intelligence. The outcome of her sojourn was the polemical book *Mother India* (1927), in which she attacked Hindu society and religion, giving depressing details about the state of women and describing grotesque rituals. Mayo described the treatment offered to women by a *dhai* (midwife) during childbirth:

> She makes balls of strange substances, such as hollyhock roots, or dirty string, or rags full of quince-seeds; or earth, or earth mixed with cloves, butter and marigold flowers; or nuts, or spices—any irritant—and thrusts them into the uterus, to hasten the event. In some parts of the country, goats' hair, scorpions' stings, monkey-skulls, and snake-skins are considered valuable applications.

British intelligence, as well as Churchill, were both delighted with the book for it portrayed Indian society as a squalid cesspool that desperately needed Britain's enlightened rule. Riots broke out in India over Mayo's controversial views, and Indian newspapers denounced the book as the worst libel. Mahatma Gandhi sent the political activist Sarojini Naidu on a popular speaking tour to the United States to refute the claims made in the book. Nonetheless, *Mother India* would remain one of the critical texts informing Americans about India for many years.

In contrast to Mayo's views, the eminent American historian Will Durant saw India differently. During his visit to India, Durant was appalled by what he called 'the most sordid and criminal exploitation' of the country by the British. Deeply moved by the plight of Indians, he wrote *The Case for India* (1930), narrating India's glorious past and its ongoing struggle for independence. Durant also pointed to Mayo's cherry-picking of facts and her flawed assessment of India.

Since the early twentieth century, the British Empire had been reorienting its relationship with its colonies. Australia, New Zealand, South Africa, and Canada had been granted dominion status, allowing them a measure of self-government, while India had been incongruously denied the same privilege. A few months before the United States entered the war, Roosevelt and Churchill had met aboard the USS *Augusta* to discuss their respective war aims. Roosevelt wasn't convinced that the United States should fight a war against fascism while turning a blind eye to colonialism. They jointly drafted the Atlantic Charter that supported the restoration of self-government to all countries occupied during the war, sending a wave of hope among the colonies. Churchill, however, backtracked later and claimed that the charter applied only to the countries conquered by the Axis powers and not the British colonies, including India.

Within days of the Pearl Harbour attack in December 1941, Japan had invaded Hong Kong and the Philippines and had driven the British out from Malaya. Two months later came Britain's epochal military defeat when Singapore, their supposedly impregnable base, fell to the Japanese and 65,000 Allied troops were forced into a humiliating surrender. Churchill called it 'the worst disaster and largest capitulation in British history'. It was a crushing blow to the British prestige and aura built over two centuries.

The Japanese had also started air raids on the overland route between Burma and China through which Chiang Kai-shek, the head of the Nationalist Government of China, was receiving arms support from the Allies. The Americans deployed General Joseph Stilwell, well known for his tough, no-nonsense demeanour and disregard for military pomp and ceremony, as the Allied chief of staff to Chiang. By March 1942, the Japanese had taken over Rangoon (now Yangon), and together with Burmese insurgents, forced the British and Chinese soldiers along with nearly 6,00,000 Indian civilians out of Burma. British civilians and administrators nabbed all the available transportation and made a quick exit, leaving everyone else to fend for themselves. General Stilwell and his remaining unit had to trek for over 200 kilometres through the harsh jungle terrain to reach India. 80,000 Indian evacuees died on the way, either falling victim to the inhuman conditions of the journey or murdered by the Burmese who had resented their presence on their land.

There was anger in India over the blatant racial discrimination in the evacuation process. Mahatma Gandhi complained to American journalists: 'One route for the whites, another for the blacks! Provision of food and even shelter for the whites, none for the blacks!' The horrific tales narrated by the evacuees led to a widespread feeling among the Indians that the Allies could not stand up to the Japanese, and that the invasion of India was imminent.

Japan had brought the war to India's doorstep. Southern India had no air defence to speak of when Japanese planes bombed Vizag (now Vishakhapatnam) and a few other coastal towns in April 1942. They also sank two cruisers, a light carrier, and a destroyer in and around the Bay of Bengal, which allowed Japanese fleets to sail unchallenged in the Indian Ocean. In December 1942, Japanese planes dropped bombs in Calcutta (now Kolkata), creating mass panic; nearly one-third of the 2 million residents fled the city.[5] The Japanese announced that they did not wish to harm the Indian people and urged them to overthrow the British. Opinions in India were divided over Japan, but one thing was clear—India's hope for seaborne security lay with America and not Britain, which had been, by now relegated to a subordinate position in the alliance. Consequently, many Indians, sceptical about Britain's future, began pulling out their savings from British-run banks.

The relentless onslaught from Japan had prompted the Americans to look at India in a new light. They realised India's significance with its unlimited workforce, vast railway network, massive grain output, and ability to produce steel and other war supplies like textiles, leather, and jute products. Roosevelt believed India could become the 'nucleus of a Far Eastern alliance'—which included China, Australia, and New Zealand—and hold out against Japan. To accomplish that goal, Roosevelt needed the Indian population to be sympathetic rather than hostile to the Allies. He therefore sent as his special representative to New Delhi, in 1942, the diplomat Louis Johnson, who started to mediate between the British and Indian leaders, openly favouring Indian independence. However, when Roosevelt tried to press Churchill for India's independence, Churchill reacted strongly, turning down the proposition.

Meanwhile, another storm was brewing in India. In August 1942, Mahatma Gandhi and the Congress leaders launched the Quit India movement. The British took an unexpectedly aggressive stance and put Gandhi, Nehru, and most of the Congress's top leadership in jail, which sparked a wave of mass political and social unrest, causing destruction of police stations, government offices, electrical installations, and train stations across India. Thereafter, the arrested leaders were entirely cut off from the outside world for the next three years until the war was over.

Amidst the turmoil, a great tragedy was about to unfold. When the war began, India was importing large quantities of rice from Burma and Thailand to meet its domestic demand, but the Japanese occupation of Southeast Asia cut off imports abruptly. With the threat of a Japanese invasion looming large, the British authorities implemented a 'scorched earth' policy whereby they removed rice stocks from coastal Bengal. Concurrently, they directed the local administration to accumulate all available rice stocks for the army. The scarcity of rice sent the prices soaring. To make matters worse, a deadly cyclone hit Bengal in late 1942 and severely damaged the rice harvest. With many unscrupulous traders resorting to speculative hoarding, the poor masses of Bengal, particularly in the rural regions, were left starving. By early 1943, famine had broken out.

For the British authorities, the priority was the ongoing war and not mitigating the famine situation. Most of the ships in the Indian Ocean were kept engaged in the war effort rather than being redirected to providing relief in Bengal. In fact, India was exporting grain to other war theatres in 1943. Offers of support from other nations were turned down even as people were dying in large numbers. Bureaucratic delays, confusion, and indifference became the order of the day. Churchill, whose racist views towards Indians were not a secret, ignored desperate pleas to provide relief and turned down requests to release ships to carry grain, going so far as to even stop a consignment of Canadian wheat from reaching India. Up to 3 million people starved to death in the Bengal famine of 1943, one of the worst catastrophes in the history of modern India.

In the meantime, Bose arrived in Southeast Asia in 1943 on board a submarine offered to him by Hitler, who had advised him to bank on Japan. Reviving the Indian National Army (INA)—which was formed by a Sikh military officer, Mohan Singh, and the Japan-based revolutionary, Rash Behari Bose—to fight alongside the Japanese for the liberation of India, Bose drew thousands of civilian volunteers from among the Indians living in Malaya, along with Indian prisoners of war captured after the fall of Singapore, making the INA 50,000-men strong. Over a period of time, however, he felt discontented because of the reluctance of the Japanese to employ the INA in crucial roles.

Towards the end of 1943, the Allies created the new South East Asia Command (SEAC), and Churchill promoted his favourite, forty-three-year-old Lord Louis Mountbatten as its supreme commander. The tall and handsome Mountbatten, with movie-star looks, was the cousin of King George VI and the great-grandson of Queen Victoria. He was married to the glamorous heiress Edwina Ashley, and the couple was popular in socialite circles in London. The decision to promote Mountbatten came despite General Montgomery, one of the most decorated military leaders in World War II, arguing that Mountbatten was 'quite unfit to be a Supreme Commander' and 'his knowledge of how to make war is really NIL'.[6]

Earlier during the war, Churchill had appointed Mountbatten as Chief of Combined Operations, skipping over many experienced officers, and the king had to turn away accusations of nepotism over the appointment. Known to be a reckless thrill-seeker, Mountbatten had sailed his warship HMS *Kelly* into a British minefield in 1941, before it was sunk by German dive-bombers. More than a hundred crew members were killed, while Mountbatten was projected as a dashing hero who stayed on the ship till the very end. He then oversaw the disastrous Dieppe Raid in France in August 1942, where around 3,600 troops, mostly Canadian, were either killed or captured in a matter of hours. At the admiralty, Mountbatten came to be known as the 'Master of Disaster'. The failures could have ruined his military career, but Churchill stood by him, and his royal connections saved him.

Mountbatten's career progression reflected a sharp downfall in the meritocracy and unforgiving standards of the British Royal Navy in the preceding centuries. In 1757, one Admiral Byng was executed on the deck of his former flagship after he was court-martialled and found guilty of 'not doing his utmost' in battle.[7]

Mountbatten arrived in New Delhi and built a lavish headquarter with a staff of 3,000, including a personal band of thirty musicians. General Stilwell, whose disdain for the British high command was not a secret, was made Mountbatten's deputy. Stilwell had a rather poor opinion of his boss and called him 'glamour boy'.[8]

With Burma under Japanese control, the overland supply route to the Chinese army had been cut off. American engineers took control of the 1288-kilometre-long Bengal and Assam Railway, and built a series of landing strips in eastern India[9] to be used by bombers as well as transport planes that airlifted supplies over the Himalayas, a route they called 'the Hump'. To mitigate the risk of American planes getting shot down, Stilwell initiated the construction of the 1722-kilometre-long Ledo Road from Ledo, Assam, to Kunming, China, which turned out to be an enormous engineering task. The road was built by 35,000 local workers and 15,000 American soldiers of whom 1,100 died. Chiang Kai-shek later had it renamed as Stilwell Road.

During the war years, India had become quite an international destination. When the Soviets started deporting Polish slave labour after the German invasion, it soon turned into a global refugee crisis. The Maharaja of Nawanagar in Gujarat sponsored a camp in Balachadi, where over a thousand Polish children were hosted. Another camp was set up at Valivade, outside Kolhapur, and it housed around 5,000 Polish refugees. India became a shelter and transit point for Jews escaping Nazi persecution together with thousands of other international refugees, such as the Maltese, Greeks, Iraqis, and Kazakhs.

The remote town of Ramgarh in Bihar had a prisoner-of-war camp for the several thousand German and Italian soldiers captured from North Africa. Around 10,000 Chinese soldiers who had escaped from Burma were also moved to Ramgarh besides thousands of American GIs (soldiers) and trainers. By 1945, over 2,00,000 American soldiers and engineers had landed in the ports of Bombay (now Mumbai) and Karachi from where they headed to Calcutta, Delhi, and other locations. Goods like refrigerators, air-conditioners, and cars followed the new arrivals in India. And entertainment options like cinemas, clubs, and restaurants started mushrooming in large cities to cater to the well-compensated American GIs.[10] Thousands of Chinese migrated to India, with many of them settling in Calcutta and opening restaurants, which probably explains the popularity of the Indo-Chinese cuisine in India.

The Tide Turns against the Axis Powers

The US industrial juggernaut was running at full force and producing more vehicles, ships, and aircraft than all the combatant powers put together. The industrial might of the United States, combined with the steely resolve of the Soviet army to defend their motherland at any cost, turned out to be the decisive factor in turning the tide against the Axis powers.

In February 1943, a Soviet counter-offensive ended the Battle of Stalingrad, considered to be one of the bloodiest battles in the history of warfare, which became a turning point in the war. The Allies then landed millions of soldiers on beaches in Europe and advanced towards Berlin, while the Soviet forces pressed forward from the east after mercilessly driving out the Germans from their homeland. In April 1945, Hitler committed suicide, while Mussolini was captured and executed. Germany surrendered unconditionally the next month.

The Japanese, however, continued to fight fanatically. The battles of Imphal and Kohima in India saw the fiercest close-quarter fighting in the war, but in the end, the British Indian Army prevailed. Fears of heavy casualties in a land invasion of Japan led the United States to use a new and more devastating weapon: the atomic bomb. Japan surrendered in September 1945, and with that, World War II was over.

Around 80 million people, or 3 per cent of the world's population, died in the six-year-long cataclysmic war, including 6 million Jewish men, women, and children who were murdered by the Nazis in the most despicable of crimes against humanity. While Britain and the United States lost over 4,00,000 men each in the war, the Soviet Union had the most staggering figure—around 20 million deaths. Author Gerhard Weinberg has called World War II 'the greatest war' since any attempt to outdo it would, most likely, not leave any survivors to document it.[11]

In India, World War II has been viewed as a distant event, largely ignoring the 87,000 Indian soldiers who lost their lives, for they were fighting for the colonial overlords and not their motherland. That said, this reasoning overlooks the fact that the war had a significant bearing on India's struggle for independence.

THE ROAD TO INDEPENDENCE

Though Britain was one of the victorious Allies, it was left a bankrupt nation with severely reduced prestige and authority. London had more than 70,000 buildings destroyed and 1.7 million homes damaged by the German blitz, and the city's residents were living under an acute rationing of food and other consumable products. The entire British industrial system was in shambles with over 2 million Britons unemployed. The British government owed an enormous debt of more than $6 billion to India and had to lobby hard to secure a $3.75 billion-loan from the United States.[12] The sun had finally set over their once-mighty empire. The United States, meanwhile, had replaced Britain as the new undisputed leader of the world.

The unwavering Churchill, who had saved Britain from the fury of the Nazis, was shocked when he was voted out in the 1945 elections as the British voters could not envisage him to be an effective leader for post-war reconstruction. His departure bolstered India's case for independence as he had vehemently opposed the idea all along.

The post-war recruitment of British men for a career in the Raj was now almost impossible as no one wanted to head to a weakening empire. British soldiers stationed in India were weary of civil peacekeeping roles and were keen to head back home. The British leaders were now contemplating exiting from India without blemishing their international prestige any further.

A poorly calculated decision made by the British authorities at this point in time was conducting the trial of three officers of the British Indian Army—Prem Kumar Sahgal, Gurbaksh Singh Dhillon, and Shah Nawaz Khan—at the Red Fort in Delhi. The three men had switched over to Bose's INA after the fall of Singapore and had been charged, subsequently, for treason. Emotions of the Indian masses were roiled up, forcing the British authorities to remit the sentences of the three men. The trio became national heroes, drawing massive crowds out onto the streets of Delhi and Lahore.[13]

In February 1946, the British authorities were shaken to the core when a naval mutiny, which received open support from industrial workers and students, broke out in Bombay. It spread to Calcutta and Karachi, where many more sailors mutinied. The loyalty of the Indian soldier, which had been the bedrock of the British Raj, was turning increasingly unreliable. In the following months, a mutiny by policemen in Bihar, during which they broke open a central armoury and went berserk, could be controlled only after military intervention.

Strikes by industrial workers, tram drivers, and railway employees had brought India to a screeching halt. Food supply was running short and black marketeering had become commonplace. Political leaders reminded people of the 1943 Bengal famine, turning the public's mood against the British rule. In Telangana, farmers armed themselves and seized land. The British officials were burdened by a shortage of resources, and were also disliked by the locals, which made their jobs and lives harder by the day.

After three years in prison, Congress leaders were finally released in June 1945. During that time, the Muslim League under Jinnah had gained significant ground. The big political question now was how and when the British should leave India, and more importantly, whom they should hand over the power to.

In July 1946, the British viceroy, Lord Wavell, invited Nehru and Jinnah to form an interim government. Jinnah's conditions were not acceptable to Wavell, who decided to form the government with Nehru alone. An infuriated Jinnah called for a series of rallies all over the country as part of Direct Action to win Pakistan. 16 August 1946 was chosen as Direct Action Day and it resulted in riots in Calcutta, leaving 5,000 people dead and over 10,000 injured. The carnage was unprecedented and a foretaste of what the Partition of the nation would later bring.

In February 1947, British prime minister Clement Attlee announced a bold plan for the British to leave India by June 1948. Attlee, not satisfied with the progress being made by Viceroy Wavell, wanted someone who could turn things around quickly. He was recommended a man perfectly suited for the job—the charming, speed-obsessed Lord Mountbatten. On 22 March 1947, Mountbatten landed in Delhi, accompanied by his wife, Edwina, and an elaborate swearing-in ceremony was held for the last viceroy of India at the Viceroy House.

Mountbatten sought to meet the leaders that he would be negotiating with over the next few months—Mahatma Gandhi, Pandit Nehru, Sardar Patel, and Muhammad Ali Jinnah—all four of them lawyers educated in England, and widowers. Mountbatten soon discovered that Jinnah was difficult to negotiate with, although one thing they agreed upon was the need for speed. Patel and Nehru, though passionately attached to the idea of a united India, eventually reached a point where they saw Partition as inevitable.

On the evening of 3 June 1947, Mountbatten, joined by the

Indian leaders, announced on a radio broadcast that power would be handed over to the Indian people by June 1948. Within a few days, however, for reasons unclear, Mountbatten changed the date to 15 August 1947, moving it forward by ten months, to the shock of everyone. The clock had started ticking for the dissection of India that was now only nine weeks away.

The Greatest Migration

There was much confusion about what Pakistan would look like and where the borders would be drawn. Around a quarter of India's 400 million-strong population were Muslims, distributed all over the subcontinent, but more prominent in the Punjab province in the west and in Bengal in the east.

Apart from the British provinces, there were 565 princely states, covering 40 per cent of India's area. They were ruled by native princes while the British Crown held suzerainty over them. Many of the princes had been living lavish, indulgent lives in their grand palaces, like the replica of the Versailles Palace built by the ruler of Kapurthala, with fleets of Rolls-Royce cars, multiple wives, or even harems. The Nizam of Hyderabad had appeared on the front cover of *Time* magazine in 1937 as the richest man in the world. The princes were anxious about losing their independence and witnessing the end of their decadent lives. When Mountbatten presented the Instrument of Accession (a legal document that enabled the princely states to accede to one of the new dominions of India or Pakistan) to the princes, some of them signed it without any protest while others had to be coerced by the tough Sardar Patel.

A respected British judge, Cyril Radcliffe, was appointed as the Joint Chairman of the two boundary commissions (Punjab and Bengal), and given only five weeks to come up with a plan for the division of India. He had never been to India, nor did he have any idea about the landscape or the people he was going to divide. The British government considered his lack of familiarity with India as a means of ensuring impartiality.

As the Partition loomed closer and the summer heat started to rise along with rumours and anxiety, tensions brimmed over into communal riots on the streets. With each passing day, the violence got worse and public order began to collapse. In the interim, government departments, libraries, and museums started preparing for the separation, making lists of items to be divided. A general rule of 80 per cent of goods going to India and 20 per cent to Pakistan was to be followed. The British India Army had to be divided too. Soldiers who were comrades in the same battalions and had fought together were now going to be split.[14]

Pakistan held its Independence Day ceremony on 14 August in Karachi and India on 15 August (midnight of 14 August) in Delhi, when Pandit Nehru delivered his famous 'Tryst with Destiny' speech in the Constituent Assembly, with over half a million people cheering outside. As the rest of the country celebrated, Punjab was burning, with Lahore as the epicentre. Calcutta, where massive riots were expected, was miraculously saved by Mahatma Gandhi, who had decided to forego the celebrations in Delhi.

No one knew where the borderlines ran because the division wouldn't be released by the British until 17 August. After the Independence Day celebrations, the extent of communal rioting and the volumes of refugees exploded, overwhelming the already inadequate infrastructure on both sides. The soldiers who had returned from the war were particularly lethal as they could orchestrate killings on a large scale.

Trains jammed with refugees travelling in both directions became the most enduring images of Partition. *Kafilas* or foot caravans comprising thousands of refugees carrying their belongings and trudging in the heat stretched for kilometres. Many of those refugee trains got ambushed, and by the time they crossed the border, they were without a sound, filled with corpses and severed limbs. In the greatest mass migration in human history, around 15 million people were uprooted and moved to the other side of the border and anywhere between 2,00,000 to 1.5 million people lost their lives.

While India was bleeding, British troops were lining up at the Gateway of India in Bombay to board ships for the homeward-bound journey. Mountbatten had instructed that British army units could not be used for internal security purposes unless there was a situation that demanded the saving of British lives. Stanford professor Stanley Wolpert writes in *Shameful Flight* that Mountbatten later admitted: 'I fucked it up'.[15]

A year after India's independence, Britain left Burma and Ceylon, and a few years later Egypt (1956), Malaya (1957), and Singapore (1963). The French lost Vietnam in 1945, Laos and Cambodia in 1953, and their Indian possessions (Pondicherry, Chandernagore, and Mahe) in 1954. The Dutch let go of Indonesia in 1949, but only after a violent struggle. In Africa, around forty countries gained independence from the British, French, Portuguese, and Belgians by the 1960s. As good as it sounds, independence did not mean prosperity for everyone as many of the newly formed nations fell in the hands of brutal dictators and corrupt political leaders.

THREE WORLDS, ONE PLANET

The war had left most of Europe and Japan in a state of ruin. The Soviet Union was badly bruised and bloodied—more than 1,700 Soviet towns and some 70,000 villages had been all but wiped off the map in addition to around 32,000 factories and 65,000 kilometres of railway tracks being entirely destroyed. All of this was aside from the social and psychological impact that the Soviet people had to deal with after having lost 20 million young men to the war.

In comparison, the United States had emerged unscathed from the war. Holding two-thirds of the world's gold reserves, and enjoying complete control over the skies and the oceans, it had 'superpower' written all over. American manufacturing switched to a peacetime mode, and consumer goods began flooding into the domestic marketplace. Returning soldiers were given home loans on easy terms, and thousands of homes were built, creating a new suburban America. Alongside the housing boom, ownership of cars, TV sets, and appliances exploded, unleashing an era of the most widespread prosperity in American history with the economy doubling between 1945 and 1960.

The United States funded the post-war economic recovery efforts in Europe with a massive $13 billion loan to seventeen countries including the UK, France, Germany, and Italy, under the Marshall Plan, which was intended to secure US geopolitical influence in the region. The Soviets rejected American financial assistance, yet they managed to turn their economic engine. A key element in their success was their massive workforce, which was mostly made up of forced labour. Around 10 million Soviet men returning from the front and at least 2 million German prisoners of war were deployed in the reconstruction efforts. Reparations from Germany, mainly seized industrial assets, helped initiate manufacturing activity. The military-industrial complex would remain a cornerstone of the Soviet economy for several decades. Armed with the atomic bomb and an advanced space programme, the Soviets now had the swagger of a superpower.

The ideological differences between the Soviet Union and the United States produced a complete polarisation between the communist and the capitalist blocs. Both the superpowers exploited local conflicts around the world and armed opposing sides in proxy wars. Their titanic rivalry came to be called Cold War, a term coined by George Orwell, the literary genius born in Motihari, Bihar. The growing paranoia led to a deadly nuclear arms race that developed into the space race, while the Olympics' arenas too, became battlegrounds. The Cold War hysteria, politics, and conspiracy theories inspired a host of novels and movies.

India during the Cold War

Months after the end of World War II, the United States and Britain were alarmed over the Soviet army troubling Turkey and Iran and were concerned about India falling under Soviet influence. The labour strikes and unemployment in war-related industries were potential targets for communist evangelists. Analysts pointed out that Soviet warships based out of Bombay or Karachi could allow them to control the strategic Persian Gulf. With the Soviet threat looming large, the Americans contemplated the possibility of having air bases in north-west India from where their warplanes could potentially bomb Soviet industrial centres.

Independent India started at a low point, saddled with fresh wounds of the Partition and millions of refugees. Civic infrastructure and administration were in complete disarray, and global experts were forecasting doom scenarios for the newly formed state that had a literacy rate barely in double digits. Churchill had earlier predicted that without the British, 'India will fall back quite rapidly through the centuries into the barbarism and privations of the Middle Ages'.[16]

By choosing a democratic path, India began a new chapter in its history that was throughout marked by inequality in terms of caste, creed, religion, and class. Under the chairmanship of the scholarly Dr B.R. Ambedkar, the Drafting Committee undertook two years of intense research and debate before the Constitution of India was adopted in 1949. Though it had borrowed provisions from the constitutions of various countries—France, Britain, the United States, Japan, the Soviet Union, Canada, Ireland, Australia, and South Africa—the constitution was still unique, covering India's social, cultural, and historical perspectives in entirety.

In the early years after independence, India's relations with the Soviet Union were not friendly, despite the fact that Nehru was influenced by the works of Marx and Lenin, and was impressed by the industrial progress of the Soviet Union. The Soviets believed that the British imperialists had simply been replaced by Indian elites like Nehru and that in the event of a war with the United States, India, being a member of the British Commonwealth, would inevitably join the Western camp. It was only when Nikita Khrushchev emerged victorious in a power struggle after Stalin's death in 1953 that India's relations with the Soviet Union opened up. Nehru visited the Soviet Union in June 1955 and addressed large audiences in Moscow, which included a young student named Mikhail Gorbachev. A few months later, Khrushchev and the Soviet statesman Nikolai Bulganin visited India, and '*Hindi Russi bhai bhai*' (Indians and Russians are brothers) became a popular slogan, much to the displeasure of the Americans.

Nehru was not drawn to the United States because of his inherent distrust of capitalists. His education at elite British institutions made him look down snobbishly at the seemingly rustic ways of the Americans.[17] He visited the United States for the first time in 1949 at the age of fifty-nine. Americans were seeking reliable allies against communism and made it a precondition before offering any economic assistance. Perturbed by Nehru's disinterest, the US State Department rejected a proposal of $500 million in financial aid to India.[18]

In 1951, Nehru launched India's Five Year Plan, which was inspired by the Soviet-style central planning model. Cambridge-educated statistician and intellectual P.C. Mahalanobis became a key person in Nehru's government driving economic reforms. Influenced by Western leftists and Soviet academicians, Mahalanobis was convinced that the government needed firm control over the economy. He conducted extensive statistical surveys and came up with the subsequent five-year plans.

India received generous support from the Soviet Union in setting up steel plants in Bhilai and Bokaro, along with the Indian Institute of Technology (IIT) in Bombay. It also received aid for development in the areas of defence, space, and atomic energy. Some of India's largest public sector companies like Oil and Natural Gas Corporation (ONGC), Hindustan Aeronautics Limited (HAL), and Bharat Heavy Electricals Limited (BHEL) were created with Soviet cooperation.

For all the camaraderie that New Delhi shared with Moscow, India's ties with the United States were not completely broken. Ample assistance arrived from American individuals, universities, and even the government. The chief engineer of the massive Bhakra

Dam, one of the largest infrastructure projects after independence, which Nehru called the 'temple of modern India', was an American named Harvey Slocum. IIT Kharagpur (1951), IIT Kanpur (1959), Birla Institute of Technology and Science (BITS) Pilani (1964), and the Indian Institutes of Management (IIMs) in Calcutta and Ahmedabad (1961) were established with support from American institutions such as the Massachusetts Institute of Technology (MIT) and the Harvard Business School.

Facing severe food shortages in the mid-60s after savage droughts, India received millions of tons of wheat from the United States. It was the Nobel Prize-winning American agronomist Norman Borlaug who solved the age-old problem of food shortages by introducing the dwarf wheat, which ushered in the Green Revolution in the late sixties. India became a food-surplus country with record-breaking wheat output.

Pandit Nehru had laid a strong foundation for modern India with the construction of dams, heavy industries, and new institutions, in addition to the ones that were a legacy of the British, but his economic vision eventually turned out to be flawed as it failed to appreciate the power of competition. The licensing requirements for the private sector handed power to bureaucrats and inspectors, and thus the infamous 'Licence Raj' was born, which made life miserable for entrepreneurs. Furthermore, archaic regulations choked India's potential, and the outcome was corruption, shoddy products, and a stagnant public sector.[19] When countries like Germany, Japan, South Korea, and Singapore were witnessing economic miracles, India was crawling at an average per capita income growth of 1.3 per cent from the 1950s to the 1980s, which has been deridingly called the 'Hindu rate of growth'.

In 1961, Nehru, joined hands with the leaders of other developing countries like Yugoslavia, Indonesia, Egypt, and Ghana, and founded the Non-Aligned Movement (NAM), under which the member countries would abstain from allying with either of the two superpower blocs and thereby exercise certain collective power. With the United States and its capitalist allies labelled as the

First World, and the Soviet Union and its communist allies as the Second World, the non-aligned countries became the Third World, a term coined by the French demographer Alfred Sauvy in a 1952 article titled 'Three Worlds, One Planet'. John Foster Dulles, the US Secretary of State, was a staunch anti-communist and took a strong dislike to Nehru's non-aligned stance.

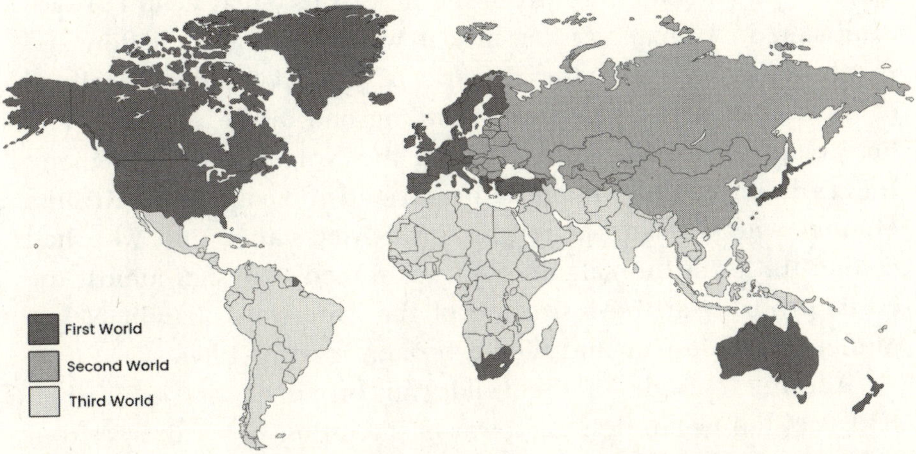

First, Second and Third World countries

The whole world watched nervously in October 1962 when the Soviets installed nuclear missiles in Cuba, just 145 kilometres from the US shores. The thirteen-day political and military stand-off, known as the Cuban Missile Crisis, was the closest that the United States and the Soviet Union came to a direct war. It was during the same short window that China attacked India through its Himalayan borders, exposing India's lack of border intelligence and defence readiness. Sardar Patel had highlighted the risk of Chinese military aggression and urged Nehru to strengthen India's defences, but Nehru had dismissed the threat as 'inconceivable'.

The Soviet Union now faced a dilemma—should it support China, its ideological sibling, or India, its friend and protégé? India reaching out to capitalist Americans for help would've meant failure for Nehru's non-aligned policy. But that was precisely how it turned out. A shaken-up Nehru frantically called President Kennedy, who did extend support, but only after the missile crisis was over.

The reasoning behind China's attack wasn't clear, but it was more than a disputed boundary issue. The conflict could have been related to India granting asylum to the Dalai Lama after the Lhasa uprising in 1959, or a cunning attempt to divert the Chinese public's attention from the disastrous Great Leap Forward campaign in China.[20] Either way, it was a deep humiliation and shock for India, given the rhetoric of India–China brotherhood of the 1950s. Nehru's personal standing had taken a beating, and he was no longer a leading voice of the Non-Aligned Movement. India's defence minister and Nehru's friend and confidante, Krishna Menon, who was known for his pro-Soviet stance and who had coined the term 'non-alignment', was forced to resign amidst the crisis, probably at the insistence of the Americans. Pandit Nehru plunged into despair and died a broken man in 1964.

Another episode of the Cold War broke out in 1971 when East Pakistan began fighting a war of liberation to break free from (West) Pakistan. The United States was providing support to Pakistan despite the Pakistani army unleashing a barbaric genocide upon the innocent civilians of East Pakistan. The war had created a crisis situation for India with up to 10 million refugees crossing the border into India by December 1971.[21] That is when Prime Minister Indira Gandhi, daughter of Pandit Nehru, decided to take action and launched an offensive against Pakistan. With support from the Soviet Union, it turned out to be a military as well as diplomatic victory for India, and the new nation of Bangladesh was born on 26 March 1971. India had thus restored some of the pride it had lost during the Indo-China War.

On a sunny day in November of 1986, I was among the thousands of school children waving flags at the India Gate lawns in New Delhi to welcome Mikhail Gorbachev, who had become the leader of the Soviet Union a year earlier. It was a time when the Soviet Union was experiencing severe economic and political stagnation due to years of excessive military spending, an inefficient command economy, and an authoritarian government. Intending to reinvigorate the economy and the communist system, Gorbachev took a bold step and set in motion radical reforms labelled as *perestroika* (restructuring) and *glasnost* (openness). Decentralisation and free-market forces were introduced along with freedom of speech, press, and religion. The outcome was, however, unforeseen: the economy deteriorated before benefits of the reforms materialised, while the freedom of expression led to criticism of the communist ideology and calls for independence. Gorbachev's decision to loosen Moscow's control over the Soviet satellite states created a fierce momentum in Poland and Hungary, and also in East Germany where it led to the fall of the Berlin Wall in 1989. The domino effect continued across the other satellite states and Soviet republics.

Meanwhile in India, the year 1991 marked a turning point. A major economic crisis was looming and India's foreign exchange reserves were down to two weeks of imports. National sentiments were outraged when tonnes of national gold reserves had to be airlifted to London and Zurich as collateral for a substantial loan from the International Monetary Fund (IMF). The astute prime minister Narasimha Rao and his Cambridge-educated finance minister Manmohan Singh turned the desperate situation into a once-in-a-lifetime opportunity, launching bold reforms that unshackled, though not wholly, India's locked-down socialist economy. Import duties were slashed, foreign investment was welcomed, and doors were opened for private players in sectors like aviation, telecom, TV broadcasting, and insurance, which were hitherto reserved for the public sector.

The very same year, a seismic global event took place as the turmoil in the Soviet Union reached a crescendo. On Christmas Day 1991, the Soviet hammer-and-sickle flag flew over the Kremlin in Moscow for the last time. The USSR had dissolved into fifteen independent countries. The collapse of the Soviet Union was hailed by the West as a triumph of democracy over totalitarianism, a victory of capitalism over communism. The United States celebrated as its formidable challenger crumbled. The Cold War was over, leading to the reformulation of political, economic, and military alliances all over the globe. It was a major shock for India as the ideological figure that India had looked up to since independence was no more. India now had to reimagine its place in the world order and make new friends and partners.

Some historians have characterised World War II as a mere extension or the 'unfinished business' of World War I. So what was the cause of World War I? While Britain and France had global colonial empires in the nineteenth century, what led to the rise of Germany, Russia, and the United States? How did Japan, an island nation at the far end of Asia, become powerful in a world dominated by the industrialised and militaristic Europeans? And where did India fit in this global contest?

2

THE EMPIRE, THE REBELS, AND THE CHALLENGERS

1840s–1920s

As long as we rule India, we are the greatest power in the world. If we lose it, we shall drop straight away to a third-rate power.

—Lord Curzon, Viceroy of India

It was the afternoon of 1 May 1851, and the streets of London were buzzing with over half a million spectators as Queen Victoria, wearing a formal pink gown, and her husband Prince Albert, rode in a procession from Buckingham Palace. The queen's arrival at Hyde Park was a magnificent spectacle where she declared the Great Exhibition to be open. A major boost to Britain's self-confidence, the gigantic exhibition was intended to showcase to the world its role as a technological force, a global leader, and a civilising power.

An enormous structure of iron and glass spanning nineteen acres, the Crystal Palace, nicknamed The Great Shalimar, was built for the exhibition. Around 19,000 exhibitors took part, and on display were gleaming steam engines, railway locomotives, electric telegraphs, and an early submarine. 6 million people flocked to the five-month-long mega event including notable celebrities of the time, such as Charles Darwin, Charles Dickens, Lewis Carroll, and Lord Tennyson.

Perhaps the most popular attraction of the exhibition was the world's largest diamond at the time, the Koh-i-Noor, which the British had acquired from the Sikhs in 1849 after the British emerged victorious in the two Anglo-Sikh wars fought between 1845 and 1849. The Koh-i-Noor now belonged to Queen Victoria, who had loaned it for the event. The India section of the exhibition attracted many viewers as it represented the culmination of years of colonisation and the reach of the British Empire.

The exhibition drew widespread acclaim, though there were critics too. The German philosopher Karl Marx, who had moved to London in 1849, called the exhibition a 'vulgar celebration of the evils of capitalism'. Visionary art critic and writer John Ruskin denounced it and concluded that 'design in the hands of a machine-minded money-seeking generation tends to take a downward curve'.

The Industrial Revolution that began in Britain in the late eighteenth century had quickly spread to continental Europe, where new methods and techniques of production and manufacturing were absorbed with natural ease. At the same time, industrialisation posed a dilemma for countries in the East, and that, in some senses, has persisted to date. It was associated with modernity, materialism, and ultimately with Western social mores, which supposedly infringed upon the deep-rooted cultural and pious traditions of the East. While many Eastern countries struggled to cope with this mega trend in their own ways, there were exceptions like Japan and Turkey, that embarked upon radical modernisation initiatives without losing their identity and pride.

THE UNCHALLENGED LEADER OF THE WORLD

By 1851, Britain had become the most powerful nation in the world, holding sway over a vast global empire that was protected by the strongest navy on the planet. Its industrial engine was firing on all cylinders, owning nearly half of the world's manufacturing capacity with explosive growth in steamships and rail and telegraph networks. London's population was approaching 3 million, making it the largest city the world had known.

There were no challengers on the horizon. The British had overpowered their closest rival, France, back in 1815 at the historic Battle of Waterloo. Spain was a has-been as its colonies in the Americas had broken free by the 1820s. The Chinese emperor had been intimidated by Britain's fearsome warships into ceding Hong Kong and opening five ports (including Shanghai) to British trade when he protested over India-grown opium being pushed illegally into his empire by the British, turning China into a nation of addicts. The largely Muslim Ottoman Empire, which had been around for four centuries, was now in a terminal decline and widely regarded as 'the sick man of Europe'.

Among Britain's colonies and imperial possessions around the world, which included Canada, Australia, New Zealand, and parts of southern Africa, the most precious was India, whose subjugation it had completed by 1849 after defeating the last challengers: the warlike Sikhs. Located strategically in Asia with a long coastline, India generated immense agricultural and artisanal output besides being a vast market for Britain's machine-made products. India also offered an endless supply of labour. Between 1830 and 1917, nearly 1.5 million Indian indentured labourers were taken to the British colonies of Mauritius, the British Guyana, Trinidad, South Africa, Malaya, Fiji, and Jamaica. Indian sepoys were a vital tool in imposing imperial control over colonies in Asia and Africa.

By the mid-nineteenth century, the 300-year-old Mughal empire in India had shrunk to a shadow of its former greatness and the then emperor Bahadur Shah Zafar was a monarch in name only, living in the Red Fort in Delhi on a pension from the British masters. The only bright spot left in the Mughal court was the poetry that the senile emperor patronised with enthusiasm.

In 1855, social reformer and civil servant Syed Ahmed Khan, who came from an elite family of Delhi, approached the famous poet Mirza Ghalib to write a *taqriz* (a traditional laudatory foreword) for a scholarly work he had completed. Ghalib wrote the taqriz, admonishing the elite imperial culture that Syed Ahmed Khan was part of, pointing to the change that was around the corner. The eminent Urdu poet Shamsur Rahman Faruqi translated Ghalib's eloquent words:

> Look at the sahibs of England.
> Look at the style and practice of these,
>
> ...
>
> What a spell have they struck on water
> That a vapour drives the boat in water!
>
> ...
>
> Oh, don't you see that these wise people
> Get news from thousands of miles in a couple of breaths?
>
> ...
>
> Go to London, for in that shining garden
> The city is bright in the night, without candles.
>
> Look at the businesses of the knowledgeable ones
> In every discipline, a hundred innovators!

The Great Rebellion

On 7 October 1857, only six years after the Great Exhibition, over 23,000 Londoners had gathered in the same Crystal Palace, which had been shifted to another location in London—not for an imperial exhibition this time, but to observe a day of mourning. Reverend Charles Spurgeon, Britain's most celebrated preacher, addressed them over the mutiny in India that had left them shocked. Spurgeon thundered, 'The sword must be taken out of its sheath to cut off our fellow-subjects by their thousands ... the religion of the Hindoos is neither more nor less than a mass of the rankest filth that ever imagination could have conceived.'[1] In other churches across Britain, a similar theme of revenge reverberated. John Ruskin dismissed Indians and their philosophy as 'childish' and restricted in intellect.[2] Charles Dickens wrote: 'I wish I were commander-in-chief in India ...I should do my utmost to exterminate the race.'[3]

The turmoil had started over cartridges for the newly deployed Enfield rifles that were purported to be greased with pork and beef fat. With an increasing number of Christian missionaries arriving in India, rumours were flying that Christianity was about to be imposed on all Indians by the British. In May 1857, soldiers of the Bengal Army mutinied in Meerut, near Delhi, ransacked the cantonment, and murdered several British officers before fleeing to Delhi. By the next day, the soldiers had secured the city and the Red Fort, and had proclaimed the reluctant eighty-one-year-old Mughal emperor Bahadur Shah as their leader.

The British policy of Doctrine of Lapse, which allowed them to unreasonably annex those Indian states where the ruler had died without leaving behind a natural heir, had contributed to the people's anger. Nana Sahib of Awadh and Lakshmi Bai, the rani (queen) of Jhansi, were among those affected by this doctrine. They would later become the leaders of the sepoy rebellion and be joined by dispossessed peasants whose lands were overtaxed by the British. Rani Lakshmi Bai had sought legal advice from the Australian lawyer John Lang, who had moved to India as a barrister and writer and had also established a newspaper, the *Mofussilite.* Lang described his journey to Jhansi and the mood of the time in his book *Wanderings in India.* When he told the queen that she didn't have much of an option, she replied, '*Mera Jhansi nahin dengee* (I will not give up my Jhansi)'.

The mutiny turned into a full-scale revolt, spreading to cities like Aligarh, Kanpur, Benaras, Allahabad, Lucknow, Jhansi, and Gwalior, albeit staying restricted to northern India. While the rebels lacked any central leadership, the British had a clear edge in organisation and communication, thanks to the newly introduced telegraph technology. The British leaders could mobilise regiments of Gurkha, Pathan, and Sikh soldiers from other parts of India that were not impacted by the rebellion. Support also arrived from outside India—from the Ottoman Empire, that was allied with the British. Delhi was finally stormed and captured by the British in September 1857, and the Mughal emperor was exiled to Burma, where he spent the last few years of his life.

British officers delivered revenge in cold blood and with an unprecedented ruthlessness that drew praise from a jingoistic press at home. The sons of the Mughal emperor were shot dead at the Khooni Darwaza (Gate of Blood) in Delhi. Rebels were strapped to cannons and blown apart. The whole population of Delhi was driven out into the open, and thousands were killed after cursory trials or no trials at all. In Kanpur, captured mutineers were forced to lick the blood of their white victims before being executed.

Shahjahanabad (the imperial capital of the Mughals built in the seventeenth century) faced large-scale demolitions and soon became the seventh ruined city of Delhi. The Scottish-born Andrew Carnegie, who made his fortune in the United States in the iron and steel industry, had visited India in 1878 as part of his world tour and wrote in his book *Round the World*: 'Delhi at last—the Rome of Asia! For eleven miles along the Imperial Way, on both sides, these ruins stretch, ending in the Kuttub Minar.... A ruin now and then is acceptable, but eleven miles of them in one or two days are rather embarrassing.'

There had been mutinies earlier by Indian soldiers, like the Vellore Mutiny of 1806 and the Barrackpore Mutiny of 1824. A conspiracy in the Bangalore cantonment in 1832 to massacre all Europeans was uncovered a day before any action could take place. However, the rebellion of 1857 was on a different scale altogether, sowing the seeds of Indian nationalism that would evolve into the independence movement.

Karl Marx and Frederick Engels, who wrote for the *New York Daily Tribune*, the paper with the largest circulation in the United States then, covered the 1857 revolt throughout. They disagreed with the assessment of the British leaders that the revolt was an isolated sepoy mutiny and believed instead that it was an insurrection by a broader section of Indian society, and part of a general anti-colonial liberation struggle of oppressed nations unfolding in the 1850s.

After the revolt of 1857, the East India Company was dissolved and the governance of India came under the direct control of the British Crown. The governor general was given the additional rank of viceroy of India, and he was to act as the personal representative of the queen. The Bengal Army was disbanded, and the British Indian Army was reorganised, inducting men from castes and communities that the British selectively labelled as martial races. The Muslim community was marginalised to an even greater extent as compared to the Hindus.[4] Thereafter, Indians were distanced from the British permanently, and the earlier romanticism towards India's antiquity and culture was replaced by authoritarian attitudes. The British ruling class retreated to segregated enclaves and elite clubs that were out of bounds for the locals. They would remain paranoid till World War II about a repeat of 1857.

The rebellion in India was not an exception. The British Empire had faced resistance in nearly every corner of the world. In the late eighteenth century, it was the rebellion by the American colonies that culminated in their independence. The Caribbean saw slave uprisings in Barbados, Jamaica, and British Guiana (now Guyana). In New Zealand, the native Maoris fought fiercely against the colonial power. In Africa, the Abyssinians, the Zulus, and the Asante people kept up their powerful resistance against the British military. In Beijing, thousands of British and French soldiers captured, looted, and burnt the magnificent eighteenth-century Summer Palace during the Second Opium War. Entire garrisons of British forces were massacred by rebels in Afghanistan and Sudan. In South Africa, the British ended up burning all of the 30,000 farmhouses of the Boer (descendants of Dutch settlers) rebels and herded their families into concentration camps, where around 27,000 of them, mostly children, died.

Was it even economically rational for the British to use coercion and violence to establish control over their colonies and protectorates? Adam Smith, the legendary Scottish economist and father of free-market capitalism, had argued that the British Empire was 'a waste of money'. It certainly seemed so in India given their massive standing army of a quarter of a million men in peaceful time, which consumed 40 per cent of their revenue. Economist Richard Cobden insisted that neither trade nor the spread of British 'civilisation' needed to be enforced by imperial structures. In May 1856, Cobden said, 'It would be a happy day when England has not an acre of territory in Continental Asia'.[5]

The rebellion in India had a profound impact on Syed Ahmed Khan, who was caught between his allegiance to the Muslim community and his high regard for the British. He endeavoured to explore Europe's progress, which was driven by knowledge, and promoted Western-style scientific education in India. Hoping for an inclusive British India where Muslim youth could progress, he founded the Scientific Society in Aligarh, modelled after the Royal Society. Khan travelled to Britain (1869–1870), which is when the queen awarded him the Order of the Star of India. Aiming to create a 'Muslim Cambridge', Sir Syed's vision was behind the setting up of the Muhammadan Anglo-Oriental College in Aligarh in 1875, which later became the Aligarh Muslim University.

Sir Syed's journey was part of a wider thought that developed in the Muslim world in the nineteenth century. An Egyptian scholar named Rifa'a al-Tahtawi (1801–1873), who lived in Paris for five years as a religious teacher, was a pioneer of the modernist awakening in Egypt that brought about a reconciliation between Islamic thought and the West. A similar figure was Jamal al-Din al-Afghani (1838–1897), who was born in Persia. During his first visit to India as a young student, al-Afghani witnessed the brutal British reprisals after 1857 and developed a lifelong loathing for the British. Straddling several countries in the Muslim world and Europe, he went on to become a highly influential political activist and journalist. Al-Afghani left a unique legacy that was a combination of encouraging pan-Islamic unity to counter European imperialism and bringing about reform of Muslim societies that was influenced by Europe.[6]

The Islamic world saw another response to European imperialism in the form of puritanical revivalist movements. Salafism developed in Egypt in the late nineteenth century and had roots in the eighteenth-century Wahhābī movement of Arabia. The Salafis believed in returning to the original political and moral practices of Islam. Similarly, in the town of Deoband, 150 kilometres north of Delhi, began the Deobandi movement in 1867, with an orthodox, anti-imperialist ideology; the origins of the modern-day Taliban can be traced to the same school of Islam.

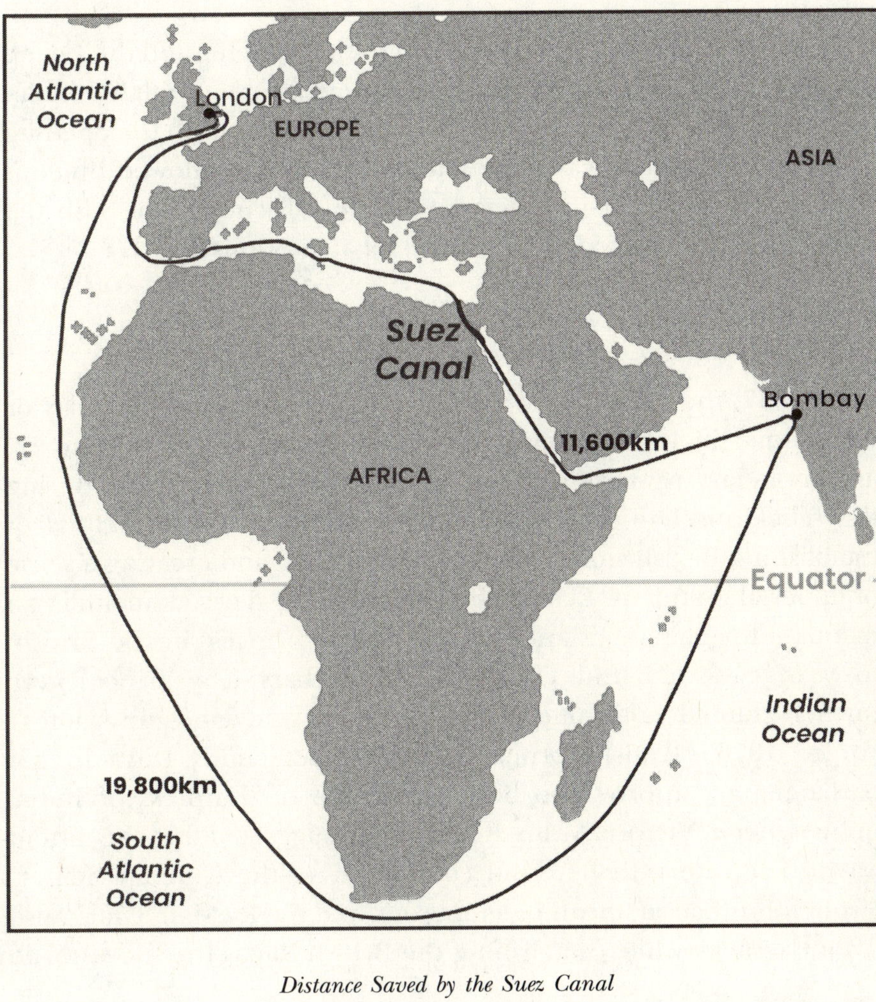

Distance Saved by the Suez Canal

Siultaneously, two other developments helped Britain strengthen its grip over India. Firstly, the opening of the Suez Canal, a 193-kilometre-long artificial waterway, in Egypt in 1869 allowed ships to travel between Europe and Asia without navigating around the continent of Africa, thereby reducing the voyage from around 19,000 kilometres to 11,000 kilometres. The average travel time reduced from over six months to two months. The second development came in 1870 with the opening of a direct submarine cable link with London. In February 1871, a telegram was cabled from Karachi that reached London in a record-breaking fifty minutes.

As a celebration of the engineering achievements and their deep impact on humanity, the renowned American poet Walt Whitman wrote his famous poem 'Passage to India'. It begins with the opening of the Suez Canal and the transatlantic cable that allowed humans to know one another in a new way, while still connecting with the ancient past embodied in the fables of mysterious India.

Pageantry Galore

After 1857, the British held several durbars (ceremonial courts or receptions) in India, granting newly invented titles, land parcels, and monetary rewards to those who had displayed loyalty during the rebellion. The durbar ceremony was nothing but a ritual of establishing British superiority over the natives and creating a sense of imperial grandeur. Elaborate protocols were devised, including a mandate for maharajas and nawabs, called 'princes' by the British, to wear jewels and fine clothes to the durbars. The princes were further granted ranks and assigned up to twenty-one-gun salutes.

In 1876, British prime minister Benjamin Disraeli got parliamentary approval to bestow the title of 'Empress of India' upon Queen Victoria, who herself had suggested it. The intent was to keep up with her rival counterparts—the German 'Kaiser' (from Julius Caesar, meaning emperor), and the Russian 'Czar' (also from Caesar)—while establishing the British Raj as the successor to the Mughals. The diminutive queen, who never visited India, was delighted with the grandiose label. The first Delhi Durbar, held in 1877, was an elaborate mass assembly to mark her coronation as *Kaisar-e-Hind,* the Empress of India.

From there on, colonial exhibitions became a regular theme in Britain. In 1886, the Colonial and Indian Exhibition opened by Queen Victoria in South Kensington in London received 5.5 million visitors. It was housed in a collection of purpose-built buildings designed in an Indian style.

In a triumphalist mood, the Empire of India Exhibition in 1895 was held at a twenty-four-acre site designed in a Mughal Indian style, aiming to project India as the product of British genius.[7] The colourful extravaganza captivated Londoners, presenting the account of Indian history from the 'Muhammadan conquest in 1024 through the Delhi Durbar of 1877'. It culminated with a 'Grand Apotheosis' when 'Britannia crowned her Majesty the Goddess of India'.

3 million people visited London in June 1897 for the diamond jubilee celebration of Queen Victoria's accession to the throne, that was combined with yet another festival of the British Empire celebrating its colonial possessions.

Two subsequent Delhi Durbars were held in 1903 and 1911 to mark the coronations of emperors Edward VII and George V. They were massive events lasting for weeks and included musical performances, lavish banquets, sporting events, and spectacular public entertainment acts. Artists, journalists, and photographers were commissioned to capture the durbar events through paintings, periodicals, photographs, postcards, and newly minted coins. In Delhi, King George V and Queen Mary appeared in the Red Fort balcony in full regalia, the king wearing the famously heavy Imperial Crown of India studded with 6,170 diamonds, sapphires, emeralds, and rubies, emulating the erstwhile Mughal emperors.

Coinciding with the durbars were famines and pestilence in India—millions perished while the British were portraying their rule as a bearer of progress and prosperity. All this while, nepotism had permeated the British Raj. Historian Jon Wilson writes in *India*

Conquered: 'Careers in the British Indian government were often transmitted from father to son. Some British elite families had four or five generations holding government office.... For each generation, the greatest concern was to maintain the institutions that supported the family business of empire.'

The Victorian era had ushered in extraordinary progress in science, technology, literature, and various forms of consumption and entertainment, but towards the end of the nineteenth century, Britain had begun to slip into relative decline. The weakening trajectory of the British Empire was hidden by the fact that it was still growing in terms of area and subjects. By 1914, the empire controlled a quarter of the world's area and a quarter of the global population, which sounds mighty impressive, although a closer look reveals that most of the territory was either the snow-covered Canadian wilderness or the arid Australian outback or vast acquisitions in Africa, while India alone, with its ocean of humanity, contributed to the population figures.

CHALLENGERS IN THE MAKING

While the prestige-obsessed British were caught up in suppressing rebellions across their global empire, steering their massive bureaucratic machine, holding durbars, and wallowing in imperial razzle-dazzle, other contenders were fast emerging on the global arena who would pose a challenge for Britain as well as for each other.

Russian Expansion and Modernisation

From a small principality around Moscow in the sixteenth century, czarist Russia had been continuously advancing eastwards. The western Europeans, however, looked down upon Russia as a backward land of Slavic peasants, more Asiatic than European. It was in 1812, that after the Russians turned Napoleon's invasion into an utter disaster, they established themselves as an eminent power.

In the following decades, Britain started to get nervous over the Russian incursion into Central Asia as it was bringing them closer to India. This British paranoia wasn't unwarranted since Russia had already made an attempt at invading India in 1801, which had to be aborted midway. Thus began the rivalry between the two empires that came to be known as the Great Game, the Cold War of the nineteenth century, where British and Russian diplomats, spies, and interlopers took part in covert missions across the buffer zones of Central Asia and Afghanistan. The game was not without dangers though, as many bold and ambitious contenders met brutal deaths.

In 1842, a pre-emptive British invasion of Afghanistan ended in a bone-chilling catastrophe when the Afghans massacred the entire British contingent of 16,500, leaving a lone survivor—an assistant surgeon named William Brydon. After all, Afghanistan has been called the 'graveyard of empires' for a reason. Nevertheless, the Great Game continued throughout the nineteenth century as Russia expanded into the mostly Muslim Central Asia, occupying Tashkent, Samarkand, Bokhara, and Khiva.

Meanwhile, another sphere of British–Russian rivalry opened up. Russia was casting covetous eyes over Turkish domains and thereby looking to take control of the Dardanelles, the strait where the Black Sea opens into the Mediterranean Sea. The British were alarmed over Russian ships gaining access to the Mediterranean Sea which was part of their principal trade route to India. The rising tensions resulted in the Crimean War (1853–1856), which was fought mainly in the Crimean Peninsula lying between the Black Sea and the Sea of Azov. France joined in to cement an alliance with Britain as well as to avenge their humiliation during the Napoleonic invasion of Russia in 1812.

Nearly 23,000 British soldiers (half of their total strength in India) were deployed from India to Crimea, and the same Enfield rifle that was behind the 1857 rebellion saw extensive action. Britain and France slaughtered the poorly trained Russian troops with long-range bombardments, exposing both their weakness in military leadership and their woefully inadequate weaponry. It turned out to be a ruinous defeat for Russia with nearly half a million soldiers dead on their own soil.

A twenty-six-year-old Russian artillery officer named Lev Nikolayevich Tolstoy was appalled by the carnage and penned a series of accounts of the siege, which were published as *Sevastopol Sketches,* whose popularity established 'Leo' Tolstoy as a literary great. Tolstoy upheld virtues like moral conduct and an age-old sense of community in Russia's villages, which he cited as the reasons behind Russia's victory over Napoleon, in his masterpiece *War and Peace* (1869). In his later years, Tolstoy underwent a profound spiritual crisis that prompted him to read Buddhist literature and a German translation of *Tirukkural,* the classic Tamil text, from where he learnt about the idea of non-violence. In *A Letter to a Hindu,* Tolstoy argued that only through the principle of love could the Indian people free themselves from colonial rule. He expressed his ideas in such works as *The Kingdom of God is Within You,* which would have a deep influence on Mahatma Gandhi.

The humiliating blow jolted Russia into competing with the industrialising European powers. Its first significant reform abolished serfdom and granted around half of the arable land to the peasants. To offset war debts and raise funds for growth, Russia sold Alaska to the United States in 1867 for $7.2 million—at just two cents an acre!

In 1860, Russia had only 2,000 kilometres of rail track, which grew to over 24,000 kilometres within twenty years. A successful bureaucrat named Sergei Witte drove further expansion of the Russian railroad network to over 56,300 kilometres by 1889. Witte also brought in foreign investment in industrial plants, introduced currency reforms, and funded infrastructure programmes.

By 1900, the Russian frontier had reached the eastern end of Eurasia, creating one of history's largest land-based empires, blessed with immense resources. Russia was now the world's fourth-largest producer of steel and the second-largest source of petroleum. Its industrial economy had progressed more in one decade than it had in the previous century, and this progress was referred to as the Great Spurt.

The West-inspired industrialisation was, however, not welcomed by everyone in Russia. Many elites and thinkers found the associated changes in the social structure unsettling; for instance, the great novelist Fyodor Dostoevsky was deeply concerned about the loss of community and moral consciousness due to the rapid modernisation and urbanisation.

America Becomes Huge and Great

It had taken the United States over 200 years to expand halfway from the eastern coast of North America, but the western half was taken in a matter of decades, reaching the Pacific coast by 1853.

The vigorous westward expansion came through means fair and foul. The purchase of Louisiana from France in 1803 was one of the largest land deals ever recorded, with $15 million being paid out for 21,44,510 square kilometres of land. In the following decades, the idea of 'Manifest Destiny' gained ground, which meant that the United States was predestined to control the whole continent from coast to coast, thanks to their inherent superiority and because God wanted it that way. This belief was reflected in the one-sided Mexican-American War (1846-48), or American invasion from the Mexican standpoint, where the United States annexed more than 1.3 million square kilometres of Mexican territory. Finally, after purchasing Alaska from the Russians in 1867, the United States was 9.6 million square kilometres in size, three times that of modern India. The world had never witnessed such a rapid supersizing of a country.

Not everyone in the United States was enthused about the Mexican-American War. Harvard-educated American author and philosopher Henry David Thoreau was arrested in July 1846 when he refused to pay his poll tax because he felt he could not support a government that was waging an imperial war against Mexico. Thoreau documented his opposition to the government's actions in his famous essay, 'Civil Disobedience' (1849). As history has shown, great ideas live long and go far. Thousands of kilometres away in Russia, Leo Tolstoy was so impressed by Thoreau's piece that he translated and published it for audiences in continental Europe. The essay would also have a profound impact on Mahatma Gandhi, who launched a movement in 1930 in India with the same name. The noble idea would later return to the United States where Martin Luther King, Jr., inspired by Gandhi's vision, would lead the American civil rights movement.

Unlike Russia, most of America was liveable. New frontier towns, cheap land, and an industrial boom attracted millions of immigrants from Europe who brought with them a spirit of hardwork and entrepreneurship. Many of them, particularly those from Scotland, Germany, and Scandinavia, were educated and possessed a variety of skills such as metalworking, engineering, beer brewing, and optical manufacturing.[8] The expansion was aided by the advent of railroads and telegraph; as of 1840, the United States had only 5,300 kilometres of railroad track, which reached 3,20,000 kilometres by 1900.[9] A similar proliferation of the road and canal network further boosted commerce, like the 584-kilometre-long Erie Canal that brought New York City to prominence.

The United States had seemingly endless land and natural resources like iron ore and coal, with none of the political constraints or cultural baggage of Europe and Asia. Gold was discovered in California in 1849, and the first oil well was drilled in Pennsylvania in 1859. The United States was all set to become an economic and industrial powerhouse.

Besides the tangible factors that drove the blistering growth of the United States, it was the ideological underpinnings of the young nation that enabled steady progress. In 1831, Alexis de Tocqueville, a young French aristocrat and political scientist who made a nine-month-long journey through the country, had astutely observed the flourishing democratic and egalitarian values in US society that prompted him to write the monumental book *Democracy in America* (1835). Tocqueville had presciently predicted that the United States would become one of the great powers in the world and would one day clash with Russia for the top spot.

And then America hit a speed bump in 1861. The northern and southern states were divided over slavery and the westward advance of the American frontier. The simmering tensions between the two led to the Civil War, where 6,20,000 men died (more casualties than all other American wars combined). The world was globalised back then as well since the same Enfield rifle that was deployed in the Crimean War and was behind the 1857 Rebellion, was used extensively in the American Civil War.

The Civil War's impact was felt around the globe. The conflict choked the traditional source of cotton for the British textile mills and the price of cotton skyrocketed, triggering a boom in places like Cairo in Egypt and Bellary in India that were engaged in the cotton trade. In Bombay, the enormous profits made by Parsi and Gujarati brokers from selling cotton were deployed in the stock market, leading to a roaring bull market. However, when the Civil War ended in 1865, cotton supply from America resumed and cotton prices in markets like Egypt and India fell, followed by a crash in share prices.

The business houses of Bombay saw their wealth evaporate, and the city's population plummeted by 20 per cent in the following years. The stock market crash of 1865 was the first of its kind in India and necessitated the formation of what is today known as the Bombay Stock Exchange, the oldest stock exchange in Asia.

America's post-war economy was soon on a recovery path, particularly in the northern states. As the nation turned into a beehive of inventions, the number of patents issued grew from around 1,000 in 1844 to 45,000 in 1897; 'inventor' became a common professional title. Among the many inventions that the United States gave the world was the aeroplane, which not only revolutionised transportation but also redefined the rules of warfare, eroding the significance of oceanic domination. By the late nineteenth century, skyscrapers started appearing in Chicago and New York City and became the symbol of America's economic success, a template that emerging cities around the world follow to date.

The Japanese Miracle

As of the mid-nineteenth century, Japan had been cut off from the rest of the world for over 200 years as its rulers, the Tokugawa *shoguns*, believed that foreign influence would corrupt their culture.

The United States, having reached the Pacific coast in an expansionist frenzy, was now looking beyond the vast ocean towards Asia. In 1853, Commodore Matthew Perry was sent to Japan to convince the Japanese, whom he considered semi-barbarous, to open trade relations with the United States. Not making progress with the Japanese authorities, Perry pulled his heavily armed warships into the Edo (now Tokyo) Bay, intimidating them into accepting the terms mentioned in the letter from his president. Well aware of the aggression meted out to the Chinese by the British warships, the Japanese grudgingly signed a treaty opening two of their ports for American ships, thus ending their 220-year-old policy of isolation. The humiliation inflicted by Perry woke up the island nation from a long slumber. The Japanese realised how far they had fallen behind and how modernisation was the only way to defend themselves from the industrialised, cannon-toting Westerners.

The *shogunate* thus began to make concerted efforts to modernise their nation. Naval students were sent to study in Western schools, starting a tradition of foreign-educated future leaders, even though there was a robust anti-Western sentiment in Japan too.

One of the leading figures in Japan at the time was Fukuzawa Yukichi (1835–1901), a philosopher, entrepreneur, and educator. He had the most significant impact as a revolutionary cultural critic and a famous writer whose books sold in millions. He headed the initiative to introduce Western ideas to increase, as he repeatedly wrote, 'Japanese strength and independence'.

Fukuzawa's autobiography is one of the most inspiring tales of grit and determination. He narrated how the Japanese started studying navigation and the science of steamships under the Dutch from 1855 onwards, and within only five years, they were ready to make a voyage across the Pacific. With Fukuzawa aboard, in 1860, the first Japanese ship reached San Francisco in what was an epoch-making achievement.

Fukuzawa travelled to several European countries and diligently noted every aspect of Western commerce, industry, society, and politics that might be of use to Japan. He published his observations in his ten-volume work *Seiyo Jijo* (*Conditions in the West*), which became a sensation overnight. From Europe as well as from his second trip to the United States, he brought a large number of Western books, which he translated and published in Japanese. Fukuzawa's idea of westernisation did not mean a slavish copying of the West, a practice he derided, rather a pragmatic view of all ideas and practices regardless of origin.

During their extensive interactions with Europe in the second half of the nineteenth century, the Japanese could not stay immune to the wave of Oriental studies as European scholars were passionately uncovering India's past, including Buddhist stupas, relics, and scriptures. With a long history of fascination with India, the Japanese referred to it as *Tenjiku,* meaning the land of heavens. India was the homeland of Buddhism, but no Japanese Buddhists had travelled to India. Professor Richard M. Jaffe describes in his book, *Seeking Sakyamuni,* the experiences of the first Japanese Buddhists who travelled to South Asia in the nineteenth century. Japanese scholars like Bunyu Nanjo and Kenji Kasahara went to England to study Sanskrit under Max Müller, the German-born philologist and Orientalist, and Indian philosophy became an area of academic interest in Japan.

In 1868, the Tokugawa shogunate was overthrown and the Meiji emperor was restored to the throne. A small group of ambitious, able, and patriotic young men spearheaded the Meiji mission to catch up with the economic, technological, and military power of the West. It was the onset of the Industrial Revolution in Japan, beginning with the manufacturing of cotton textiles and silk. A new Western-based education system was implemented wherein thousands of students were sent to the United States and Europe; more than 3,000 Westerners were hired in Japan to teach modern science, mathematics, technology, and foreign languages. The first railway line was opened between Tokyo and Yokohama in 1872, and by 1890 the country had more than 2,250 kilometres of railroads. Its cotton textiles were now competing successfully with British products in China and India. Japan had become an outstanding example of large-scale industrialisation outside of Europe.

The modernisation of Japan also entailed a major shift in the dietary patterns of its people. For over a thousand years, the Japanese people had tabooed eating meat, consuming a vegetarian diet in line with the tenets of their national religions of Buddhism and Shintoism, besides it being a result of the practical limitation imposed by a shortage of lands conducive to rearing animals for meat. But now, inspired by the meat-loaded diet of the tall Westerners, they shunned their age-old tradition and took to eating beef, which was seen as a step towards progress and civilisation.

It was towards the end of the nineteenth century that the idea of pan-Asian unity was born, and one of its earliest proponents was the Japanese art historian and scholar Okakura Kakuzo. The opening phrase of his most influential work, *The Ideals of the East* (1901), 'Asia is one' was often quoted by intellectuals and statesmen. Okakura called India and China 'the two mighty civilizations', and Buddhism 'the great ocean of idealism, in which merge all the river systems of Eastern Asian thought'.[10] But the hopes of pan-Asianist romanticists like Okakura quickly came to an end as Japan turned into a European-style imperial power, unleashing aggression over fellow Asian nations.

Rising imperial ambitions over Manchuria and Korea brought Russia and Japan on a collision path. The whole world took notice when Japan dealt a mighty blow to Russia in 1905 at the Battle of

Tsushima Strait (which divides Japan from Korea), considered one of the greatest naval victories in history. Before the conflict began, Japan was no match for Russia's mighty fleet of warships and its million-man-strong army. Like Perry, who looked down upon the Japanese as primitive beings, the Russians called them 'yellow apes'. Under the command of the outstanding Admiral Togo, however, the Japanese destroyed the Russian naval force, sinking six of their battleships and killing 5,000 sailors. The white man wasn't invincible any more. US president Theodore Roosevelt called it 'the greatest phenomenon the world has ever seen'. Indian freedom fighter Lala Lajpat Rai, who visited the United States in 1916, wrote in his book *The United States of America: A Hindu's Impressions* that 'The Jap has to be tolerated (in America) because he is "a citizen of a country which recently whipped one of the great powers".'

It was the first time an Asian power had defeated a Western one, and the news sent a wave of excitement through China, Vietnam, Indonesia, India, Persia, Egypt, and Turkey. Students and revolutionaries from all over Asia flocked to Japan, hoping to find support and encouragement for their nationalist movements. Among them were nationalists like Sun Yat-sen, the head of the revolutionary army of China, and Rash Behari Bose, the Bengali revolutionary, who were convinced that under Japan's leadership, Asia would be able to challenge Western hegemony.

Italy and Germany Are Born

Italy was a motley of states bounded by culture and language that were witnessing a wave of nationalism as a reaction to French domination. Political activist and revolutionary Giuseppe Mazzini founded the Young Italy movement in 1832 and inspired a generation of young nationalists around the world. Under leaders like Giuseppe Garibaldi, Italy was unified by 1861. Mazzini and Garibaldi had a deep influence on Indian independence leaders and provided a template for movements like Young Bengal and Mahatma Gandhi's Young India.

Likewise, Germany, as we know it today, did not exist until 1871. The German realm was a collection of around 300 individual states that shared little more than a common language. After an earlier attempt at unifying the states in 1848 fell apart, the charismatic statesman Otto von Bismarck, also known as the Iron Chancellor, orchestrated the unification of Germany after winning a nationalistic war against France in 1871. On 18 January 1871, Germany became a nation state for the first time in history.

The newly born entity got down to business right away, absorbing new industrial technology with gusto. The tariff barriers put in place by Bismarck after 1880 provided the embryonic German industry with the necessary protection from foreign competition. Thus began what has been called the Second Industrial Revolution, where Germany came to rival Britain as Europe's primary industrial nation.

An entirely new industrial sector, automobile manufacturing, was born after an engineer named Nickolaus Otto built the first practical internal combustion engine in 1876, and a decade later Gottlieb Daimler and Karl Benz developed the first petrol-driven car. Between 1880 and 1910, Britain's share of global trade fell from 23 to 17 per cent. Its global industrial capacity by 1910 was 15 per cent, compared to the United States' 35 per cent and Germany's 16 per cent. Iron and steel, machinery, power generation, and chemicals had replaced cotton textiles as the symbols of industrial and economic supremacy. On the eve of World War I, German steel output was double that of Britain. Germany was producing more than half of the world's electrical goods; its chemical industry dominated the world market for synthetic dyes with three firms—BASF (Badische Anilin und Soda Fabrik), Bayer, and Hoechst—producing 80 per cent of the world's supply of dyestuffs.[11]

How did Britain fall behind Germany and the United States?

Without the trappings or the burdens of a global empire weighing them down, Germany and the United States could devote their energies to real progress. Since they industrialised later, they were able to model their factories after those of Britain, thus making more efficient use of their capital and improving upon the known methods.[12] They also had more abundant and cheaper supplies of energy and raw materials. While the United States saw rapid growth in patents leading to more innovation, the British patent laws remained expensive and cumbersome. The profits earned in the first phase of the Industrial Revolution had turned the British entrepreneurs and wealthy class into risk-averse rent-seekers at a time when the labour unions had created an unproductive bargaining situation.

In response to the import tariffs imposed by Germany and the United States, Britain imposed similar protectionist tariffs, though over time they made the British industry less competitive. During the downturns, Britain could further squeeze a largely unprotected India, but this ease of exploitation only added to its complacency.

Education was also a determining factor. Germany was one of the first European nations to have free and compulsory public education, a resolve that would have a profound impact on their economic progress.[13] While institutions in the United States and Germany concentrated on science, technology, and vocational training, the British institutions focused on high social status and non-technological education, producing gentlemen and not practical men.

UNINDUSTRIAL INDIA

Other than the cotton mills that came up around the 1860s in cities like Ahmedabad, Bombay, and Nagpur, deploying spinning and weaving machines imported from London, British India possessed no engineering, machine-tool, or chemical industries. Britain had restricted India to being a primarily agricultural state. Some even gave a racial justification for this lack of industrialisation. Sir Richard Temple, the former governor of Bombay, claimed in 1881 that 'the Hindus are not a mechanical race'.[14] Author Gurcharan Das has pointed out that unlike how things panned out in Britain, the United States, Germany, and Russia, where the railways were a key contributor to their industrialisation, India under the Raj remained unindustrialised.[15] Rail transport, often trumpeted as one of the main benefits of British rule in India, was primarily intended to transport raw materials like cotton and indigo to the ports, and military supplies to the cantonments. Besides, it benefitted the British steel and rail industries, and the British financiers who were guaranteed a higher return than the prevailing interest rates, the cost of which was borne by the already poor Indian taxpayers.

Likewise, British policies on education were drafted in tune with their colonial needs, and that resulted in abysmal literacy rates in British India: less than 6 per cent by 1901 and less than 15 per cent by 1947. In contrast, the native rulers of princely states like Baroda, Travancore, and Mysore promoted education with a reformist zeal, launching initiatives like free and compulsory primary education for children.

One of the first leaders of India's independence movement, Bal Gangadhar Tilak (1856–1920), who pioneered the idea of *Swaraj* (self-rule), was also a founder of two newspapers—the *Mahratta* in English and *Kesari* in Marathi. What is lesser known is the fact that the two papers extensively covered global trends around science, technology, and industry. Thomas Edison appeared regularly in their articles, and a common theme was the 'internationalization of the world'. The *Mahratta* called for the necessity of technical education in India and increasingly looked to the United States, and not Britain, as the leader. The *Kesari* assessed Germany as the place for producing scientists and the United States as the place for producing technologists.[16]

India had abundant iron ore reserves and yet had to import iron. The credit for the creation of the steel industry in India goes to the visionary industrialist and entrepreneur Jamsetji Tata (1839–1904) and his son Dorabji Tata. Having established cotton mills in the 1870s, Jamsetji visited every important exhibition on industry and technology, like the ones in Paris, Chicago, and Dusseldorf, and carefully examined technologies that could be applied in India. In the 1890s, he decided to build India's first steel mill and got the go-ahead from the British only because they were falling behind Germany and the United States in steel output. The first steel plant was opened at Jamshedpur in Bihar (now part of Jharkhand) in 1907, using American know-how. It is interesting to note that precisely a hundred years later, in 2007, the Tata group acquired UK's Corus Steel for $13.5 billion (and Jaguar Land Rover for $2.3 billion in 2008).

From the 1880s, Jamsetji had been exploring the possibility of setting up a university in India that would conduct research at the highest level. His dream came true in 1908 when the Indian Institute of Science was established in Bangalore. The *Mahratta* saw the institute as a virtual declaration of scientific and industrial independence for India.

THE INDO-IRISH CONNECTION

In South Asia, the term 'Britisher' is used commonly and taken to mean a homogenous group of people who came from Britain, overlooking the fact that there were many Irishmen who were an integral part of the British Empire. The relationship between the Irish people and the British Empire, however, had its share of contrasts that are worth exploring.

Back in the sixteenth century, Ireland became England's first colony and ultimately a training ground for the Empire. The ideas and policies relating to land ownership, education, and Anglicisation that were fashioned in Ireland were applied to India and vice versa. English philosopher John Stuart Mill wrote in an article in 1848, 'Those Englishmen who know something of India are even now those who understand Ireland best'.

Many Irishmen served loyally in the Empire and earned fame, like John Nicholson, who is known for his crucial role in suppressing the 1857 rebellion in India, and Arthur Wellesley, the first Duke of Wellington, who is widely considered one of the leading military and political figures of the nineteenth century. Roughly half of the European soldiers in the British Indian Army during the nineteenth century were Irish, and around one-sixth of the candidates admitted to the Indian Civil Service were graduates from Trinity College in Dublin.

Then there were those Irish who opposed British imperialism, some mildly, and some vehemently so. Thomas Henry Kavanagh, the hero of the siege of Lucknow in 1857, was critical of the British administration and regretted the subsequent segregation of Indians and the whites.[17] With the rise of Irish nationalism from the 1880s, the British government started to have concerns about the loyalty of Irishmen in India. It was around the same time that Indian nationalists began looking up to Ireland for inspiration. Irish politician Frank O'Donnell, in his maiden speech in the House of Commons in 1874, criticised the British government's response to the Bengal famine (1872–1873), a catastrophe that resonated with the Irish who had witnessed over a million deaths during the Irish Potato Famine (1845–1849). O'Donnell founded the Constitutional Society of India, aimed at establishing home rule for Indians.

Political leader and social reformer Gopal Krishna Gokhale, a mentor to Mahatma Gandhi, looked up to the Irish Home Rule Movement. He travelled to Ireland in 1894 and arranged for Irish nationalist Alfred Webb to serve as the president of the Indian National Congress (INC). Meanwhile, Dadabhai Naoroji, the first Indian to be elected to the British Parliament, spoke in favour of Irish Home Rule, while also campaigning for India's cause. The Irish nationalist Maud Gonne cited Naoroji's book, *Poverty and Un-British Rule in India* (1901), on the drain of wealth from India to England, suggesting that it equally applied to Ireland; she labelled Queen Victoria as the 'Famine Queen'.

The illustrious activist Annie Besant (1847–1933), though born in London, was proud of her Irish roots. She took an interest in theosophy and moved to India, where she became the president of the Theosophical Society. Her interest in education led to the founding of the Central Hindu College, which became the nucleus of the Banaras Hindu University. Mahatma Gandhi once said that Besant had awakened India from a deep slumber. She was an avid supporter of the Irish and Indian cause of self-rule and became involved in the Indian nationalist movement, launching the Home Rule League along with Bal Gangadhar Tilak in 1916. A year later, Besant was elected as the first woman president of the Indian National Congress.

During World War I, Besant's clarion call of 'England's need is India's opportunity', echoed the Irish slogan 'England's difficulty is Ireland's opportunity', which had become popular among Irish nationalists. The US-based Ghadar (revolt) Party, a group of expatriate Indians, who were supported by Irish-American nationalists, made an elaborate plan along with Indian revolutionaries based in Japan and India for a coordinated rebellion in February 1915. The plot was, however, foiled as British spies had infiltrated the movement.

The British were also able to thwart the attempts of Germany to provide military support to Irish nationalists during World War I. Nonetheless, the Irish nationalists staged a rebellion in Dublin during the Easter week in April 1916 to end the British rule in Ireland. The Easter Rising was swiftly suppressed by the British, and more than 2,000 Irish people were killed or injured. Later, there would be repercussions far away in India. In June 1920, around 300 Irish soldiers in the Connaught Rangers, protesting against martial law in Ireland, mutinied in Punjab. The rebellion was quelled and 88 mutineers were court-martialled while one Private James Joseph Daly was executed. Daly was hailed as a martyr by the Irish nationalist groups.

A best-selling book titled *My Fight for Irish Freedom* (1924), written by the Irish revolutionary Dan Breen, was translated into Hindi, Punjabi, and Tamil and became a source of inspiration for Indian freedom fighters. In 1930, Bengali nationalists attempted to replicate the Easter Rising in an event known as the Chittagong Armoury Raid on Good Friday. Subhas Chandra Bose said, 'In my part of India—Bengal—there is hardly an educated family where books about the Irish heroes are not read and, if I may say so, devoured.'

The Irish revolutionary leader and statesman Eamon De Valera, also known as the founding father of the Republic of Ireland, was a hero and mentor to Indian nationalists as he stood for India's cause. In a speech addressed to the Friends of Freedom for India, an organisation affiliated with the Ghadar Party, in New York in 1920, he said: 'We of Ireland and you of India must each of us endeavour, both as separate peoples and in combination, to rid ourselves of the vampire that is fattening on our blood and we must never allow ourselves to forget what weapon it was by which (George) Washington rid his country of the same vampire. Our cause is a common cause.'

THE WAR TO END ALL WARS

At the dawn of the twentieth century, nationalistic jingoism was sweeping through Europe, prompting statesmen to indulge in military bravado. Britain's paranoia over Russian expansion was replaced by the threat of a rising Germany under Kaiser Wilhelm II, who happened to be the eldest grandchild of Queen Victoria and the first cousin of King George V. The Kaiser, who was fascinated by British ships as a young boy while visiting his grandmother, was an ardent fan of the books written by an American naval officer named Alfred Mahan. One of the foremost thinkers on naval warfare, Mahan published his landmark book *The Influence of Sea Power upon History* in 1890. The arguments and strategies outlined by Mahan immediately drew the attention of most major navies, ultimately provoking a naval arms race between Britain and Germany. As a countermeasure to Germany's alliance with Austria-Hungary, the British formed an alliance with the French in 1904, and three years later, the Triple Entente—an association of Britain, France, and Russia—was created.

As of 1914, Europe had not seen a major war for a hundred years. The trigger for World War I came in the month of June when the Austrian archduke Franz Ferdinand, a close friend of the Kaiser, was assassinated by a Serbian nationalist, and that led Austria to declare war on Serbia. While Germany backed the Austrians, Russia, eager to defend the Slavic identity and to restore its lost prestige after the humiliating defeat in the Russo-Japanese conflict in 1905, came to the aid of Serbia. In the absence of any global institution or agency that could mediate and diffuse the crisis, where diplomats and political elites had clearly failed, it rapidly snowballed into an all-out war between the two alliance groups—the Central Powers (comprising Germany, Austria-Hungary, the Ottoman Empire, and Bulgaria) and the Allied powers (comprising Russia, Britain, France, Italy, and Japan). Expected to be over in a few months, the ruinous war went on for four years, and came to be called the Great War.

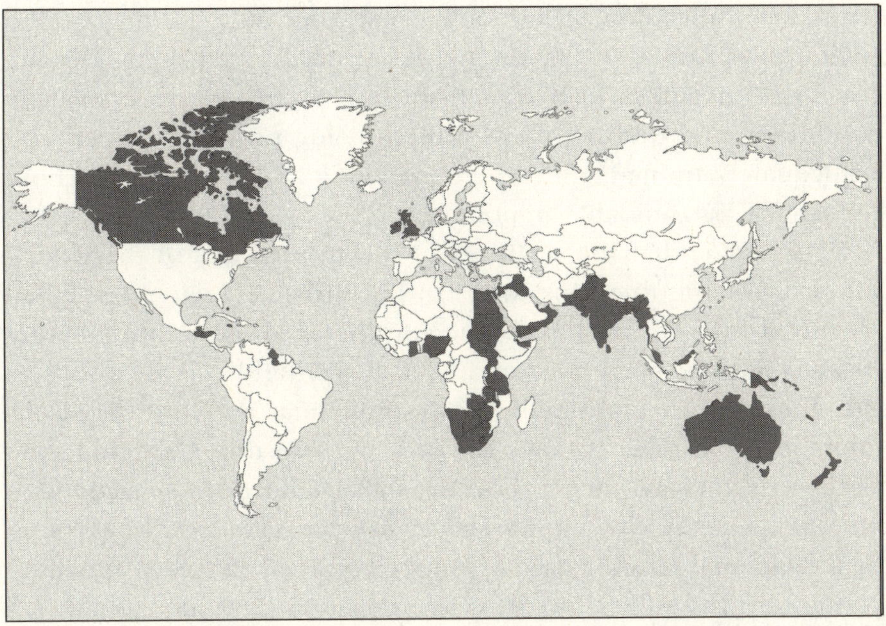

The British Empire in 1914

At the start of the war, Britain had a small, professional army of 2,50,000 Regulars (7,00,000 including Territorials and Reservists) compared to Germany's massive conscript army of

4.5 million. Compared to the other colonies and dominions of the British Empire, India would provide the largest volunteer force of around 1.3 million soldiers, along with an enormous £100 million as contribution for the war effort. The maharajas and nawabs of India, eager to demonstrate their loyalty to the British Crown, also offered generous support in the form of money, troops, and horses. With the memories of the 1857 rebellion still alive, the British administration treaded with caution while ramping up the army in India, closely monitoring any rumours or hostile propaganda. Indian soldiers—predominantly Punjabis, Pathans, Gurkhas, Jats, Garhwalis, Rajputs, and Dogras—boarded ships from ports in Bombay and Karachi, and headed westwards to faraway battlefields in France, Belgium, Egypt, Mesopotamia, Palestine, and Turkey. Mostly illiterate, they were enthused about going to vilayet (foreign lands, often meaning Britain or Europe), but little did they realise what the war was about or the mayhem that awaited them. Despite having no experience in trench warfare or the extreme weather conditions, and despite many of them being poorly equipped and inadequately trained, they fought valiantly and were able to hold up against a formidable opponent.

The war ended the myth about the invincibility of the British Empire. For the first time in centuries, British citizens were killed by enemy fire on British soil. The empire faced several humiliating defeats, like the surrender of 13,000 British and Indian troops to the Turks at Kut-al-Amarah in Mesopotamia, and the disastrous attempt to invade Turkey. Devised by Winston Churchill, the Gallipoli campaign turned into an abject failure when faced with an unexpectedly defiant Turkish army commanded by a young general named Mustafa Kemal. Trapped on the beaches in appalling conditions, the Allied forces suffered around 2,50,000 casualties.[18] The Turkish triumph came within a decade of Japan's crushing victory over Russia.

The United States, which had long held an isolationist policy and had been neutral during the ongoing war, joined the Allied powers in 1917 after several American ships travelling to Britain were sunk by German submarines. The face-off between the United States and Germany was, however, not unexpected. Alfred Mahan had taken note of the waning power of the British and had predicted that Germany's rising demographic and industrial growth and its impending quest for world domination would, at some point, lead to a clash with the United States.

Instead of the quick victory that the Germans had hoped for, the war turned into a protracted, gruelling conflict. Britain and France, with their vast colonial empires and greater depth of resources, proved to be better suited to the long war. Over time, Germany began to run out of steam against the fierce combined resistance of the French forces, Russia's massive war machine, the might of the British Royal Navy, and the arrival of American soldiers on the battlefield.

Struggling with shortages of food and clothing besides the falling morale of civilians and soldiers, Germany realised that it was no longer possible to win the war. By the time the guns went silent in 1918 and the Allied powers emerged victorious, more than 16 million people were dead, including nearly 72,000 Indian soldiers. This industrial war, fought with airplanes, submarines, and tanks, was far more calamitous and consequential than any other war, profoundly changing the way nations looked at technology. It ended four monarchies—German, Ottoman, Austro-Hungarian, and Russian—and paved the way for new nation-states, marking the beginning of the end of colonialism in Asia and Africa. Who would have imagined that twenty years later, another war would erupt that would far eclipse the Great War, killing five times more people.

India after the Great War

Indian political leaders had widely supported the war effort, hoping their allegiance to the Empire would be subsequently rewarded either with greater autonomy or with a gradual shift towards self-rule. Instead, within months of the end of the war, the British authorities imposed the repressive Rowlatt Act that severely curtailed the civil liberties of the Indian people and allowed the government to arrest individuals without any warrant. It was followed by the brutal Jallianwalla Bagh massacre in Amritsar in April 1919, where General Reginald Dyer ordered his troops to open fire on unarmed Indian civilians, slaughtering hundreds and injuring over a thousand people. It left a permanent scar on the nation's psyche, becoming a turning point in the struggle for independence.

Before the recovery from World War I could begin, an even greater devastation swept through the globe. An outbreak of influenza in 1918, commonly known as the Spanish Flu and which most likely originated in the United States, soon turned into a pandemic with the infected troops returning home. In India, as the ships docked in Bombay and soldiers boarded trains to their towns and villages, the disease spread like jungle-fire. The pandemic struck in progressively deadlier waves and infected about 500 million people worldwide, about one-third of the global population, of which around 50 million were dead by 1920. The death toll in India ranged between 10 and 20 million. Aptly referred to as a 'forgotten pandemic', it is puzzling how such a catastrophic episode of history managed to escape the world's collective memory, only to be revisited a century later with the outbreak of COVID-19 in 2020.

The Khilafat Movement

The entry of the Muslim Ottoman Empire in the war as an ally of Germany triggered anxiety among the British authorities regarding the loyalty of Indian Muslims. The Ottoman sultan Mehmed V, as caliph of Muslims the world over, even declared holy war on the Allies, urging all the Muslims in British, French, and Russian dominions to rise up. As the war progressed, Germany and the Ottoman Empire astutely engaged in a propaganda campaign to instigate Indian Muslims to rebel against the British, but other than a handful of incidents of mutiny and defection, they failed to ignite any such uprising.

After the war was over, the Ottoman Empire was to be partitioned into areas of British and French control and influence, sowing the seeds of strife and unrest in the Middle East that have lasted to date. The partition decision aroused fears of disunity among the Muslim community since the Ottoman sultan was seen as the community's overarching leader. Thus began an agitation by Indian Muslims called the Khilafat Movement (1919–1924). Bolstered by Mahatma Gandhi's support, the combined Non-Cooperation and Khilafat movements became the first all-India agitation against the British rule as well as a symbol of Hindu-Muslim solidarity. Ironically, it was the same Khilafat Movement that contributed to reinforcing the Muslim identity in India that prompted a counter movement among the Hindus, thereby marking the beginning of Hindu-Muslim polarisation.

In the interim, the modern nation-state of Turkey was born in 1923, headed by its national hero Mustafa Kemal, who drove the occupying forces out of his homeland and came to be known as Ataturk—Father of the Turks. Embarking upon one of the boldest modernisation drives ever, he declared Turkey a secular state and abolished the Islamic caliphate and Shariah (Islamic law). Women were legally empowered. The fez was outlawed, and veils for women and turbans for men were discouraged, while Western clothing was encouraged; the Arabic alphabet was replaced by the Latin one.

With Kemal abolishing the Ottoman sultanate in 1922, and the caliphate in 1924, the Khilafat Movement lost its footing and quickly dissipated. Kemal was initially popular in India among the Muslims as well as the Hindus for having boldly defied the imperialist powers, but after his modernist policies, his popularity started to wane, especially among the orthodox and older Muslims.

COMRADES AROUND THE WORLD

Though Victorian England had proved its technological might to the world, the Industrial Revolution had not worked out for everyone. A large number of men, women, and even young children performed brutally repetitive work for long hours in noisy, smoke-belching factories—many of them dying due to lung diseases, while the factory owners reaped handsome profits and joined the established land-owning elites. As the Industrial Revolution swept through continental Europe, building fortunes for a few capitalists and bankers, millions were pushed into a life of drudgery.

Karl Marx and his friend, Friedrich Engels, who was the son of a textile firm owner with factories in Germany and Britain, were moved by the plight of the working classes. They believed that exploitation and misery of the working class were endemic to capitalism, and proposed communism, an antithesis of capitalism, and a revolutionary ideology that envisioned a classless society where all the goods and the means of industrial production—such as mines, mills, factories, and railroads—would be publicly owned and run for the benefit of all.

The core idea of communism is an old one. Christianity, Islam, Judaism, and other religions called for egalitarianism, universal sharing, and redistribution of resources for the happiness of all. Philosophers in the sixteenth and seventeenth centuries spoke about such a utopian society. However, it was the Industrial Revolution that was behind the rise of modern communism. *The Communist Manifesto* published by Marx and Engels in 1848 had minimal impact initially, but over the years it turned into one of the world's most influential political documents. Ironically, both Marx and Engels had relocated to London, the epicentre of the Industrial Revolution, where they could freely critique the revolution, unlike in Germany or France. Probably, that very freedom of expression explains why the Industrial Revolution had occurred in Britain in the first place.

John Ruskin too, was outraged and wrote four essays in 1860, condemning the prevailing conditions. They were combined into a book called *Unto this Last,* where he offered a compelling vision of a better society that provided equality and justice for all. It had a transformative impact on Mahatma Gandhi, who translated it into Gujarati in 1908 under the title of *Sarvodaya* (*Well-being of All*).

Somehow, however, communism never took off among the

masses in industrial Britain. Instead, it ended up flourishing in an unlikely country—the primarily agricultural and feudal Russia, where World War I had taken a heavy toll on soldiers and peasants, with food riots breaking out in several Russian cities. Under the leadership of the revolutionary Vladimir Lenin, the Bolsheviks seized state power in October 1917. Lenin then became the premier of a new government based on *soviets* or workers' councils. Private mills, mines, factories, and estates of wealthy landowners were seized and redistributed among the peasants. With the USSR as the centre, communism spread to eastern Europe, Asia, Africa, and later crossed the Atlantic to reach South and Central America (Cuba, Chile), covering a third of the world's area.

Pandit Nehru had closely followed the developments in Russia and had studied the works of Marx and Lenin, which had influenced his views. He travelled to the Soviet Union for the first time in November 1927 along with his father, sister, and wife to attend the tenth anniversary celebrations of the Bolshevik Revolution. The Soviet model left him impressed, and he saw it as a compelling alternative to Western imperialism. Marx and Lenin inspired many other prominent freedom fighters like Lokmanya Tilak, Subhash Chandra Bose, Veer Savarkar, and Bhagat Singh.

When the Great Depression hit the US stock market in 1929, it wiped out millions of investors. Over the next ten years, nearly half of the American banks failed, industrial output crashed, and some 15 million Americans were left unemployed. When a big question mark hung over the fate of the capitalist system, the USSR appeared as a beacon of hope, a better society with its stable economic and political system.

Worth mentioning here is the eventful life of a lesser-known Indian leader named Narendranath Bhattacharya (1887–1954). In his early years as a revolutionary, Bhattacharya was sent on a mission to Indonesia to procure arms. From there he proceeded to Japan and America under a new name—Manabendra Nath Roy. After reading about Marxism in the New York City Public Library, Roy moved to Mexico where he became one of the founders of the

Mexican Communist Party, the first communist party to be set up outside the Soviet Union. Roy's name finally reached Lenin's ears, who invited him to Russia and mentored him personally. Roy was subsequently elected a member of the presidium of the Communist International (Comintern) and sent to China. In October 1920, he issued a manifesto along with a few other comrades in Tashkent, Uzbekistan, calling for the creation of a communist party in India. It was during the rise of Joseph Stalin that Roy fell out of favour and left the mainline communist movement.

Over the years, communism engendered many theoretical debates and evolved into many variants, including some extreme forms like Maoism and Naxalism in India. It turned out that societies with rampant poverty and oppression were most conducive to the communist philosophy. Far from the imagined utopia, the outcome of the communist ideology was authoritarian, repressive regimes, and a staggering 120 million deaths in the twentieth century.

The British victory over France at Waterloo in 1815 was a pivotal milestone that propelled them to the top of the world order. How did they manage to subdue a European powerhouse like France? Industrialisation was undoubtedly a key driver behind the rise of Britain. While everyone agrees that the Industrial Revolution began in Britain in the second half of the eighteenth century, there is a clear lack of consensus on what caused it. Did the subjugation of India have anything to do with it?

3

A TALE OF TWO RIVALS

1700s–1820s

English is just badly pronounced French.

—Georges Clemenceau, French statesman

They were the best of friends. They were the best of enemies. Allies in both the world wars and the Crimean War (1853–1856), Britain and France go way back—nearly 2,000 years when both were imperial provinces of the Roman Empire. The Duke of Normandy (France) invaded England in the year 1066, starting a period called Norman England and bringing French culture to the island. Consequently, around half of modern English words are derived from French. Over the ensuing centuries, the British and the French fought many wars, including the never-ending Hundred Years' War (1337–1453). During the European Enlightenment of the seventeenth and eighteenth centuries, British philosophers were strongly influenced by the intellectual milieu of France, and vice versa.

In the second half of the eighteenth century, a momentous period in world history, Britain and France were involved in a series of wars that were fought around the globe. India and the Americas were the principal theatres of these wars and saw their fortunes diverge sharply. With French assistance, the North American patriots won independence from Britain, their controlling parent. The French Revolution followed soon, where the masses removed the French upper classes in the most violent manner. Around the same time, India was subjugated by a few thousand British men, while the Industrial Revolution was unfolding in Britain. The world would never be the same again.

A GLOBAL RIVALRY

By 1700, France had a population of around 20 million, which was four times that of England, and a proportionately large economy, while possessing the strongest army in Europe. The English were naturally anxious about their powerful neighbour dominating continental Europe. They had historically relied on Scottish soldiers and were worried about a potential alliance between Scotland and France that would have been disastrous for England. Scotland, on the other hand, with only 1 million people, feared getting swallowed and anglicised by England.

Colonies in the New World

England's colonial pursuits in North America were more enthusiastic vis-à-vis France. By the early eighteenth century, it had thirteen well-established colonies along the eastern coast of North America. With a combined population of around 2.5 million people, the colonies generated vast amounts of tobacco, indigo, timber, rice, codfish, and later cotton. The English had established several colleges and universities, which continue to be top-ranked globally to date—Harvard College (1636) was the first one, followed by College of William & Mary (1693). Yale College was established in 1701 and was named after Elihu Yale, who had built a fortune serving in the British East India Company for twenty years, becoming the first president of Fort St. George in Madras (now Chennai).

New France, in comparison, had only 70,000 people, but it had a much larger area to the west of the English colonies, thus blocking their westward expansion. The French were mostly engaged in fur trade, bartering with Native American tribes with whom they had established amicable relations. They had not encouraged large-scale emigration as they were concerned about depopulation in France. Contrarily, the British had allowed their needy and aspirational folks to pursue international opportunities, while simultaneously getting rid of the unwanted and rebellious parts of their population. In his book *The Rise & Fall of the British Empire*, historian Lawrence James attributes the willingness of the English people to emigrate to an old tradition of craftsmen and labourers moving around England looking for work.

Scotland, Europe's poorest independent country then, had watched with envy as England and other European nations had amassed enormous wealth through their colonies overseas. In the 1690s, driven by nationalistic fervour and hoping to catch up, the Scots invested en masse in an ambitious scheme whereby a new colony was to be established on the strategic isthmus of Panama between North and South America. Within two years, however, the overhyped and ill-conceived venture ended up failing miserably, leaving half of the colonists dead and the Scottish economy in ruin. Desperate for economic security, the kingdom of Scotland entered into a union with England and Wales in 1707, under the name of Great Britain. Through the union, the English built political safeguards against France while the Scots gained stability and access to global opportunities.

Trading Companies in the Old World

In India, the Compagnie Française des Indes Orientales (French East India Company) had its base in the coastal town of Pondicherry, which lay between two British posts—Madras (Fort St. George) and Fort St. David (near the town of Cuddalore, Tamil Nadu). The French had also acquired Chandernagore, few kilometres north of British Calcutta. Unlike the British East India Company (EIC), which was a joint-stock company held by shareholders, the Compagnie remained under the firm control of the French government and was run by aristocrats whose raison d'être was power rather than profit. Located next to each other, the British and the French posts were never far from getting embroiled in a conflict.

After only a few decades of its establishment in India, the Compagnie was floundering and on the verge of a collapse, until Joseph Francois Dupleix arrived in India in 1721. Born into a wealthy family, Dupleix was ambitious and hardworking, and he grew the volume of French trade in India immensely while generating a fortune for himself on the side. The EIC officials envied his panache and saw him as their arch-rival. Dupleix envisaged acquiring for France vast territories in India, for which he built an army of native troops.

In 1742, the War of Austrian Succession broke out in Europe with Britain and France on the opposite sides, bringing the conflict into India. Dupleix's large, well-trained native force, supported by a French fleet out of Mauritius, forced British Madras into a surrender. He was now in supreme command and sent an expedition against Fort St. David (1747). But the French invasion was repelled, and a young British officer named Robert Clive came to be noticed for playing his part in the British victory.

Unlike Dupleix, Clive was born into a poor family in Shropshire, England. A troublemaker from an early age, Clive was expelled from three schools and had developed a reputation for being violent and quarrelsome. At one point, he led a gang that terrorised the town's shopkeepers into paying them protection money. A career in India was a good option for such unworthy men in Britain, which is why Clive's father had shipped him to India at the age of eighteen as a clerk and bookkeeper for the EIC. Desperately unhappy after arriving in India and suffering from depression, Clive tried to shoot himself twice.

The war in Europe ended in 1748, and Madras was restored to the British, but Dupleix did not give up on his aggressive plans and started taking sides in local rivalries. His contenders won virtually all of southern India and reciprocated with land grants and loot. Dupleix had reached a peak and for some time seemed well placed to take control of other parts of India. He even started dressing like an Indian prince. The British camp was disheartened; it wasn't a great situation to be in after having been around in India for nearly 150 years. Clive returned to his clerical duty.

Much of what we know about Dupleix and Pondicherry in those decades is through the diary of the Hindu merchant Ananda Ranga Pillai (1709–1761) who maintained it faithfully for twenty-five years. Pillai had risen to a position of great influence as an interpreter and the chief agent for the French colony. He admired Dupleix and was a keen supporter of his imperial ambitions, preferring his rule over that of the Marathas or the Muslim powers of South India. He wrote in his diary, 'If his (Dupleix's) courage, character, bearing, greatness of mind, and skill in the battlefield, were put to the test, he could be compared only with the Emperor Aurangzeb, and Louis XIV; and not with any other monarch.'

In 1751, the Nawab of Carnatic, a French ally, besieged a British-supported ruler at the fortress of Trichinopoly (now Tiruchirappalli) when Clive turned the tables, outmanoeuvring his opponents. This feat proved to be a watershed in the British contest with the French. As Clive's stars kept rising, Dupleix's ambitious schemes continued to fail. Dupleix was asked to return to France in 1754 where he found himself financially ruined and died in obscurity. French historians have insisted that it was Dupleix who invented the strategies of indirect rule and the induction and training of native troops, which Clive would later emulate. It was Dupleix's ambition that inspired the British to embark upon a career of conquest in India.

World War Zero

Concurrently, in North America, a skirmish broke out between the British and the French in May 1754. A small group of British soldiers from the colony of Virginia, under the command of a tall, well-built young officer named George Washington, attempted to expel the French from a disputed territory and ended up killing several of their men. This skirmish sparked off a war that came to be called the Seven Years' War (1756–1763) and was fought around the globe; some historians have called it World War Zero.

While Britain's Prussian allies helped contain France in Europe, British naval strength enabled them to seize Quebec, Montreal, and Louisbourg in North America. When word about the war reached India, the British forces captured French Chandernagore and Pondicherry.

With the Treaty of Paris (1763), France had lost its colonial empire. In North America, they ceded Canada and the lands east of the Mississippi River to Britain. French Louisiana (most of today's central United States) and New Orleans went to Spain as compensation, while France retained the sugar-rich islands of Guadeloupe and Martinique in the Caribbean. In India, the French were permitted to return to their posts but forbidden from maintaining any troops. Voltaire, the most influential French writer and philosopher of his time, played down the loss of French territory in North America as a 'few acres of snow', but deeply lamented the loss of India, reflecting the wider sentiment in France.

Many men from the dismantled French army in India joined the forces of native rulers as mercenaries, while some even moved to the EIC. One such French soldier was Claude Martin, who rose to the rank of major general in the EIC army. He spent twenty-four years of his life in Lucknow, where he became the richest European and left a substantial legacy in the form of writings, buildings, and educational institutions, like the prestigious La Martiniere school.[1]

The United States is Born

The Seven Years' War had created a massive war debt for the British, and they looked for ways of recovering it from their American colonies, like imposing a sugar tax or stamp duty. These burdensome measures had created deep resentment in the colonies. When the king allowed the EIC to dump its surplus tea from Asia directly in the American colonies and undersell colonial merchants, the colonists were enraged. Fearing a repeat of EIC's acts of exploitation in India, the colonists boarded three British ships in the Boston harbour on a cold December night in 1773, and emptied 342 chests of EIC tea into the water in an act of protest which came to be known as the Boston Tea Party.

Estrangement continued to grow between the colonies and the British Crown, ultimately spurring a colonial rebellion led by George Washington. The French, who were resentful over losing their vast colonial possessions, saw the rebellion as an opportunity to get even with the British. In 1778, they formally recognised the United States as a sovereign nation and declared war on Britain. The Spaniards and the Dutch followed, making things worse for the British. Finally, the combined Franco-American army under the command of General Washington surrounded the British army, led by General Charles Cornwallis, at Yorktown, and the French navy cut off any relief. Cornwallis surrendered in October 1781 and another Treaty of Paris was signed in 1783, which formally ended the War of American Independence. Britain handed all the land east of the Mississippi River to the United States, doubling the size of the newly created nation.

An independent state born out of opposition to an all-powerful colonial empire, the United States had set a precedent for similar movements in the rest of the Americas against the Spanish and the Portuguese empires.

The Land Down Under

The loss of the American colonies was a big blow to the British and it left King George III in shock for several months. That was when the Pacific region came into focus with Australia emerging as the alternative to American colonies for dumping convicts, who were crowding prisons in Britain. The first fleet of eleven ships arrived in Australia in January 1788. Britain and France already had an intense rivalry going on to the Pacific and had been sending exploratory expeditions to the Pacific Ocean since the 1750s. James

Cook, the British navigator, cartographer, and captain in the Royal Navy, turned out to be the most accomplished of all the explorers of the Pacific and claimed Australia and New Zealand for the British Crown. Here again, compared to the French, the British were far more active as colonisers.

The French Revolution

As the eighteenth century drew to a close, the French monarchy was facing an unexpected foe that was even more formidable than Britain—its own people. By helping the American colonies break free from Britain, France had avenged its earlier losses but had gained little else. The mountains of war debt and years of mismanagement by the monarchy had bankrupted the nation, leaving the masses deprived and hungry. Showing utter disregard for the misery of their subjects, King Louis XVI and Queen Marie Antoinette continued with a lavish lifestyle of elaborate rituals and extravagant expenditure on fashion and luxuries at Versailles, a few kilometres south of Paris.

Amidst the rumblings of discontent in Paris, however, the city was bursting with intellectual energy as thinkers and scholars were vigorously debating new ideas in salons. In that era of enlightenment, reason and science began to question the age-old class divide between the nobility and the poor, just when the notion of individual rights arrived from the United States as an inspiration.

As the price of bread spiralled out of control, hunger and desperation gave way to rage, and riots broke out. The French Revolution (1789–1799) turned into the bloodiest uprising Europe had ever known, but it was one of the most significant events in history that would have repercussions not only in Europe, but in other societies throughout the world. The absolute monarchy that had ruled France for centuries was overthrown violently by the masses; Louis XVI and Marie Antoinette were guillotined, sending shock waves throughout Europe and the rest of the world. French society underwent an unprecedented transformation as aristocratic privileges and hierarchy were replaced by the new principles of equal opportunity, freedom of speech, and democracy.

The French nation was now hungry for a hero and it found one in a young and ambitious artillery officer named Napoleon Bonaparte, who had risen through the military ranks and seized political power. Napoleon would go on to become a national hero in France and one of the greatest military generals and statesmen in history.

The Egyptian Campaign

A paragon of optimism and confidence, Napoleon strode with élan and led daring war campaigns in Europe, forcing France's adversaries into submission. Gauging that the time was not yet ripe for a duel with Britain, France's ultimate enemy, Napoleon planned an invasion of Egypt to disrupt British trade routes and, in consequence, threaten their possessions in India. In May 1798, an armada carrying 30,000 troops sailed from France to Egypt.

For centuries, Egypt had been ruled by the Muslim Mamluks, whose outdated army was no match for Napoleon's modern weaponry. The Mamluk forces were overwhelmed within two hours of battle, losing nearly 6,000 men while the French had only thirty casualties. Napoleon's army entered Cairo the next day, and thus began a three-year-long French occupation of Egypt, marking the beginning of European incursions into the Middle East. 'I was full of dreams,' Napoleon later mused, 'I saw myself founding a new religion, marching into Asia riding an elephant, a turban on my head, and in my hand the new Koran.'

The French invasion of Egypt set off alarm bells in London and British India, prompting plans to counter the threat. Within months, Napoleon's dreams of conquering Asia were abruptly halted when the British admiral Horatio Nelson, who once famously said to a naval recruit, 'You must hate a Frenchman as you hate the devil', tracked down the French fleet east of Alexandria in August 1798 and destroyed it in a daring attack. More than 3,000 French sailors were killed or injured, while another 3,000 were taken prisoners. Napoleon's propaganda machine, nonetheless, managed to portray the disastrous campaign in Egypt as a grand success to the French people.

When the Russian Czar Turned His Gaze to India

After the debacle in Egypt, Napoleon soon got another opportunity to threaten British India. In the year 1800, Paul I, the impulsive and tyrannical czar of Russia, suggested to Napoleon a joint invasion of India. Paul proposed that a force of 35,000 Russian Cossacks would advance across Central Asia and a French army contingent would meet them in Astrabad (modern-day Gorgan, Iran). The combined force would then trek through Persia and Afghanistan into India, and unleash a massive onslaught against the British. While the czar was bubbling with enthusiasm over his audacious and clever scheme, Napoleon was not convinced. Doubting the czar's understanding of the 2,000 kilometre-long long route from Astrabad to the Indus and the logistical complexities involved in the suggested undertaking, he turned down the proposition. Nevertheless, undeterred by Napoleon's refusal, Paul decided to go alone. In January 1801, a 22,000-strong Cossack army embarked upon the bold expedition. Shortly into the journey, however, they received news of the czar's assassination and had to abort their mission and retreat. The soldiers were fortunate, as without the requisite knowledge of the harsh terrain and conditions that lay ahead, the contingent would have certainly perished en route.[2]

The Final Lap

While Britain dominated the oceans, France was the unmatched power on the European continent—a juxtaposition that has been referred to as the whale versus the elephant. In 1804, at age thirty-five, Napoleon crowned himself the emperor of France at the Notre Dame cathedral in Paris. The next year, he began planning a bold invasion of Britain with 2,000 warships carrying 2,00,000 soldiers. Although the British were poorly defended on their land, they had the world's greatest navy protecting the English Channel, which ultimately forced Napoleon to forsake his plans.

In October 1805, while Napoleon was preparing to fight the combined forces of the Austrians and the Russians, Admiral Nelson, in an encore performance, led his fleet to one of the greatest victories for Britain, wiping out Napoleon's fleet off the Cape of Trafalgar in south-west Spain. Though Nelson lost his life in the battle, the triumph cemented his position as one of the greatest heroes in British history. Never again would the French challenge the might of the British navy, which would dominate the world's oceans for a century.

Lacking the naval strength to successfully take on the British, Napoleon now turned to economic warfare. He imposed an embargo on the European nations under his control against trade with Britain, which came to be known as the Continental Blockade. In Asia, he used the Dutch island of Java as a springboard for attacking British ships, which left Lord Minto, the then governor general of India, a worried man. Minto appointed an EIC administrator named Stamford Raffles as his agent to prepare the way for a naval invasion of Java, which was launched in June 1811 from Malacca. Java fell without a struggle. Eight years later, Raffles would found Singapore, his long-envisioned port at the strategic exit of the Strait of Malacca.

Russia had agreed to be part of Napoleon's Continental Blockade, but later reneged from the treaty. Incensed at this betrayal, and suspecting its alliance with Britain, Napoleon led an army of 6,00,000 men—*le Grand Armee*, the largest in the history of Europe up to that time—into Russia in 1812. Napoleon had prophesied that the invasion would be over in twenty days, but things turned out differently. As the icy Russian winter set in, the campaign began to flounder and his forces began retreating. The invasion ended in a catastrophe with barely 1,00,000 soldiers making it out of Russia. Napoleon later admitted that the Russian campaign was his greatest mistake. From then on, his empire began to crumble as much of Europe united against him.

Napoleon's storied military career came to an end in June 1815 at the Battle of Waterloo, near Brussels, where he was crushed by a coalition force commanded by Arthur Wellesley, the Duke of Wellington, alongside the Prussian army. Napoleon was exiled to one of the remotest places on the planet, St. Helena, a tiny island in the South Atlantic Ocean, where the once-great emperor lived out the rest of his days in boredom and despair. Waterloo ended any hopes of France challenging Britain again and paved the way for Britain to become the world's first superpower.

Meanwhile, in Latin America, where the American and French revolutions had inspired independence movements, it was the Napoleonic invasion of Spain and Portugal in 1808 that gave the final impetus to those endeavours for freedom. Within a short span, between 1810 and 1824, most of the nations—Mexico, Chile, Argentina, Colombia, Venezuela, Brazil, Ecuador, Peru, and Bolivia—gained their independence.

In the decades following Waterloo, the French recovered, but instead of challenging their old rival, they chose to become a political ally, joining the British in the Crimean War against Russia and the Second Opium War against China. They resumed their colonial ambitions, beginning with the invasion of Algeria in 1830, and later with incursions into Indo-China (Vietnam, Cambodia, and Laos) and other parts of Africa.

BATTLEGROUND INDIA

While the European trading companies had a presence along the coasts of India in the seventeenth century, the vast Indian subcontinent was ruled by the Mughal emperors out of their imperial capitals of Delhi and Agra. For them, these trading companies were small fish lurking on the coasts. Nonetheless, the emperors had taken note of the Europeans' naval firepower and were often impressed by the demeanour of the Western visitors to their courts. They also appreciated the inflow of European bullion, which helped them fund their war machine.

After Mughal Emperor Aurangzeb's death in 1707, the political landscape changed drastically as the empire started to disintegrate and regional nawabs and rajas began squabbling over territory. Sensing an opportunity, the Persian conqueror Nader Shah descended through the Khyber Pass into the plains of India in 1739 and crushed the Mughal army. This was followed by his triumphant march into Delhi and unrestrained plunder for two months. He returned to Persia with a caravan of thousands of horses, camels, and elephants laden with gold and silver. He also carried back with him the famed Peacock Throne that was studded with precious stones and said to cost up to four times as much as the Taj Mahal, along with the famous Koh-i-Noor diamond and its sibling, the Darya-i-Noor. A few years later, when Nader Shah was assassinated, his cavalry commander and protégé, Ahmad Shah Abdali, was elected by the Afghan chiefs as shah. Abdali founded the Durrani Empire and acquired the Koh-i-Noor, which would remain in the possession of Durrani rulers for over six decades until it was given to the Sikh ruler Maharaja Ranjit Singh as a gift.

Also known as the founder of modern Afghanistan, Abdali raided India several times, sacking the key Mughal cities of Lahore, Delhi, and Agra, among others. The already waning Mughal prestige was now left in tatters.

As the Mughal power was fading, the Maratha Empire kept expanding under a string of capable leaders and generals such as Baji Rao, whom General Montgomery, of World War II fame, called one of history's greatest cavalry generals.[3] At its peak, the Maratha Empire stretched from Attock on the Indus River till Thanjavur in southern India. Dismayed at the loss of Mughal domains to the ever-growing Maratha Empire, Shah Waliullah Dehlavi, a prominent Islamic scholar of Delhi, invited Abdali to fight the Marathas. In a historic battle, the two forces met at Panipat in 1761, where Abdali handed a shock defeat to the Marathas. Henceforth, the dominance of the Maratha Empire ended and gave way to a loose confederacy of various Maratha factions in Maharashtra, Baroda, Nagpur, Indore, and Gwalior.

British Rule Begins

Before the Seven Years' War had reached the shores of India, another storm had been brewing in eastern India. The nawab of Bengal, India's richest province, died in 1756 and was replaced by his headstrong, twenty-year-old nephew Siraj ud-Daula. A dispute with the British about fortifying Calcutta provoked Nawab Siraj ud-Daula to gather a large army and capture the fort there. The Company officials in Madras were incensed and started planning a retaliatory expedition for Bengal. In the meantime, Clive struck a deal with Mir Jafar, the nawab's uncle and also the general of his army, who held his own ambitions to rule the province and was thus ready to betray the nawab. It is to the credit of Jafar, who played his part in the fixed match, that Clive's 3,000 troops prevailed over the nawab's army of 50,000 men at at the Battle of Plassey (1757). The nawab fled from the battlefield and the battle was over, becoming a turning point in India's history. As agreed, Clive enthroned Jafar as the new nawab of Bengal, while Siraj ud-Daula was captured and executed.

Soon, a hundred boats loaded with treasure were sailing downriver to the EIC headquarter in Calcutta, just like Nader Shah's caravan loaded with treasures had exited from the Khyber Pass a few years earlier. As a personal gift from Jafar, Clive received £234,000 in cash, along with land grants and an annual pension of £27,000, while the Company received £3 million annually for three years. It was around this time that the Indian word 'loot' entered the English language. George Bruce Malleson, in *The Decisive Battles of India* (1883), described Plassey as the most unheroic English victory.

The EIC's run continued with a decisive victory over the combined forces of the states of Bengal, Awadh, and the Mughal emperor, which gave them the *diwani*—the authority to raise taxes—of Bengal, Bihar, and Orissa (now Odisha). It was the first time in

250 years that a European trading company had advanced inland. British 'rule' in India had begun. When the Company employees saw the early revenue figures in 1765, they were dumbstruck. From then on, the EIC started paying for Indian goods with the taxes collected from India, putting an end to the eastward flow of bullion, which had been a cause of worry in the West since the days of the Romans.

Clive returned to England at age thirty-five, the richest man in Europe. He bought tens of thousands of acres of land, built an opulent house, collected fine art, bought seats in the Parliament for himself and for his family and friends.[4] While a noble in Britain could live well on £800 a year, even junior company employees were returning with fortunes. The nouveau riche returnees were derided for the vulgar display of their new-found wealth and were called *nabobs* (from nawabs). A deluge of job applications followed for a career in India, with many offering large bribes.

Not only England, but also Scotland, especially the city of Edinburgh, started to see riches pouring in from India. English and Scottish remittance agencies that assisted in transferring funds from India to England and Scotland opened in Bengal, Madras, and London. Edinburgh was transformed with the new estates and mansions that began to dot the city, as well as with the emergence of new suburbs.[5] At the same time, Glasgow, Scotland's other major city, was witnessing a similar economic boom built on its tobacco trade with America, paving the way for the Scottish Enlightenment, an intellectual revolution where greats like Adam Smith and David Hume pioneered world-changing ideas.

Being over six months of travel away from Britain, India was wide open to exploitation and manipulation by EIC employees. Between 1765 and 1770, they raised the taxes in Bengal by three times from the already high rates imposed by the erstwhile nawab. The poor masses were pushed into starvation as famine hit Bengal in 1770, killing 10 million from its population of 30 million. Adam Smith denounced the Company as a 'bloodstained monopoly that was burdensome, useless and responsible for massacres in Bengal'.

A few years later, Clive died in England under mysterious circumstances, most likely having committed suicide. His reputation remained under a cloud.

The Mysore Wars

Meanwhile, in southern India, Hyder Ali, a commander in the service of Mysore's Hindu Wodeyar king, usurped the throne in 1761 and declared himself the sultan. Hyder established his capital at Seringapatam (modern-day Srirangapatnam) near Mysore and became a major challenger to the EIC forces. Impressed by the French military methods, Hyder became an ardent student of French tactics and recruited their artillery experts. Realising the need for a navy to survive against British dominance, he started building one. He employed a Dutch shipwright named Joze Azelars, who designed and built several warships, and recruited European mercenary sailors including a commander named Stannett. The navy was meant to open further communication links with the French and boost Mysore's maritime trade.

While Bangalore (now Bengaluru) is known to many Americans today as the outsourcing destination, not many know of nearby Mysore or Seringapatam. However, over two centuries ago, when American patriots were fighting for independence, Mysore, Seringapatam, Hyder, and his son Tipu Sultan were familiar references in American newspapers and everyday conversations. Mysore, it is said, was one of the first states to recognise the newly independent United States. In 1781, the Pennsylvania legislature readied a warship named *Hyder Ally* to demonstrate their support for Mysore against their common oppressor. Philip Freneau, the 'Poet of the American Revolution', wrote a poem in honour of the ship:

From an Eastern prince, she takes her name,
Who, smit with freedom's sacred flame
Usurping Britons brought to shame,
His country's wrongs avenging.

In 1782, triggered by the ongoing American Revolution, a powerful American-allied French navy fought a series of battles against the British navy in the Indian Ocean. Combined with Hyder's forces, this joint attack could have seriously jeopardised the British foothold in South India, but the British fleet was able to defend against the attack. Hyder died in December 1782, and the next year the Treaty of Paris was signed, which prevented any French fleet from challenging the British in the Indian Ocean again.

Mysore's war against the British was continued by Tipu Sultan, who built one of the most technologically advanced fighting forces on the Indian subcontinent, and continued to invest in his navy and in innovations like the lethal, iron-clad Mysore Rockets. It was Hyder and Tipu's openness to learning from the French that made them the most potent threat to the British.[6]

Looking beyond India for alliances, Tipu sent a high-powered delegation to Constantinople in 1785, seeking military assistance from the Ottoman sultan against the British. However, the sultan was unable to offer any help as he depended on British support against the Russians. Hoping to build a front against the British, Tipu then reached out to King Zaman Shah of Afghanistan, the grandson of Abdali, as well as the Shah of Persia, appealing to their religious sentiments. In 1787, Tipu dispatched a mission to Versailles, seeking an alliance with Louis XVI, proposing that 10,000 French soldiers be based in Seringapatam. Louis XVI accepted all the lavish gifts but could not offer any help as France was going through the most turbulent times. He would be beheaded in a public square in Paris a few years later.

In the British camp, meanwhile, General Cornwallis got a chance to redeem himself after the humiliating surrender to Washington in America. In 1786, he accepted the appointment as governor general and commander-in-chief of the EIC in India. Having learnt a hard lesson in America, Cornwallis ensured that a settled colonial class did not emerge in India by imposing measures like banning employment in the EIC of the offsprings of those British men who had taken Indian wives.[7] From there on, Indian mistresses and wives were replaced by memsahibs, allegedly snooty British women, who further distanced their men from the natives. After a disappointing campaign against Tipu Sultan in 1790, Cornwallis allied with Mysore's enemies (the Marathas and the Nizam of Hyderabad), and in 1792, defeated Tipu, seizing half his kingdom and taking his two young sons as hostages.

Cornwallis returned to Britain in 1794, and a few years later he was appointed the lord lieutenant and commander-in-chief of Ireland (1798–1801). His appointment came just before the outbreak of the Irish Rebellion of 1798 against the British Government, but he managed to suppress it. He was instrumental in achieving the passage of the Act of Union (1801), which created the United Kingdom of Great Britain and Ireland, thus ending the nominal independence of Ireland. Under Cornwallis, Irish Catholic tenants lost control to Protestant landowners, similar to the Zamindari system that he had introduced in India under the Permanent Settlement Act (1793). After Zamindari, two more land revenue systems were introduced in India by the EIC–Ryotwari and Mahalwari. These systems would ultimately turn into instruments of exploitation leading to large-scale dispossession and rural indebtedness.

In the meantime, Tipu had been exchanging letters with Napoleon, seeking French support for defending Mysore against the British, and Napoleon had assured 'Tippoo Sahib' that a large force would be dispatched from Egypt to India to help him drive away the British. The new British governor general, Richard Wellesley, was concerned over Tipu's attempted liaison with the French and the Ottomans. Wellesley was an aggressive expansionist and a staunch Francophobe, even though he was married to a glamorous French woman. He wrote to the Ottoman sultan in Constantinople to discourage Tipu from his stance. The sultan wrote to Tipu in 1798, warning him against the French, the enemies of Islam, who had invaded Egypt without any justification.

After his men intercepted Tipu's letters to Napoleon, Wellesley had enough pretext to launch an offensive. Under the command of his younger brother, Arthur Wellesley, the future victor at Waterloo, and General Harris, a large army of 21,000 soldiers was mobilised, and it stormed Seringapatam on 4 May 1799. Tipu was killed, and his death was followed by a customary plunder of the city by the winning troops. For the EIC, the victory yielded a massive cache of jewellery, arms, cash, and souvenirs. The storming of Seringapatam remained one of the most dramatic battles for the British and was captured in many paintings and written accounts.

After the defeat at Waterloo in 1815, France abandoned any military ambitions in India, restricting itself to the management of its small ports. Mauritius and a few other islands were handed over to the British. With the French out of their way, the British continued with aggressive expansion. By 1818, they had overpowered the weakened and divided Maratha confederacy through diplomacy and wars, thereby gaining control over a large part of India.

THE STUDY OF INDIA—FOR RIVALRY, CURIOSITY OR CONTROL

In the wake of European merchants, who mostly stuck to the coastal trading ports, came Jesuit missionaries who ventured deep into India, meeting the locals, understanding the cultures and customs of the land, and documenting their observations. In 1718, Abbe Bignon, librarian to the king of France, invited French missionaries active in Asia to collect and send back manuscripts and ancient texts, in an attempt to create an Oriental section in the Royal Library in Paris. Hundreds of manuscripts in Sanskrit and Tamil started arriving at the library, turning into a rich collection. By the mid-eighteenth century, the French were clearly ahead of the British in their exploration of Indian texts and culture, as the British were still focused on trading.

The French were also ahead in mapmaking. In 1752, geographer and cartographer Jean-Baptiste Bourguignon d'Anville, whose maps were known for accuracy and were keenly tracked by the British, made the first map showing India as a whole. The British geographer

James Rennell later used details gathered from extensive surveys and projected them over d'Anville's map of India to construct his map of 'Hindoostan' in 1782, which was the first nearly accurate map of India.[8]

Besides the competition over territory and trade, an intellectual rivalry had arisen between Britain and France over uncovering India's (and the Orient's) antiquities, where Paris-born scholar and linguist Abraham Hyacinthe Anquetil-Duperron established an early lead. In 1755, he travelled to India at the age of twenty-four, hoping to learn Sanskrit from the Brahmins of Varanasi, a feat no European scholar had achieved. However, the timing of his adventure was not in his favour. He had planned to travel from the French trading post of Chandernagore in Bengal up the Ganges to Varanasi, but he found himself caught in the turmoil between the British and the nawab of Bengal. After an agonising escape to Pondicherry, Anquetil decided on an alternative plan—to head to Surat in Gujarat and learn ancient Persian from the Parsis, a community of Zoroastrians who had fled their ancestral home in Persia centuries ago. His bad luck, however, continued as Surat was captured by a British fleet in 1761, although by then he had managed to acquire over 200 ancient Persian and Sanskrit manuscripts. He was allowed to return to Europe on a British ship, but his journey was marked throughout by harassment, which turned him into a life-long detractor of the British Empire.

Warren Hastings, the first governor general of Bengal, who professed, 'I love India a little more than my own country', had a practical problem at hand. Vast regions of India, teeming with millions of people, had to be administered by a handful of British officers, for whom Indian languages, customs, and traditions were altogether alien. That being so, Hastings encouraged the study of ancient Indian texts among British scholars, who approached the Brahmins, a small minority group who were the sole authorities in Sanskrit works. The colonial scholars thus learnt about India from a Brahminic perspective. Nathaniel Halhed published *A Code of Gentoo Laws,* which came to serve as a foundation for Company-administered Hindu courts, and Charles Wilkins began translating the *Bhagavad Gita.*

Meanwhile, Anquetil created a sensation in Europe when he published a French translation of the Zoroastrian *Zend-avesta,* a millennia-old collection of scriptures central to Zoroastrianism. Until then, the Hebrew scriptures were considered to be the most ancient religious texts.

In another work, Anquetil criticised the British portrayal of Asian empires and societies as inherently despotic and oppressive, arguing that it was nothing but a means for men like Warren Hastings to justify their rapacious rule. Citing Mughal chronicles, he showed that the Mughal Empire did have governing rules, and it was the British who had actually introduced despotism in India.

When Anquetil disparaged the scholarship of some of the learned members of the University of Oxford,[9] one person took serious offence at his words—a scholar named William Jones who wrote an anonymous letter to Anquetil, expressing his indignation in harsh words. Known as 'Oriental Jones', he had mastered thirteen languages, including Persian and Arabic, which he had learnt from a man called Mirza, a Syrian at Oxford.[10]

As chance would have it, in 1784, William Jones was posted as a judge for the EIC in Calcutta, which would become his home for the next ten years until he died in 1794. Within months of his arrival, Jones founded the Asiatic Society of Bengal, which became a repository of the linguistic, cultural, and historical legacy of India. He spelt out his personal objective in a letter: 'It is my ambition to know India better than any other European ever knew it.' In his sixth anniversary discourse, pronounced before the members of the Asiatic Society, Jones said: 'By united efforts, the French have compiled their stupendous repositories of universal knowledge; and by united efforts only can we hope to rival them, or to diffuse over our own country and the rest of Europe the lights attainable by our Asiatick Researches.'

Jones's translation of Kalidasa's fifth-century masterpiece *Abhijnana shakuntalam* made him a national hero in Britain.

The popular press repeatedly described him as the scholar who had established intellectual superiority over rival Anquetil and France. His attempts at comparing Indian and Greek religion and mythology kindled the romantic imagination in Europe. Jones is widely recognised for his observation that Sanskrit had a strong resemblance to Greek, Latin, and Persian, and is also credited for establishing that the 'Sandracottos' mentioned in ancient Greek texts was none other than Chandragupta Maurya who founded the Maurya Empire in the fourth century BCE. We shall visit this topic in detail in Chapters 9 and 10.

In the interim, Anquetil continued his research in Paris and published *Historical and Geographical Research on India* (1786) and *India in Rapport with Europe* (1798). He introduced to the Europeans another Eastern gem—a Persian text called *Sirr-i-Akbar* or 'The Great Secret' that he translated to French and Latin. *Sirr-i-Akbar* itself was a seventeenth-century Persian translation of the ancient *Upanishads* by Dara Shikoh, the scholarly son of the Mughal emperor Shah Jahan. The text was brought to France by Francois Bernier, who had served as a physician in the Mughal court. Anquetil's translation of *Sirr-i-Akbar* remained the only one for a long time and it deeply moved the German philosopher Arthur Schopenhauer. It was the works of Anquetil and other such scholars that helped crystalise Voltaire's belief that the accomplishments of the ancient East could rival or even supercede those of the Greco-Roman civilisation.

The British scholars may have seen Anquetil as a rival, but ended up emulating his image as an Orientalist-adventurer; Anquetil's spirit of inquiry became a key feature of the imperial vision of the British. Their military victories over the French in India brought them increased access to native elites, manuscripts, and other resources, putting their scholars at a distinct advantage over the French. EIC employees posted in all corners of India started gathering and submitting reports about inscriptions, monuments, manuscripts, and coins that the Asiatic Society could collate and publish.

Notwithstanding that the French state had lost out in the colonial competition in India, its intellectuals were unexpectedly successful at constructing a scholarly conception of India and its past. In 1814, they created the first chair of Sanskrit at the College de France, and the Société Asiatique was founded in 1822. Paris became the mecca of Indology where aspiring German Indologists headed to learn Sanskrit. To European scholars and romanticists, India became the cradle of civilisation, an inspiration for another Renaissance that would be different from the earlier Greco-Roman Renaissance.

Abbe J.A. Dubois, a French missionary who arrived in India in 1792, saw the region in a different perspective. He spent thirty years in the deep hinterlands and wrote a highly influential book called *Hindu Manners, Customs and Ceremonies.* In spite of being filled with disdain for the conditions and ignorant practices prevalent in India, his work was a unique and detailed record of Hindu rituals of various castes.

Since Indians lacked the tradition of recording events chronologically and writing history in a way the Europeans were familiar with, they were deemed to be an ahistorical people. British historian James Mill completed his colossal *History of British India* in 1817 after a twelve-year effort. He never visited India and relied much on the works of Dubois, and the accounts of British men returning from India. His book popularised the image of an India that was mired in ignorance and superstition, a land that was perpetually backward and inferior as a civilisation. It became the most important book at the East India College (later Haileybury) where the civil servants and other officers were trained before heading to India.

Initiatives of documenting customs and manners, translating Indian literature, interpreting archaeological finds, and writing history would become a blueprint for the future British rule over the entire Indian subcontinent. In a similar move, when Napoleon invaded Egypt in 1798, he brought with him more than one hundred savants to study the ancient land—its antiquities, artefacts, natural specimens, and music. The scholarly initiative formed the basis for the nineteenth century's most significant publishing project, the *Description de l'Egypte.*[11]

Were the French and the British merely trying to establish their lead in the field of Oriental studies or was there an ulterior motive? Edward Said, professor at Columbia University, asserted that there was indeed an ulterior motive. In his groundbreaking book *Orientalism* (1978), he argued that the colonising West (primarily Britain and France) created the false and romanticised notion of the Orient to subjugate and control it, portraying Eastern societies as exotic, yet primitive and inferior, thereby providing an implicit justification for its imperial ambitions. From Professor Said's perspective, the real British rule in India began not with Clive's war at Plassey, rather with Hastings's and Jones's 'study' of India.

The Orientalist perspective shaped not only the European conception of India, but also the way Indians viewed their own culture and history. Historian Romila Thapar writes in *The Penguin History of Early India*:

> A dichotomy in values was maintained, Indian values being described as 'spiritual' and European values as 'materialistic', with little attempt to juxtapose these values with the reality of Indian society. This theme has been even more firmly endorsed by a section of Indian opinion during the last hundred years. It was a consolation to the Indian intelligentsia for its perceived inability to counter the technical superiority of the west, a superiority viewed as having enabled Europe to colonise Asia and other parts of the world.

Given the prevalence of the Orientalist discourse and the manipulative tendency of the colonial masters, it is tempting to paint all the Westerners in India with one stroke. But that would be unfair to the soldiers, administrators, and scholars who toiled for years to uncover the past for the sake of nothing other than sheer curiosity and passion, men like Alexander Cunningham, James Prinsep, and Aurel Stein, whom we shall meet in later chapters.

REVERSE TRAVELOGUES

The second half of the eighteenth century saw a unique new development: Indian travellers heading to the West and writing what came to be called 'reverse travelogues'—accounts describing what the West was like to Indian eyes. These travel accounts help us draw a meaningful and qualitative comparison of the cultural, political, and economic situation in the West vis-à-vis India, which is something that economic historians otherwise derive based on speculative assumptions.

One of the earliest reverse travelogues is an account in Persian called *Shigurf Nama-i Vilayat*, translated as *The Wonders of Vilayet*. It was written by Mirza Sheikh I'tesamuddin, who was born in 1730 to an elite Muslim family of Bengal. I'tesamuddin began his career as a munshi to Mir Jafar, the nawab of Bengal, and later entered the service of the EIC, where he got an opportunity to travel to England via France in 1766, and returned to India after three years.

I'tesamuddin's account starts with his enthusiasm for the journey, which was mixed with frightful anxiety over leaving his homeland. He was very observant in describing different kinds of ships and noticed that the Europeans were superior in the art of navigation and were constantly trying to improve their skills. I'tesamuddin was much taken by London, which he described as 'no city on earth as large or beautiful'. The British Museum, which was fairly new, having opened its doors in 1759, left him thoroughly impressed. He marvelled at the treatises in Arabic, Greek, Syrian, and Chinese, and the versions of the Persian *Zend-avesta*, and the Vedas, besides the many other curiosities he saw in the museum. He also visited Oxford University, which he referred to as an 'ancient madrasah'.

I'tesamuddin's sadness over the passing away of the glory days of the Mughals somehow did not cloud his perception of the British people. For him, the journey to vilayet was an enriching experience that brought him closer to understanding the powerful Europeans who had successfully charted the seas and subjugated India.

Another such early traveller to Europe was Mirza Abu Taleb

Khan. He recorded his three years in Europe in his memoir *Masir Talib fi Bilad Afranji,* translated as *The Travels of Taleb in the Regions of Europe,* which is even more detailed than I'tesamuddin's account.

Taleb was born in Lucknow and had spent years in the service of the Muslim governors of Bengal and Awadh. In the 1790s, however, as fate would have it, he ended up in Calcutta, unemployed and depressed. Seeing him in such a miserable state, his Scottish friend, Captain David Richardson, asked Taleb to accompany him to Europe at his expense. They set sail from Calcutta in February 1799 in a Danish ship called *Christiana.* After spending a few months in Cape Town, they boarded a British ship called *Britannia* that took them to Ireland, where Taleb met Lord Cornwallis, whom he had known in India. Taleb described his experience of attending a performance in Dublin of the British siege of Seringapatam in 1799: 'The representation was so correct, that everything appeared natural; and the conclusion was very affecting.'

Dubbed as 'the Persian prince', Taleb was presented to the king and the queen in London. In his account, he described the city thus: 'London is the capital of the Empire, and the largest city I have ever seen. It consists of three towns joined together, and is twenty-four miles in circumference... The shops are in regular rows; and are very rich, extensive, and beautiful, beyond anything I can describe. The greatest ornament that London can boast of is its numerous squares... Of the many admirable institutions of the English, there was none that pleased me more than their Clubs...' Besides praising the virtues of the English, Abu Taleb did not hesitate in writing about the vices of his imperial patrons, whom he considered highly materialistic, and therefore unfit to rule a spiritual country like India.

The late eighteenth and nineteenth centuries saw many more Indian travellers who crossed the oceans and wrote about faraway lands, like the Patna-born Sheikh Din Muhammad (anglicised to Sake Dean Mahomet) who introduced Indian cuisine and shampoo (from the Hindi word *champo,* which means massage) baths to England and became the first Indian to write a book in English—*The Travels of Dean Mahomet.*

THE UNITED STATES MEETS INDIA

The newly born United States was ready to enter the East Indies trade as it was no longer prohibited by the EIC's commercial monopoly. In its early days, the United States had a fragile economy and produced little other than tobacco, raw metals like iron and lead, lumber, butter, cheese, and beef.

Sailing from Philadelphia, *United States* was the first American ship to reach the shores of India, landing in Pondicherry in December 1784. The residents of the French colonial settlement looked curiously at the ship's unfamiliar flag with its thirteen stripes, wondering which country it belonged to. The commandant of Pondicherry received the Americans graciously, extending all the privileges to them.[12]

To American merchants departing from the ports of Philadelphia, Salem, Boston, New York, and Providence, the voyages to the other side of the globe were an opening to an alien realm beyond Europe, an opportunity to learn about their young nation's place in the world. Mostly travelling to the teeming coastal cities of Pondicherry, Calcutta, Madras, and Bombay, they wrote journals recording their observations and experiences in India. They frequently referred to the racial order of British India, at times sympathising with Indians as fellow victims of colonial oppression, while at others reaffirming their superiority. The sight of beggars and poor natives living in squalor or the practicing of bizarre ritulas like the *sati,* the burning of a widow on her husband's funeral pyre, left them dismayed. They also noticed the skills and business acumen of the Indians whom they interacted with—translators called *dubashis* (meaning someone who is well-versed in two languages), clerks called *sircars,* and moneylenders and merchants called *banians.*[13] In 1791, one Captain John Gibaut brought to Salem, Massachusetts, an Indian man as a servant. His name is not recorded, but he was from Madras and was, possibly, the first Indian to set foot on American soil.

Americans returned home with stories of their adventures

and 'curiosities'—miniature statues of Hindu gods and goddesses, strange Indian objects, musical instruments, hookahs, and paintings and prints made by European as well as Indian artists. Though no one in the United States knew how to play the musical instruments brought from India or had any knowledge about the legends and rituals associated with the statues of the Hindu gods and goddesses, there was deep fascination towards them. In 1799, a group of mariners established a museum in Salem, housing such objects and curiosities. A merchant named Jacob Crowninshield brought the first elephant from India to New York and sold it for $10,000. The elephant's new owners took it on a tour, charging 25 cents per person for the privilege of viewing it.

From personal experience, in 1995, while getting ready to depart for America, I was advised by friends and family to carry some ethnic Indian souvenirs or miniature idols, like Nataraja or Ganesha, as Americans were supposedly 'crazy' about them. It turned out to not be the case, and over time I forgot about it, until I stumbled upon engrossing accounts of American merchants from the late eighteenth century.

The British initially saw the Americans as new competitors but realised that they brought with them valuable silver that would help them finance their war machine. That being so, the British did not exclude the Americans but restricted their participation in the Indian trade. In 1792, Benjamin Joy was appointed as the first official representative of the United States to India by President Washington and sent to Calcutta. Joy stayed there for three years but struggled to obtain official recognition from the British authorities. Several other American consuls followed, yet the British did not formally recognise them until 1851.

During the Napoleonic wars, American vessels prospered as neutrals, carrying much of the international trade, although there was always a possibility of getting caught in the crossfire. From 1795 through 1805, the total American trade with India exceeded that of all the continental European nations put together, and Elias Hasket Derby of Salem, who traded in a wide range of commodities including tea, coffee, sugar, rum, and cotton, supposedly became America's first millionaire. The duties levied on the Indian imports helped finance an American Industrial Revolution, funding the construction of mills, canals, railroads, and steam-powered vessels.

American merchants developed close relations with several Indian businessmen, like the Parsi trader Nusserwanjee Maneckjee Wadia, who was a well-respected name in Bombay. The modern-day stereotype of Bengalis as a people who look down upon commerce is probably a product of the post-Independence decline in Bengali entrepreneurship, as history shows otherwise. Calcutta was a bustling trading centre that American merchants flocked to. The millionaire Bengali merchant Ramdulal Dey (1752–1825) was the most prominent and wealthiest of the specialists in the American market. In his honour, a Boston merchants group named one of their ships *Ramduloll Dey,* and another group presented Ramdulal with a life-size portrait of their national hero, President George Washington.[14]

When the Boston merchants active in the coastal trading centres were trying to make sense of the complexities of India, there was one Boston-born individual who saw India up close and personal. David Ochterlony had arrived in India in 1777 as an eighteen-year-old cadet commissioned into the EIC army in Bengal. He saw action in the wars against Mysore and the Marathas, and rose through the ranks to become a major general in 1814 before subsequently attaining the powerful position of the British resident to the Mughal court in Delhi. Ochterlony embraced the Mughal culture and was reputed to have taken thirteen Indian wives. Every evening, he would take his wives on a procession around the walls of the Red Fort, each one seated on the back of her own elephant. People in Delhi knew Ochterlony as 'Loony Akhtar' (meaning crazy star), although he liked to be addressed by his Mughal title, Nasir-ud-Daula (meaning Defender of the State).

Along with the souvenirs, American merchants brought home translations of Indian literature that engendered a deep fascination towards Indian religions and philosophies in New England cities such as Boston, Salem, Cambridge, and Concord, all of which had a thriving literary culture. The essayist and philosopher Ralph Waldo Emerson was drawn to Raja Rammohan Roy's writings and to ancient Sanskrit texts. Emerson's neighbour was the other American icon, Henry David Thoreau, who discovered Sanskrit literature in Emerson's library. Thoreau's favourite was the *Bhagavad Gita*, of which he wrote, 'The reader is nowhere raised into and sustained in a higher, purer, or rarer region of thought than in the Bhagavad Geeta'. In *Moby Dick* (1851), considered to be one of the greatest American novels, writer and poet Herman Melville mentioned the engraving of the fish incarnation in the Elephanta caves (near Bombay) and depicted the great whale as the *Matsya* or the fish avatar of the Hindu deity of Vishnu.

Of all the stories about the Americans who came to India, the story of Josiah Harlan appears to be the most fascinating. Born in Pennsylvania in 1799, Harlan was a voracious reader of the classics from early days and was also something of a dreamer who had become obsessed with the story of Alexander's conquest of Persia and India. He was further intrigued by the stories of India told by his older brother Richard, who had travelled to Calcutta in 1816. In 1820, young Harlan left Philadelphia, employed as supercargo on a ship bound for Canton (now Guangzhou) and Calcutta. From there on, his spirit for adventure took him through an incredible journey over the next two decades—to Burma as a surgeon, to Maharaja Ranjeet Singh's court in Lahore as his physician, and to north-west India and Afghanistan as a militia leader during the Great Game. Believe it or not, Harlan was even proclaimed as a prince of the Ghor province (where Muhammad Ghori came from) in Afghanistan! Despite his swashbuckling adventures, Harlan remained unknown in America and died in obscurity in San Francisco in 1871.[15]

The American trade with India started to wither once they lost their uniquely neutral position after the Franco-British rivalry was over in 1815. In parallel, the burgeoning machine-made products in the United States and Europe, supported by protective tariffs, had weakened the world market for Indian products. As America's focus shifted to continental expansion and domestic issues, India gradually faded away from its memory for over a century, until the onset of World War II.

MACHINES DIVIDE THE WORLD

Compared to the upheaval in France in the late eighteenth century, Britain was stable, politically and socially. Britain also provided far greater freedom to its citizens, unlike the other European monarchies, more so since the Glorious Revolution of 1688 that had reduced the power of the British monarch. British people could freely assemble, express, debate, criticise, write, explore, take risks or be entrepreneurial.

Tinkering with machines had started in the British mines that were beset with the problem of water infiltration. Thomas Newcomen built the first practical steam engine in 1712 that could pump water out of the mines. Scotsman James Watt improved upon Newcomen's engine and devised a much simpler and more efficient engine in 1760. Watt soon became a national hero; his engravings sold widely, promoting the virtues of hard work and inventiveness.

Britain was blessed with vast reserves of iron and coal, the necessary ingredients for industrialisation, with coal being relatively close to the surface, and therefore easy for miners to find and extract. It helped that capital was cheaper in Britain than in the rest of Europe, and the rule of law ensured that inventors' patents were protected along with investors' rewards.

As of the mid-eighteenth century, India was known around the world for its textiles—fine muslins, chintzes, and calicoes, or *indiennes* as the French called them—made by artisans who had honed their skills over generations. These textiles became popular in Europe as they were cheaper, more durable, and easier to colour and wash than the wool or linen that was produced locally. By 1766, cotton cloths constituted more than 75 per cent of the EIC's total trade.

The concerned indigenous wool and linen producers in Britain had been agitating for long and finally convinced the government to impose several tariffs on Indian textiles. In 1721, a ban was imposed on the import of cotton garments from India, though the importation of raw cotton was still allowed. France also imposed similar restrictions. A new indigenous industry producing cotton cloth started emerging in Britain and France. The French and the British EIC officials keenly investigated the manufacturing techniques of the Indian artisans. Despite this rapid appropriation of Indian techniques, they struggled to compete with the high-quality yet cheaper Indian garments.

With wages in Britain as high as six times those in India, there was a clear incentive to mechanise the spinning and weaving process.[16] In 1764, Englishman James Hargreaves invented the spinning jenny, a machine that could produce multiple spools of threads simultaneously. In a little over a decade, there were over 20,000 spinning jennies in use across Britain.

More inventions continued to improve and further automate the process of weaving cloth. The productivity increased 370 times, which made British machine-made cloth much cheaper than the Indian products. The amount of raw cotton used by British mills in hubs like Lancashire and Yorkshire went up from 2 million pounds in 1760 to over 350 million in 1850,[17] much of it coming from the American South where the invention of the cotton gin by Eli Whitney had sped up the processing of raw cotton by 300 times.[18] Textiles became synonymous with the Industrial Revolution. Around this time, London was booming and overtook Paris as Europe's largest city.

No doubt the British people were inventive, but there was more to this 'revolution' as Harvard professor Sven Beckert has argued in his insightful book, *Empire of Cotton: A Global History*. He says that 'Europeans became important to the worlds of cotton not because of new inventions or superior technologies, but because of their ability to reshape and then dominate global cotton networks'. He has coined the term 'war capitalism', referring to slavery, armed trade, the imposition of unfair trade policy and tariffs on Indian products, and forcing their machine-made cotton products on India duty-free.

The revolution ruined India's thriving textiles industry and impoverished millions of artisans, while the British exports to India skyrocketed. The EIC increasingly resorted to violence and corporal punishment, and the oppressive taxes administered by their collectors turned rural India into the gloomiest part of the world. The Indian weavers' share of the cloth sales went from one-third to one-seventeenth. By 1795, the EIC itself recorded 'unprecedented mortality among the weavers'.[19] Governor General Lord William Bentinck commented in 1835: 'the misery hardly finds a parallel in the history of commerce. The bones of the cotton-weavers are bleaching the plains of India'.

Britain's new industrialised economy was booming by the early nineteenth century, thanks to the windfall gains from India that made up almost a third of their national savings. Before the Industrial Revolution, there were modest wealth gaps between countries, for the economic output of a nation was mostly a function of its population. However, that correlation was disrupted after the introduction of machines. Western Europe and North America became industrialised, wealthy economies, leaving heavily populated India, China, the Islamic world, and other parts of Asia and Africa far behind.

By the time England started its colonial expansion in the seventeenth century, Spain and Portugal already had burgeoning global empires. Why did England arrive late to the party? And how did the English manage to survive and excel in spite of such intense competition? Who were the first Englishmen to reach India, and what were their experiences like?

4

RISE OF THE RAINY LITTLE ISLAND

1550s–1720s

I have already joined myself in marriage to a husband, namely the kingdom of England.

—Queen Elizabeth I

Nearly three hours south of Washington, DC, is a place called Jamestown, which was the first permanent English settlement in the Americas, established in 1607. American archaeologist William Kelso says Jamestown 'is where the British Empire began'. In an intriguing twist of fate, British general Cornwallis had surrendered to George Washington in 1781 in Yorktown, which is only thirty kilometres away from Jamestown, ending a significant chapter in the history of the British Empire.

Alternatively, one could argue that the British Empire began in the port town of Surat in Gujarat, where a merchant ship of the English East India Company first landed in the year 1608. Historian John Keay believes there's yet another candidate for 'where the British Empire began'—a tiny speck of an island, about three kilometres long and less than one kilometre wide, called Pulau Run in the middle of the Banda Sea in eastern Indonesia.[1] In what would seem an unimaginable deal today, in 1667, the Dutch had handed over Manhattan to the British in exchange for Pulau Run. Why would the Dutch opt for a trade like that?

To explore the genesis of the British Empire, we have to go back to the sixteenth century, when England was ruled by a remarkable queen.

THE PIRATE QUEEN

In November 1558, Elizabeth Tudor, the tall and well-poised twenty-five-year-old daughter of former king Henry VIII, became the queen of England. Her birth had been a great disappointment to her father as he had wanted a male heir. Before Elizabeth turned three, Henry had her mother, Anne Boleyn, beheaded for she had failed—in Henry's eyes—to produce a male heir. Labelled as an illegitimate child, Elizabeth had a troubled childhood. Her ascension wasn't easy either as she had to survive violent opposition and imprisonment for a year in the Tower of London during the reign of Queen Mary I, her half-sister. Queen Elizabeth would have to carve out her place in a cut-throat world dominated by male monarchs.

Her grand coronation ceremony and the festive mood on the streets of London in January 1559 masked the fact that the England she inherited was destitute and bankrupt, with a national debt of £3,00,000, an astronomical sum at the time. Increase in taxes due to a series of wars that Henry VIII had fought against France and Scotland, coupled with poor harvests and rapid inflation caused by the heaps of silver and gold brought from the New World into Europe had led to rampant poverty.

England's population was around 3 million at the time while London had 70,000 people, which made it the sixth-largest city in Europe after Paris, Antwerp, Lisbon, Venice, and Naples. English towns were dirty, smelly, and crowded. One could see dead bodies lying around during an epidemic of influenza or plague. Religion was a matter of life and death, and people were hanged or burnt alive for certain forms of heresy. The body parts of traitors were displayed over the gates of London as a warning.[2]

The population was growing rapidly, but the employment opportunities not so much. The wool and cloth industry, the mainstay of English manufacturing and exports for centuries, had been faltering due to stiff competition from its continental counterparts and other geopolitical developments. England's trade with Antwerp, the leading commercial port of western Europe, where English merchants traded wool and cloth for Asian luxury products like spices brought by the Portuguese, had collapsed in 1549 when the Portuguese traders closed their establishment. England's economy had suffered another serious blow in January 1558, when the port city of Calais (France), England's last outpost in continental Europe through which wool and cloth were profitably exported, fell to a surprise French attack.

To add to the misery, the English nobility and wealthy merchants, who owned most of the agricultural land and lived in palatial estates and castles, had been dispossessing tenants to run their farms with hired hands. That being so, the dislodged peasants, along with the jobless cloth workers, wandered in market towns and seaports looking for work, many turning to begging.

England was a military and economic underdog compared to the mighty Spain, France, Portugal, and Venice. Elizabeth's court was considered crude in contrast to that of Philip of Spain, and the English people were deemed to be impolite and rough.

But there were a few bright spots too. To begin with, the uniquely advantageous location of England. The narrow English Channel was a natural barrier against invading armies from Europe, reducing the need to maintain a large, standing army. Elizabeth's grandfather, Henry VII, had initiated a programme of building warships that Henry VIII carried forward, building up to forty ships for the Royal Navy. England had no shortage of either entrepreneurs who were willing to invest their capital on risky but potentially lucrative ventures, or of young men who were known for their daring and navigational skills, ready to go deep into the dangerous oceans for trade or even theft. Then there were the intellectually curious individuals, many of them graduates of Oxford and Cambridge, who kept abreast with the latest developments around the world.

The Quest for Asia

The sharp decline in cloth exports, along with the loss of imports of spices, prompted London's merchants to search for new markets for English products and to reach the source of Asian goods. A commercial venture was established in 1552 with a rather fanciful name—The Mysterie, Company, and Fellowship of Merchant Adventurers for the Discovery of Regions, Dominions, Islands, and Places Unknown. The next year, the company launched its first expedition, to seek a Northeast Passage (along the Arctic coasts of Norway and Russia) to Asia, with Sir Hugh Willoughby as the leader of the mission, and an outstanding navigator named Richard Chancellor as the chief pilot. Two of the three ships—with Willoughby on one of them—disappeared somewhere near the Norwegian coast, only to be found with frozen bodies of the crews in the following spring by Russian fishermen. Meanwhile, Chancellor continued the voyage and reached the town of Arkhangelsk along the northern coast of European Russia. From there, he made the overland journey of nearly 1,000 kilometres by a horse-drawn sleigh to Moscow, where he was received cordially. Chancellor managed to establish trade links with the Russians, selling English broadcloth to them and buying hemp, furs, and hides. On his return to England, The Muscovy Company was established in 1555 and was granted a monopoly of Anglo-Russian trade.

In 1558, Anthony Jenkinson, an enterprising merchant of the Muscovy Company, made his first expedition to Russia and met with Ivan the Terrible, the first czar of Russia. When Elizabeth was being crowned, Jenkinson had reached Bukhara in Central Asia and was negotiating trade deals and exploring future opportunities.[3]

When Jenkinson set sail from London again in 1561, he carried a letter from Queen Elizabeth for the Persian king. It was Elizabeth's first letter to a Muslim ruler, a letter that was not easy to write since no one in her court knew much about the religious or political situation in Persia; they did not even know the name of the king of that faraway ancient land. What the letter described was not the dominions of the Persian ruler, but the Achaemenid Empire of Persia from the sixth century BCE!

After a longer stay in Moscow due to delayed approvals to proceed further, Jenkinson finally reached the court of the Safavid Shah Tahmasp at Qazvin (150 kilometres north of modern Tehran) in 1562. Had Jenkinson arrived a few years earlier, he would have met Humayun, the second Mughal ruler of India, who had been provided refuge by Shah Tahmasp for ten years after he was chased out of India by Sher Shah Suri in 1544. With the help of the Safavids, Humayun was able to recover Delhi and Agra in 1555. Jenkinson had awkward moments in Tahmasp's court, where nobody had heard of his country 'England', its queen or its 'famous city' of London.[4] When his efforts to obtain the trade approvals from Tahmasp did not yield any results, he decided to return home. Nevertheless, he wrote an insightful account of Persia that was the earliest description of the religion, politics, and people of the region by an Englishman.

India, or *Ynde* (*Inde*), as it may have been called in England due to the ever-increasing French influence over the island nation since the fifteenth century, was even further east of Persia and mostly beyond the English imagination, although the English merchants in Seville, Spain, were aware of Portugal's India links. Jenkinson found out that the overland routes to China and India were well-known but impassable due to wars and banditry along the way.

For England, Russia may have come closer to home, but the original mission of finding a sea route to the most prized markets of Asia, where the Portuguese held a monopoly on the spice trade, remained unfulfilled. Nor did England have access to the New World, where Spain had earned a windfall of precious metals. A daring navigator named Martin Frobisher was enlisted by the English merchants to make a renewed attempt at finding a marine route to Asia, this time from the north-west (along the northern coast of Canada). Equipped with the best marine technology available at the time, Frobisher mounted three epic voyages in the 1570s. He reached as far as what is today north-eastern Canada, but his mission changed course when he found what he thought were gold deposits on his second voyage. In a frenzy over gold that lured many investors, including Queen Elizabeth, he made further voyages carrying home hundreds of tons of the ore that eventually turned out to be nothing but worthless rock. Frobisher's unsuccessful expeditions bankrupted his investors and ended the hopes the English merchants had of finding a northern sea route to Asia.

Rivalry with Spain

Spain, the most powerful nation in Europe then, and also staunchly Catholic, was the greatest threat to England, where Protestantism had been growing rapidly since the 1520s. In Europe, an alternative to fighting wars was intermarriage among the royalty as a means of forging political alliances. King Philip II of Spain had married Mary I in 1554. When she passed away in 1558, Philip was anxious to marry Elizabeth, intending to bring her (and England) into the fold of the Catholic Church while also ensuring safe passage for Spanish merchant ships through the English Channel. However, to his great irritation, Elizabeth refused his proposal.

In 1570, when the Pope realised that Protestant England was unlikely to become Catholic again, he called for Elizabeth's removal, provoking Catholic Spain's antagonism towards her. England was politically and economically isolated, and their merchants were barred from trading with the Netherlands, which was under Spanish control. Several of Elizabeth's courtiers, like the hawkish Humphrey Gilbert, were of the opinion that she should take an aggressive stance towards the Iberian power. However, lacking the resources to confront Spain, Elizabeth found an alternative path—piracy or 'privateering', as it was called, as a naval strategy. The privateers enlisted by her were called Sea Dogs, who intercepted Spanish vessels, seized treasures, and raided their Caribbean colonies, while the queen denied her involvement. Annoyed with the growing menace of her Sea Dogs, King Philip called her 'the Pirate Queen'.

At the same time, the increasingly Protestant Netherlands drew the wrath of Philip when it rebelled against the Spanish rule. A vicious war went on for decades, with the Spanish army ravaging towns and massacring thousands of Dutch people. Antwerp was sacked by the Spanish army in 1576, and things got worse four years later when Spain took over Portugal and closed Lisbon to Dutch merchants. Antwerp's economy tanked, and the city turned into a war zone due to the relentless assault by the Spanish army. Half of Antwerp's population fled north to Amsterdam, changing its fortunes overnight.

Elizabeth and the Islamic World

In a lesser-known countermeasure against Spain, Elizabeth reached out to the Ottoman Empire, which was the chief rival of Spain and covered a vast area stretching from the modern Middle East and North Africa to Eastern Europe. In doing so, Elizabeth hoped to defend England as well as open its doors to a lucrative trade with the Ottomans.

In her letters, she addressed the Ottoman sultan as an exalted ruler of an empire and described herself as the queen of not only England, but also Ireland and France. Though she tried to overstate her authority and position herself on their side as a common enemy of Catholicism, England was, in reality, an obscure and faraway island of fishermen and wool merchants, an insignificant entity for the powerful Ottomans. The Ottoman sultan Murad III was not inclined to launch an attack on Spain without any strategic gains; nevertheless, he was convinced enough to allow trade with England and gave her merchants the same rights he had earlier granted to the French merchants.

Coincidentally, while Elizabeth was writing letters to the Ottomans, Akbar, the Mughal emperor in India, was also engaged in diplomatic exchange with them over trade and pilgrimages to Mecca and Medina. Istanbul was, therefore, a common factor between India and England, although no direct communication had taken place between the two as yet.

Elizabeth issued patents to Sir Edward Osborne, Richard Staper, and a few others to trade, and the Turkey Company was born in 1581. The company established factories (trading centres) in commercial hubs besides Istanbul such as Aleppo, Alexandria, Mosul, and Smyrna, places where they had never gone before. Oriental luxury items like silks, carpets, wines, and spices started flowing into England, much to the delight of those who could afford them. The Ottomans, meanwhile, wanted scrap metal to make weapons, which England provided. As a political gesture, Elizabeth had metal stripped from deconsecrated Catholic churches and their bells melted to make arms for the Ottomans. When the charter of the Turkey Company expired, it was merged with the Venice Company and renamed as the Levant Company in 1592. The venture was an immediate success.

Elizabeth also initiated diplomatic and trading ties with the ruler of Morocco with an understanding of providing and receiving military support against Spain when needed, and The Barbary Company was thus set up in 1585. English merchants began travelling to cities like Marrakesh and importing sugar, currants, and sweet wines. After three decades of trading with Islamic nations in North Africa and the Middle East, Elizabethan England had developed a curiosity towards the Muslims, who were addressed by various names—Mahometans, Ottomites, Saracens, Moors, Pagans, Turks, and Persians. As new theatres were mushrooming in London throughout the 1580s and 1590s, more than sixty plays were inspired by themes from the Muslim world.

Queen Elizabeth's Men

Elizabeth's reign was meritocratic, where she rewarded those who demonstrated loyalty to the Crown and the nation through their skills and talents, regardless of their social background.

One of the most extraordinary figures of the time was John Dee, a Cambridge-educated mathematician, geographer, and astrologer who enjoyed strong support from Elizabeth; she sought scientific as well as astrological advice from him and called him 'hyr Philosopher'. Somewhat eccentric yet well-travelled and extremely well-read, Dee had amassed the most extensive library in England at the time with over 3,000 books and 1,000 manuscripts in some twenty-one languages, eclipsing the collections at Oxford and Cambridge. It was he who coined the term 'British Empire', mentioning it several times in his book *The Perfecte Arte of Navigation,* and proposed that a navy ought to be established to protect England's foreign interests. He was also instrumental in laying the groundwork for the voyages of Richard Chancellor, Martin Frobisher, and many others, personally instructing captains and pilots in the principles of navigation and providing them with maps.

Another remarkable scholar was the Oxford-educated geographer and writer Richard Hakluyt, noted for his voluminous writings and promotion of the overseas expansion of England. Hakluyt is known for his work, *The Principall Navigations, Voiages and Discoveries of the English Nation* (1598) that provided almost everything known about the early English voyages to North America. Based on primary sources, such as the journals of explorers, and reports and sailing directions by seamen, Hakluyt's book became an authoritative guide for navigators and merchants.

The most flamboyant and daring of all of Elizabeth's Sea Dogs was Francis Drake. Raised in a poor family, Drake had no formal education and no seafaring experience. He struck terror into the hearts of the Spaniards, who called him 'El Draco' (the Dragon), raiding and destroying their ships in the Atlantic and the Caribbean. Although Drake was deemed to be a fearsome pirate, he had also built a reputation for treating captured enemies humanely, earning respect from all corners.

In 1577, Drake set out with five ships and 164 men on a daring mission to circumnavigate the world. They sailed all the way down to the southernmost tip of South America, where a passage is named after him, before heading north into the Pacific Ocean along the west coast of New Spain (Mexico) and North America, and then sailing westwards towards Asia. After sixty-eight days in the Pacific Ocean, they reached a group of islands called the Maluku (Moluccas, Indonesia)—the fabled Spice Islands, fulfilling a long-standing dream of English merchants and explorers to reach Asia by sea. The local sultan was delighted to receive Drake and agreed to grant England the monopoly of the spice trade in return for protection against the Portuguese.

Drake's arrival in Plymouth after the three-year-long voyage was greeted with mass jubilation. The first Englishman to circumnavigate the world, Drake had boosted the morale of his fledgling island nation. He had also brought with him an astonishing bounty of gold ingots, silver bars, pearls, and emeralds plundered from Spanish vessels and ports en route that amounted to £1,26,000—about half the English government's annual revenue. A fuming King Philip sent his men to Elizabeth, demanding that she hand over Drake and the bounty to them, which she promptly refused. Instead, she bestowed a knighthood on the undaunted adventurer.

With tensions between Spain and England rising, Elizabeth sensed that war was on the horizon. She authorised pre-emptive raids on Spanish colonial ports and outposts in the Caribbean, which were led by none other than Sir Francis Drake. Commanding a fleet of twenty-nine ships in 1586, he wreaked havoc, assaulting the town of Santo Domingo (The Dominican Republic) and burning and looting much of Cartagena (Colombia) before he was paid a hefty ransom. A year later, Drake destroyed a hundred Spanish ships in Cadiz, Spain.

An enraged Philip launched a massive invasion of England in 1588 with his 'Invincible Armada' of 130 massive ships carrying 18,000 soldiers and 7,000 sailors, the greatest naval force in the world at the time. Pitted against the armada were England's smaller but heavily armed warships, like the *Revenge* commanded by Drake and the *Triumph* led by Frobisher. Legend has it that Drake was playing a game of bowls when he was informed that the Spanish armada was approaching, to which he replied that there was enough time to finish the game and defeat the armada. Helped by an unexpected storm at sea, the swift and persistent English navy destroyed the armada. England was now a world-class naval power. The Moroccan ruler Ahmad al-Mansur and the Ottoman sultan Murad III came to regard Elizabethan England as a rising power on the world stage. With Elizabeth's support, the Dutch also started to score victories over Spain.

Over the next decade, the conflict continued until Spain's economy started to fall apart. Elizabeth's death in 1603 brought to an end an extraordinary forty-five-year reign that came to be called the Golden Age of England. Her successor, King James I, immediately opened negotiations for peace with Catholic Spain and signed a peace treaty in 1604, finally ending the enmity between the two nations. Simultaneously, England's alliance with the Islamic world (Morocco, Turkey) was over, although their engagement with the Mughal Empire of India was about to begin.

THE FIRST ENGLISH AND DUTCH TRAVELLERS TO REACH INDIA

As of the 1570s, any Englishman or Dutchman looking to travel to India would have had to board a Portuguese vessel. The first known Englishman to set foot in India is believed to be a Jesuit priest named Thomas Stephens who arrived in Goa in October 1579. He wrote a letter to his father—the first known account of India by an Englishman—that was published in Richard Hakluyt's *Principall Navigations, Voiages and Discoveries of the English Nation.*

Stephens described the Indians thus: 'The people be tawny, but not disfigured in their lips and noses? They that be not of reputation, or at least the most part, go naked, saving an apron of a span long, and as much as a breath before them, and a lace two fingers broad before them, girded about with a string and no more?'

The coastal city of Goa was the capital of the Portuguese *Estado da India* and a cosmopolitan centre where students from Portugal,

China, East Africa, Armenia, and all over the Indian subcontinent came to attend Jesuit schools. Things changed within a year of Stephens's arrival as Philip II of Spain occupied the throne of Portugal in 1580. Portuguese Goa got involved in the Spanish Inquisition that incited attacks on Hindus, Muslims, and Jews.

After learning Marathi and Konkani besides Portuguese, Stephens wrote the *Krista Purana* (*The Christian Puranas*), an epic 11,000-line poem about the life of Jesus Christ in a mix of Marathi and Konkani, which became very popular among the local population. He also wrote the first Konkani grammar book and continued to live in the village of Rachol in Goa till his death in 1619.[5]

With the sea route via the Cape of Good Hope becoming unsafe for English merchants after the Spanish occupation of Portugal in 1580, they began contemplating a land route to India from Syria. John Newberry, a Levant Company merchant who had travelled to modern-day Syria, Iraq, and Iran, believed that commerce with India via the land route was a feasible option. In November 1582, Newberry visited John Dee to gather information for an overland expedition and later consulted Richard Hakluyt as well, who provided him with Stephens's letter. A reconnaissance mission was planned and funded by the Levant Company. Besides Newberry, the party consisted of traders John Eldred and Ralph Fitch, a painter named James Story, and a jeweller named William Leeds. The inclusion of Leeds is explained by the fact that the Golconda mines of India were the only source of the finest and the largest diamonds in the world until the eighteenth century. These men carried with them letters of introduction from Queen Elizabeth addressed to the Mughal Emperor Akbar.

The party sailed from London in February 1583 in a ship called *Tiger* and reached Aleppo (Syria) in May and from there they moved to the port town of Basra (Iraq) in August. While Eldred stayed in Basra, the rest of the party embarked for Ormus island (Hormuz in Iran), where they landed in early September. A group of Italian merchants operating in Ormus got suspicious of their arrival, and all of them were arrested and shipped to Portuguese Goa, where they spent a month in prison.[6]

The Englishmen were fortunate to have found two friends in Goa—one was their fellow countryman, Father Thomas Stephens, and the other was a young Dutchman named Jan Huygen van Linschoten, who was an assistant to the archbishop of Goa. Stephens and Linschoten were able to exert some influence in the prisoners' favour, and since they all professed to be good Catholics, they were released just before Christmas Day of 1583, based on a personal bail by Stephens.

Within a few days, the situation was grim again as per the instructions coming out of Lisbon for the Portuguese officials in Goa. Alarmed at the possibility of getting arrested, the four Englishmen decided to escape from Goa and slipped over the border into the territory of the sultan of Bijapur. James Story stayed back in Goa and married a local woman, but from there on, his whereabouts are not known.

Newberry, Leeds, and Fitch made it to Bijapur and from there they travelled further ahead to Golconda, looking for precious stones at both the places. Passing through Ujjain, they reached Agra where they found out that Akbar was in Fatehpur Sikri, which was another thirty kilometres away. At Fatehpur Sikri, the three separated—Leeds entered the services of Akbar and nothing is known beyond that; Newberry decided to return home via Lahore and was never seen again.

Fitch managed to survive. He travelled and explored eastern India, sailing on the Yamuna and the Ganga, stopping in Allahabad, Benaras, Patna, and all the way to Chittagong (Bangladesh). From there on, Fitch proceeded to Pegu (Myanmar) and Chiang Mai (Thailand). He then returned home via Cochin–Goa–Basra–Aleppo, finally reaching London in April 1591, eight years after he had left the city. Fitch seems to have followed an itinerary similar to that of a Venetian merchant named Cesare Federici, who had travelled through Asia from 1563 to 1581. Federici's account, titled *Viaggio* (*Travel*), was published in Venice and later an English version had appeared in London. Fitch may have imitated Federici's writing style, but his travel account is an intriguing first-hand record of life in India 400 years ago. He wrote:

> Agra is a very great citie and populous, built with stone, having faire and large streetes, with a faire river running by it, which falleth into the Gulfe of Bengala. It hath a faire castle and a strong, with a very fare ditch. Here be many Moores and Gentiles. The king is called Zelabdim Echebar (Jalaluddin Akbar); the people, for the most part, call him the Great Mogor. From thence we went for Fatepore (Fatehpur Sikri), which is the place where the king kept his court. The towne is greater than Agra, but the houses and streetes be not so faire. Here dwell many people, both Moores and Gentiles. The king hath in Agra and Fatepore 1,000 elephants, thirtie thousand horses, 1,400 tame deere, 800 concubines; such store of ounces, tigers, buffles, cocks, and haukes, that is very strange to see. He keepeth a great court, which is called Dericcan (Darikhana). Agra and Fatepore are two very great cities, either of them much greater than London and very populous.[7]

In a reversal of fortunes, Agra is today a dusty, crowded town that tourists visit to check the Taj Mahal off their list and try to get out as soon as they are done. London, on the other hand, is among the greatest cities in the world.

Fitch's account remained popular for many years. In fact, Shakespeare alluded to his adventures in the famous play *Macbeth* (1606). Neither Fitch nor anyone else in England could have imagined in their wildest dream that one day their nation would be ruling over the entire Indian subcontinent and that it would be the crown jewel of their global empire, where the sun would never set.

As Fitch was exploring India, Linschoten, the Dutchman who helped the English party in Goa, found something that would change the course of history for the Dutch and the English. Since Vasco da Gama's discovery of the sea route to India a century ago, the Portuguese had gathered copious information required for a safe oceanic voyage to the East. They kept this information closely guarded as a national secret since it was highly coveted by their European rivals, who wished to enter the lucrative trade.

Enter Linschoten. He managed to pull off one of the most extraordinary episodes of corporate espionage in history. Abusing the trust put in him by the Portuguese, who probably did not even see the Dutch as a threat, Linschoten managed to meticulously copy the Portuguese maps, their valuable sailing instructions, historical records, and nautical data like currents, deeps, islands, and harbours.[8]

On his return to the Netherlands, he sold the story of his travels to a publisher in Amsterdam, who published it in 1596 in an elaborately illustrated book called *The Itinerario.* It talked about a variety of things, such as Linschoten's journey, the countries in the East Indies, the numerous remote islands that dotted the entire region, the non-Christian cultures, Goa, and the exotic spice trade with prices of various spices and commodities. Linschoten confirmed the rumours in Europe about the Portuguese *Estado da India* becoming weak and the loosening of Portuguese control in Indonesia. *The Itinerario* became an instant sensation and a bible to merchant groups who wished to enter the Asia trade.[9]

COLONISATION OF NORTH AMERICA

The rivalry with Spain had severely impaired England's economy and worsened unemployment. Richard Hakluyt characterised English trade as 'beggarly' and proposed that England should seek opportunities in America, which was endowed with an abundance of fish, timber, furs, and food crops. Setting up colonies there could generate large-scale employment for farmers, fishermen, shipbuilders, and several other trades; moreover, the colonies could serve as launching pads to attack the Spanish fleets, he argued.

Hakluyt's advice made sense. Considering her nation's economic and social situation, Elizabeth began promoting colonial ventures, granting monopolies to her trusted men. But only few colonisation options remained in America. South and Central America were already taken by the Spanish and the Portuguese, leaving North America and a few small islands in the Caribbean. Even North America was partially occupied: the northern regions along the Atlantic seaboard (modern Canada) were claimed by France while Spain had laid claim to the southern regions. What was left for the English was the region in the middle—what is now the East Coast of the United States. It wasn't a coveted land even a century after the discovery of the New World. There were no signs of gold or silver; it was too far north for crops like sugar to be grown as they required warm weather, and too far south for the best furs to be found there. The English, as latecomers, did not have much option other than to settle for this unwanted part of the continent.

After the treaty with Spain in 1604, hostilities had reduced and the English were now looking to shift from plundering Spanish possessions to setting up permanent establishments. A group of English merchants formed a joint-stock company called the Virginia Company (named after their 'virgin queen') that was granted a charter by King James I to establish a colony in North America. Three ships, the *Susan Constant*, the *Goodspeed*, and the *Discovery*, sailed from England in December 1606 and landed in Virginia in April 1607, where the settlement was named Jamestown after the king.

Jamestown had nearly everything going wrong from the get-go. Besides the lurking danger of attacks from Native Americans, it was a swamp and a breeding colony for malaria-causing mosquitoes. 67 of the original 105 colonists were dead within nine months. The morale was at an all-time low as the colonists continued to dig, looking for gold where none was to be found. Conditions of the colony kept worsening, and by winter it reached a terrible state of starvation, where the survivors ended up devouring their horses. That is when one of the seasoned leaders of the colony, John Smith, took control. Unlike his peers, Smith brought in rigorous discipline and pushed the colonists towards practical means of survival in the wilderness. The number of deaths reduced and the colony survived.[10]

Unable to find gold, the colonists discovered the value of tobacco, which the Native Americans had smoked for centuries. Once introduced in Europe, it became a popular product and provided the settlers with a cash crop they desperately needed to sustain. Soon, large tobacco plantations emerged and the Virginia colony started to thrive. The tobacco output multiplied by leaps and bounds, reaching a point where it contributed up to a fourth of the overall British Crown's custom revenue.

In 1630, a group of English Protestants, known as the Puritans, seeking greater religious freedom, decided to settle in the New World. Around 1,000 Puritan men, women, and children arrived in America in June, and established the Massachusetts Bay Colony. Most of them were either tradesmen or skilled craftsmen and were better educated than the average English person. New towns were founded, each one of them with a church and a school, reaching a point where the Puritan communities in New England had the highest literacy rates in the Western world in the seventeenth century. Several of the influential colonists were Oxford and Cambridge graduates who were keen to establish a college in their new homeland; Harvard College was thus founded in 1636 in the town of Cambridge.

Free from the barriers of religion and class, the colonies of Jamestown and Massachusetts Bay survived and flourished due to a strong work ethic and a sense of community and self-sufficiency, laying a template for the future generations and for hundreds of new towns across North America. Tocqueville wrote: 'The whole destiny of America is contained in the first Puritans who landed on these shores'.

The Dutch did not want to stay behind. They commissioned the English sailor Henry Hudson, who headed an expedition to America in 1609, reaching the island of Manhattan and then sailing north for 250 kilometres up the river that is named after him. More Dutch expeditions explored the area, which became the colony of

New Netherland. In 1625, the colonists founded New Amsterdam at the southern tip of Manhattan Island as the colony's capital, with a fort to protect the harbour and the precious fur cargoes. A year later, they bought the whole island of Manhattan from a group of Native Americans for only sixty guilders!

With New Netherland sandwiched between the English colonies of Virginia and New England, rivalry between them was a given. A series of Anglo-Dutch wars were fought in the second half of the seventeenth century, where England faced the most humiliating naval defeats in its history. Anglo-Dutch settlement treaties were signed where colonial possessions around the world were exchanged. The highly productive colony of Suriname (on the northern coast of South America) went to the Dutch while New Amsterdam came to the British and became New York City, and New Netherland became New York, thereby earning the British a contiguous presence on the East Coast. Now, coming back to why the Dutch had traded Manhattan for the tiny island of Pulau Run, the single reason was nutmeg. It grew nowhere else in the world and could be bought for a pittance in the Banda Islands, but once it reached Europe, its value went up a whopping 32,000 per cent!

EARLY DAYS OF THE EAST INDIA COMPANIES

After England defeated the Spanish Armada in 1588, the Atlantic routes controlled by Spain started to soften. James Lancaster, who had served under Drake as a commander, was granted permission by Elizabeth for a reconnaissance voyage. He sailed from Plymouth in April 1591 with three ships to the East Indies, reaching the island of Penang (in current Malaysia) in June of the following year. Plundering Spanish and Portuguese ships on the way, he returned to England in May 1594, completing one of the earliest English expeditions to Asia.

In the meantime, a Portuguese ship called *Madre de Deus* (Mother of God) was returning from her second voyage to Asia in August 1592 when it was captured by Sir Walter Raleigh and the Earl of

Cumberland. It was bigger than any ship that they had ever seen and was laden with chests filled with jewels and pearls, gold and silver coins, fine cloth and tapestries, and tons of exotic spices. The spectacularly precious cargo left the Englishmen bedazzled, opening their eyes to the vast riches that lay in the East.[11]

The Dutch, whose trade in Europe was tormented by Spanish embargoes, were also keen to explore possibilities in Asia. In 1592, two Dutch navigator brothers, Cornelis and Frederik de Houtman, were sent by Amsterdam merchants to Lisbon to gather intelligence on the Spice Islands. They were arrested for attempting to steal secret details of voyaging from the Portuguese merchants but later managed to be released and returned to Amsterdam in 1595. Meanwhile, Linschoten had returned from India to Amsterdam with valuable information on how to get to Asia. With the collective stolen knowledge at hand, they concluded that Bantam (in present-day Indonesia) provided the best opportunity to buy spices.

The Dutch Compagnie van Verre was founded in 1594 and their first trading expedition to the East Indies, commanded by the de Houtman brothers, left Amsterdam in April 1595 with four ships and 249 men. It turned out to be a rough start for the Dutch as the voyage, beset with blunders, mutiny, and scurvy, failed miserably. A second expedition commanded by Jacob van Neck returned with vessels full of spices, a highly profitable voyage with 400 per cent returns, paving the path for their Asian enterprise.

On hearing about the highly profitable Dutch ventures, London merchants were motivated to emulate their success. The trigger came in 1599 when the Dutch merchants raised the price of pepper. They had also petitioned Queen Elizabeth around the same time to purchase several English ships for their ever-expanding trade in the Indies. The angry London merchants decided that they should secure their own supplies of spices and made a compelling case to the queen for a charter. A meeting was held on 24 September 1599 at Founders Hall at Lothbury Street, London, where the letter of Thomas Stephens, along with the maps and records produced by Linschoten, the account of Ralph Fitch, and the capture of the

Madre de Deus cargo, were part of the agenda.

On 31 December 1600, Elizabeth signed the charter creating The Company of Merchants of London Trading to the East Indies, or the East India Company, with Thomas Smythe as the company's governor. Smythe also served as the governor of the Virginia Company and the Muscovy Company at various times. A total of 218 merchants raised £70,000, which allowed the EIC to buy three ships, the *Susan,* the *Hector,* and the *Ascension.* Some of the investors had also invested in the Virginia Company. Richard Hakluyt became the first historiographer of the English EIC, and Ralph Fitch was hired at some point as a consultant for his invaluable experience of faraway lands.

The first voyage began on a cold day in January 1601 with a fleet of five ships, under the command of James Lancaster, sailing down the Thames River to the open sea. England was still at war with Spain and Portugal, and no landing was to be made in India. The objective of the company was to reach the Spice Islands.

Fighting wretched conditions and afflicted with scurvy, the fleet reached Sumatra eighteen months after leaving London. While the local ruler was delighted to see a new foreign trading entity as the Portuguese were unpopular throughout the region, the residents of the hot and humid Sumatra did not have a real need for English goods like woollen vests and wrought iron. Not making any commercial progress, Lancaster decided to raid and loot a Portuguese ship loaded with merchandise before heading home. When they reached London, their voyage was deemed worthwhile, if not profitable, and Lancaster was knighted. The second voyage was more fruitful, bringing in profits at just under 100 per cent. Compared to the Virginia Company that, while claiming ownership of swathes of American land, had a longer and somewhat unpredictable profit cycle, the EIC offered its investors quicker and more reliable returns.

In the meantime, the Dutch merchants realised that having five different trading companies was inefficient and decided, therefore, to consolidate them. The Vereenigde Oost-Indische Compagnie

(VOC) or the Dutch East India Company was thus founded in 1602, with a trading capital of over £5,00,000 (as against the EIC's £30,000, which was the largest sum ever invested in an English venture).

With Portugal's hold over the Spice Islands shaky, as Linschoten had reported, the determined and ruthless Dutch started to soon dominate the maritime trade in Asia. They began by sinking a Portuguese fleet in a full-scale naval battle in the Bay of Bantam, and in 1605, wrested the Portuguese fort of Amboina (part of modern Indonesia), strategically situated between tiny islands that produced nutmeg and cloves. To finance growth, the Dutch invented the idea of making the shares of a joint-stock company tradable, which is the genesis of modern stock markets around the world. Soon, the Dutch economy became the most sophisticated in Europe. By 1610, while the English had sent out only seventeen ships to Asia, the VOC had sent sixty, and these returned with massive cargoes filling up huge warehouses in Amsterdam with Oriental merchandise that included pepper, cloves, mace, nutmeg, and Indian fabrics embroidered in Mughal style.

As compared to the political and military support that the VOC received from the Dutch government, the EIC was by and large on its own. In 1623, matters came to a head when the Dutch executed eighteen English agents suspected of spying in Amboina, for they had zero tolerance towards any such activity. The massacre caused deep outrage among the English merchants who lodged a strong protest with London, but ultimately, there were no reprisals. Instead, the English were virtually eliminated from the Moluccas and had to relocate their base to India.

The aggressive Dutch also drove the Portuguese out of Ceylon (Sri Lanka) and Cochin, and built an elaborate trade network stretching from the Persian Gulf to Japan. They would have dislodged the Portuguese entirely from the subcontinent had Goa not been so well-defended. Not only would the Portuguese survive in Goa for three more centuries, but they would outlive the Dutch and even the British in India.

The booming VOC trade turned Amsterdam into a great

entrepôt, generating enormous wealth and fuelling the Dutch Golden Age that saw the construction of mansions, canals, churches, and harbours, and the blossoming of art and science. The most prominent icon of that prosperous era in Dutch history was the painter Rembrandt, considered to be among the most celebrated artists in European history. Rembrandt acquired Mughal paintings that arrived in the Netherlands on VOC ships and became one of the earliest European admirers of Mughal art. He made around twenty-five drawings based on Mughal miniatures from India that are known to be among his most compelling works on paper.

THE GAME OF THRONES IN INDIA

Seventeenth-century India was marked by a mingling of world views and intense competitions as diverse entities and individuals—Indians, Persians, Turks, Ethiopians, Armenians, Jews, Portuguese, English, Dutch, French, and Danes—jostled over trade, territory, and power.

When the Mughal Emperor Akbar died in 1605, his eldest son Salim inherited one of the wealthiest empires in the world, ruling over roughly a hundred million people, a quarter of the world's population. The Mughal capital of Agra had a population of 7,00,000, which was several times that of any of the European cities. Salim adopted the name *Jahangir* (Ruler of the World) and married an exceptionally beautiful, widowed Persian woman, to whom he gave the title of *Nur Jahan* (Light of the World). Jahangir's excessive consumption of alcohol and opium, coupled with his disinterest in administration, paved the way for Nur Jahan to become highly influential at the Mughal court.

Lesser attention has been given in history books to the Habshi or the Siddi people who were brought to India as slaves from Abyssinia (Ethiopia) and the Horn of Africa by the Arabs. In the seventeenth century, they were recruited by the Muslim rulers of Gujarat, Bengal, and Deccan in their militaries. Compared to the New World colonies of the Europeans, the Muslim kingdoms of

India offered far greater opportunities to the African slaves. Siddis started as bodyguards or soldiers who could go on to attain freedom, advance to the rank of a commander, and even become governors.

The most famous Siddi was Malik Ambar. Born as Chapu in Abyssinia in around 1548, he was sold into slavery at a young age and sent to Baghdad, where he was converted to Islam and renamed. After being sold repeatedly, he ended up in the Deccan region of India where he joined the Ahmadnagar Sultanate. He rose to the position of a commander and built a large army of over 50,000 soldiers, a fifth of them Africans. In time, he became the regent, effectively ruling Ahmadnagar until he died in 1626. For three decades, he thwarted the repeated attempts made by the Mughal emperors to control the Deccan region. Jahangir had become bitterly obsessed with Malik Ambar, but could never subdue him. Malik Ambar's island fortress of Janjira, on the west coast of India, remained unbreached for centuries.[12]

The English East India Company was founded in 1600, although it wasn't until August 1608 that they made their first landing in India when their ship, the *Hector*, dropped anchor near Surat, Gujarat. Its captain was the ambitious, beer-guzzling William Hawkins, who had been a merchant in the Levant. While the native merchants looked at the ship from an unfamiliar European nation with inquisitiveness, the aggressive Portuguese went ahead and attacked it, confiscating its goods. Sensing danger to his life, Hawkins slipped out of Surat and reached Agra. Hawkins was a trader and not a diplomat, and though he did not have any striking gifts for the emperor, yet Jahangir was impressed by the Englishman, especially because he was able to speak in Turkish. Jahangir offered to keep Hawkins in his court as a resident ambassador and presented him with a Christian Armenian girl named Mariam from his harem to marry. Despite the warm welcome, Hawkins gradually fell out of favour with Jahangir due to intrigues in the Mughal court against him. His attempts to obtain an approval for trade failed and he departed from Surat along with his Armenian-Indian wife, who is said to be the first person from India to have reached England.

In September 1612, another fleet of the English EIC, led by Captain Thomas Best, landed in Surat. This time around, the English were better prepared. Captain Best encountered the Portuguese fleet at Suvali, a small town near Surat, destroying three of the Portuguese galleons. His belligerence left the Mughal governor of Gujarat in awe, who promptly reported it to the emperor. Henceforth, Jahangir was more favourable towards the bold and fearless English merchants, and that marked the beginning of their ascent. Another reason for Jahangir's leaning towards the English was to safeguard the passage of Muslim pilgrims to Mecca via the Arabian Sea that was controlled by the whimsical Portuguese, who were unchallenged in the waters.

The Mughal court was divided over the Europeans. Jahangir's son, Khurram, favoured the Portuguese while another faction supported the English. Sensing the fluctuating moods of the Mughal court, the EIC's directors urged King James I to send a special ambassador. After much brainstorming, it was agreed that Sir Thomas Roe, a tall, well-spoken man with a commanding presence, would be sent to India.

Roe landed in Surat in September 1615 with a mission to conclude a commercial treaty with the Mughals. Jahangir was fascinated by his personality and offered him a gracious reception. Roe's journal paints a captivating picture of the Mughal court as a site of daily drunkenness and revelry, with Jahangir often ending the night dead-drunk. He also described a variety of other things like the misery of the peasants, how unsafe the highways were, and the general inefficiency and corruption of the local administrators. About the legal system of the Mughals, Roe noted: 'They have no written law. The King by his own word ruleth'.[13] He remained in India till 1619, and though he failed to secure a commercial treaty, he was able to obtain a *firman* (edict or order) that entailed permission to trade in India along with certain privileges, a landmark in the history of the EIC in India.

Business in seventeenth-century India was no less competitive than it is today. With mercantile traditions going back centuries, the

Indian market was dominated by several wealthy native merchants, like the Surat-based Jain merchant Virji Vora, who ran a business empire that traded in indigo, pepper, and cotton. As a banker, Vora lent considerable sums to the European trading companies and could negotiate very favourable terms from them.[14] Another merchant named Abdul Ghafur possessed some twenty ships, ranging between 300 and 800 tons each, and conducted a volume of trade that was equivalent to the whole of EIC's annual trade volume. Then there were others like Bhimji Parekh and Shantidas Zaveri who did wholesale business with Persia, Arabia, and East Africa and who had excellent relations with the Mughal headquarters in Agra and Delhi. Networks of such Gujarati traders extended to faraway lands, from the Philippines to Russia, and the *sarafs* (Gujarati moneylenders) lent capital at competitive interest rates.[15]

It was in the seventeenth century that the British merchants met the Parsis, a small and inconspicuous community that had been living in and around Gujarat for centuries since their escape from Persia after the Muslim conquest. The British merchants came to realise and appreciate the work ethic, diligence, and integrity of the Parsis and gave them a more substantial role as their agents. The fortunes of the Parsis grew along with the British, and over time they became wealthy and influential businessmen engaged in finance, shipbuilding, and the cotton and opium trade.

Then there was the Armenian merchant community which had flourished under the Mughal emperors. Akbar had encouraged the Armenians to settle in cities like Agra and Lahore and build their churches. He even married an Armenian woman. The Armenians were able to connect with the European trading companies and helped them with their knowledge of the vernacular languages and local business practices.[16] As the seventeenth century drew to a close, Armenian merchants were present in such European cities as Amsterdam and London where they were prominent merchants and freighters for the trading companies.[17]

Other European nations too were drawn to the lucrative trade with India. The Danish king's resolve to improve Denmark's economic situation led to the founding of the Østindisk Kompagnior, the Danish East India Company, in 1616. Two years later, a young admiral, Ove Gedde led the first Danish voyage to India, landing at the Coromandel Coast where he secured the rights to build a fort from the ruler of Thanjavur. Fort Dansborg was built at Tranquebar (Tharangambadi), 120 kilometres south of Pondicherry, and stands to date. The Danish Company, however, remained a fringe player and its fortunes rose temporarily whenever the dominant powers went to war.

The French arrived late in India. Jean-Baptiste Colbert, the finance minister to King Louis XIV, founded the Compagnie des Indes Orientales or the French East India Company in 1664. It was the letters of men like Francois Bernier, the French physician who served the Mughal emperors, and the precious stones merchant Jean-Baptiste Tavernier who brought the famous Le bleu de France or the Hope diamond to France, which had sparked off the idea of a French trading company. Bernier gave detailed descriptions of the economic conditions and the religious and social customs of India in his influential work *Travels in the Mogul Empire* (1671).

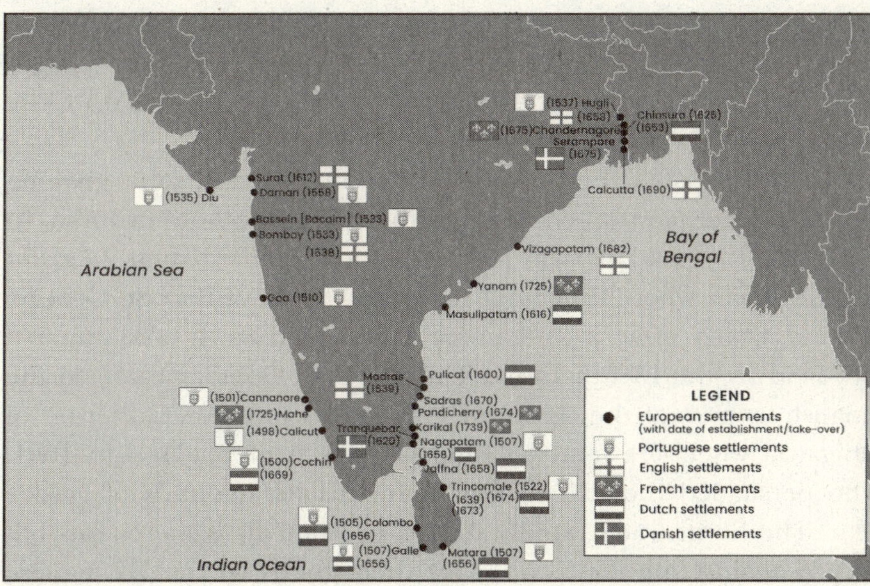

European settlements in India

The English Versus the Dutch

Political allies, yet fierce commercial rivals, the English and the Dutch followed different trajectories. The Dutch operated on a far more sophisticated financial system that allowed their government to borrow from its citizens. They had also earned the trust of financiers across Europe by repaying loans promptly, all thanks to highly profitable voyages. As a result, their companies enjoyed interest rates as low as 4 per cent compared to the hefty 10 per cent paid by English companies. Where the Dutch focused on rarer spices with high margins, the English traded in lower-margin, high-volume commodities like cotton textiles.

The Dutch were far ahead of the English in the initial decades, and yet in the long run, it was the English strategy that proved to be more resilient. The scarcity-based Dutch trade had a finite upside and required a significant investment to enforce the undersupply against rampant smuggling and espionage. Over a period of time, the social status and the exotic quotient of spices started to diminish, while stimulants like tobacco, tea, and coffee became a rage in Europe. The Dutch had concentrated so much effort on the spice trade that when the demand pattern changed, they were caught off-guard. From there on, Amsterdam's golden age started to lose its sheen.

In comparison, the business of the English EIC kept growing steadily as they continued to strengthen their foothold in India. In 1640, local Nayak rulers in southern India granted them land on the east coast where they built the trading post of Fort St. George, around which grew a settlement called Madras. It was the first site held by the EIC in India. The island of Bombay came to the English as part of the dowry of Portuguese princess Catherine of Braganza when she married King Charles II of England in 1661, who persuaded the EIC to rent it for just ten pounds of gold a year. The Surat trade rapidly shifted to Bombay as merchants felt secure against the confiscation of their goods by the Portuguese or the Mughal agents as was the case in Surat. In 1690, the EIC commander Job Charnoc decided on an unlikely village called Kalikata as their base for trade in Bengal. It was renamed Calcutta (now Kolkata), and would go on to become the 'second city' of the British Empire.

At the dawn of the eighteenth century, the EIC could boast of an enviable command over the seas, a flourishing trade in cotton textiles that eclipsed its spice trade in profitability, and three large Presidency towns of Calcutta, Madras, and Bombay on the east and west coasts of India. By 1720, the EIC had overtaken the Dutch VOC, which was on the wane, having faced mounting losses and rampant corruption among its employees. In 1741, the Travancore king Marthanda Varma's army defeated the VOC, resulting in the complete eclipse of Dutch power in Malabar. One of the VOC's employees stole some nutmeg and clove seedlings, which were then successfully replanted in Mauritius and Réunion. The swelling supplies sent the prices of the precious spices crashing down. What had started with espionage ended with the same. Before long, the once-mighty VOC was technically bankrupt and it was dissolved in 1800.

THE KNOWLEDGE DIVERGENCE

Europe had been witnessing a burst of intellectual curiosity since the onset of the Renaissance in the fourteenth century. The Italian genius Leonardo da Vinci (1452–1519), best known for his masterpieces, the *Mona Lisa* and *The Last Supper*, had conceived things like a helicopter and an armoured vehicle, centuries ahead of time. The oceanic discoveries in the late fifteenth century had introduced the Europeans to unknown lands and human populations as well as to old civilisations with different ways of life, that further aroused their curiosity and gave them a comparative perspective. Sailors venturing into the vast oceans found it imperative to study the heavens to locate themselves. Knowledge was now being acquired by experience rather than through an exposure to and an accumulation of myth, tradition, rumour, or speculation.

By 1450, there were only about 50,000 books in all of Europe, most of them controlled by the Church. German craftsman Johannes Gutenberg's invention of the movable-type printing press in 1450 revolutionised book production and made books affordable for the masses. By the end of the century, there were printing presses in 280 towns in Europe that had printed around 20 million books on an endless variety of subjects. Englishman William Caxton learnt the printing process in Belgium and brought it to England in 1476. His standardisation of the English language created a literary culture that spread widely. In Elizabethan England, people were reading books on a diverse range of subjects like gardening, anatomy, medicine, adventure, literature, seafaring, and social etiquettes, to name a few. England's literacy rate kept rising steadily: from 10 per cent of its male population in 1500 to 25 per cent in 1600, and from 1 per cent of its female population to 10 per cent in the same period.

By 1500, Europe had around seventy universities—England had two, Spain nine, France thirteen, and Italy twenty—thereby creating a vast network of knowledge creation and sharing.[18] European nations may have been perpetually at war with each other, but there was always room for ideas and curious minds to move around. It helped that Latin was the common language across Europe, for it made wandering scholars feel at home in the classroom.

It may have been a coincidence, but parallel to the knowledge explosion, was a religious upheaval that was unfolding all across Europe. Learned men had begun to question the Catholic Church's nearly absolute control over the people and the governments. In 1517, Martin Luther, a German pastor, penned a document attacking the Catholic Church's corrupt practices and posted his *95 Theses* on the church door in the town of Wittenberg. Luther argued that the Bible, and not the pope, was the central means to discern God's word. Helped by Gutenberg's printing press, a movement for religious reforms, known as the Protestant Reformation, began to spread rapidly across western and northern Europe, further contributing to the rising literacy rates and removing the barriers to intellectual progress.

An obscure Polish priest and astronomer Mikolaj Kopernik, better known as Copernicus, who attended the University of Bologna in Italy, posited that the planets revolved around the sun and not the earth, as was believed by virtually everyone until then. The Scientific Revolution is said to have begun when his book *On the Revolutions of the Heavenly Spheres* was published in 1543. The same year, Belgian anatomist Andreas Vesalius published one of the most influential books on human anatomy. Other great scientists, astronomers, philosophers, and physicians simultaneously emerged in Germany, Denmark, France, and Italy.

From across the channel, the English statesman and philosopher Francis Bacon devised an investigative method to test hypotheses by observing, measuring, and experimenting, rather than by using logic-based arguments. He published *Novum Organum* (*New Instrument*) in 1620, a treatise formulating the basics of the modern scientific approach. William Gilbert, the personal physician to Queen Elizabeth and a part-time scientist, published *De Magnete*, a book on magnetism and electricity, which is recognised as one of the greatest works of scientific discovery. His book influenced the Italian astronomer Galileo Galilei, who became one of the tallest figures of the Scientific Revolution.

In 1608, Hans Lippershey, a German-Dutch spectacle maker, invented the telescope, and within months, telescopes were being made and circulated across Europe. At the other end of the observation spectrum, the invention of the microscope made it possible for the human eye to view an entire world of microorganisms, which had previously been invisible. The leap from naked-eye vision to device-aided vision allowed the Europeans to explore remote corners of the earth, catch sight of new worlds beyond our planet, and solve biological mysteries. The early breakthroughs inspired an avalanche of discoveries and innovations in Europe that allowed it to assume the throne of scientific progress.

Author Steven Johnson has linked the era of the Scientific Revolution to the advent of coffee houses. The first documented coffee houses, *kaveh-kanes*, had opened in 1554 in Istanbul, from where the merchants brought the concept to Italy, France, Germany, and England. Europeans were soon addicted to the beverage and coffee houses became the intellectual hubs where philosophers, scientists, and inventors would hang out, sharing and debating their ideas. In an interesting argument, Johnson states that until the arrival of coffee, the beverage of choice in the English society was alcohol, and as the English suddenly switched from a depressant like alcohol to a stimulant like coffee, voila!—their minds became supercharged after a long slumber.

The Scientific Revolution and India

In the sixteenth and the seventeenth centuries, the East was the land of plenty compared to the West. European nations, other than Spain, were no match against the vast empires of the Mughals, the Ottomans and the Mings when it came to wealth, manpower, military strength, and the ability to build grand imperial structures. British economist Angus Maddison estimated that in 1600, India's share of the world Gross Domestic Product (GDP) stood at 23 per cent, as large as all of Europe put together. But by the time the British departed from India in 1947, its share had dropped to just over 3 per cent. No doubt the British colonial rule was exploitative and left India impoverished; however, lesser emphasis has been placed on the role of Europe's knowledge revolution in ensuring its future economic success and on understanding India's inability to catch up with this knowledge revolution.

Europeans like Sir Thomas Roe and Jean-Baptiste Tavernier had brought telescopes to the Mughal court, and yet the new scientific device hardly created any stir in India, which is surprising because astronomy, timekeeping, and calendars were essential to Muslims as well as to Hindus. Many other European merchants and diplomats brought compasses and terrestrial globes for Mughal emperors, princes, and nobles, who received them as novelties, ignoring their practical use and making no attempts to manufacture them. Highlighting the profound ignorance of anatomy among the Indian medical practitioners, Francois Bernier wrote:

> It is not surprising that the Gentiles understand nothing of anatomy. They never open the body either of man or beast, and those in our household always ran away, with amazement and horror, whenever I opened a living goat or sheep for the purpose of explaining to my Agah [assistant] the circulation of the blood, and showing him the vessels.[19]

Likewise, spring clocks remained expensive gifts for the Mughal royalty and were never made available to the masses, whose daily lives had forever been guided by the movement of the sun and the moon, and whose awareness of time was based on abstract cosmological concepts. Assessing the poor response to clocks, the EIC had resolved in 1613 to not send any more of them to India. By contrast, towns in Europe had public clocks sitting high on towers since the fourteenth century. These early communal machines were egalitarian in nature and inculcated a sense of and respect for time, as noted by the American historian Lewis Mumford, who called the clock 'an essential machine for the industrial age'.

The European Jesuits brought printed books to the Mughal court, but printing did not take off in India until the British introduced it in the nineteenth century. The disinterest and callousness towards the printing press were not only due to the Mughal elite's obsession with calligraphy. It could have also been a result of the ulema, the Muslim clergy, and the administrators not wanting the masses to acquire knowledge, similar to the ancient Vedic elite memorising texts instead of writing them down.

The Mughals, no doubt, deserve the credit for extraordinary achievements in architecture, art, and poetry. The artists in Akbar and Jahangir's ateliers incorporated Western techniques in their works, like the use of light, shade, and perspective; their ability to replicate Western art left European visitors like Thomas Roe astounded. The Mughal nobles and intellectuals were aware of European scientific thought, but they failed to appreciate the scale of disruption that the Scientific Revolution was about to bring. When Shah Jahan was building the Taj Mahal (1631–48) and the city of Shahjahanabad (1638–48), the English Puritans were founding Harvard University (1636). Around the same time, the world-famous Bodleian Library at Oxford was being built under the patronage of Sir Thomas Bodley, a diplomat in Queen Elizabeth's court. In 1645, a number of English natural philosophers, inspired by Francis Bacon's 'new science', established an informal group that would meet at various locations in London and Oxford and exchange ideas. It came to be known as 'the Invisible College' and is said to be the precursor to the Royal Society which was established in 1660.

While Akbar had shown remarkable openness in integrating non-Muslim subjects into his empire, and a tremendous curiosity towards various religions, encouraging vibrant debates on spiritual themes where he invited scholars and theologians of various faiths, his efforts seem to have had an opposite effect. His liberal attitude did not sit well with the ulema, who pushed for more orthodox measures and a greater emphasis on Quranic studies.[20] By the time Aurangzeb came to power after executing his scholarly brother Dara Shikoh and began imposing increasingly puritanical edicts, the English physicist and mathematician Isaac Newton was publishing his work *Principia Mathematica* (1687), one of the most important works in the history of modern science.

Scholarly pursuits remained within reach of only a few Mughal nobles, who also maintained personal libraries, while there were hardly any channels for curiosity to percolate down into the rest of the society, as had been the case for ages in India. Bernier and Roe wrote about the stark inequality that existed in the Mughal Empire between the ruling elites and the impoverished masses, who had no means or incentive to follow any creative or scholarly pursuits or even to improve their farming techniques and means of production. Where Europe had a vibrant ecosystem of universities and intellectual societies, Mughal India lacked the existence of institutions that were conducive to intellectual inquiry.

The colonial game had started with the discoveries of America and the oceanic route to India by Spain and Portugal respectively. Was it a coincidence that both the discoveries took place within a few years of each other? How was the economic and political environment in Europe at the time? How did the Portuguese establish a foothold in India? And why did the Spaniards not come to India when other Europeans did?

5

THE OCEANS CONQUERED

1410s–1540s

To boldly go where no man has gone before

—opening narration, *Star Trek*

The 1490s were a momentous decade in human history. In 1492, the daring Italian explorer Christopher Columbus set sail from southern Spain, determined to find a direct sea route to Asia, and stumbled upon a previously unknown continent—the Americas. Five years later, the Portuguese explorer Vasco da Gama departed from Lisbon, and rounding the Cape of Good Hope, landed in Calicut (now Kozhikode), becoming the first European to reach India by sea. For the first time ever in history, both hemispheres of the world were interlinked by ships and trade.

The path-breaking discovery of new sea routes heralded an era of rapid globalisation and flourishing colonial empires for Spain and Portugal, radically altering the orientation of global trade and interaction. The Silk Road network, which stretched from China to Europe and which had been the world's most important system of communication and commerce up until that point,[1] faded into insignificance, and central Eurasia lost its economic vigour. On the other hand, the Atlantic seaboard of Europe was transformed from a peripheral backwater into a powerful hub of trade and commerce.

Europe was on its way to becoming the new centre of the world.

How European expansion came about is an intriguing tale of adventure, ambition, curiosity, need for survival, and intense competition.

PRELUDE TO THE AGE OF EUROPEAN EXPANSION

For ages, among the most sought-after and aspirational commodities in Europe were spices like pepper, cinnamon, nutmeg, mace, and cloves, all of which came from the bountiful and fabled lands of the East. The reader may well wonder why the Europeans were so enthused about acquiring and using spices when all they supposedly ate was bland food. Well, back in those days, spices served multiple purposes—they were used to preserve food, to suppress the foul taste of stale meat, to enhance the flavour of wine, to cure a variety of ailments, to summon the gods, and sometimes were simply served as condiments. Above all, spices were seen as a marker of status, given how expensive they were. The price of pepper could go up to fourteen times between the Malabar and Alexandria, up to eighteen times by the time it reached Venice, and up to thirty times in London.[2]

For merchants, spices were the ideal commodity as they were extremely durable, had high value-to-weight ratio, and could be easily transported, stored, and repackaged into smaller sizes. The wealth of European merchants, cities, and nations depended on their access to and control of supply lines from the East. The Genoese and Venetian merchants regularly received cargoes of Eastern goods from ports in Egypt, the Levant, and the coastline of the Black Sea, though the life and culture of the East remained a complete mystery to them. It was in the late thirteenth and fourteenth centuries, that European friars, monks, and merchants, including the world's most famous traveller Marco Polo, made path-breaking journeys to Asia. Their riveting accounts of the 'enigmatic Orient' were widely relished in Europe.

The travel trend continued well into the fifteenth century,

keeping the allure of Asia alive in the European mind. One of the prominent travellers of this period was Niccolò de'Conti—a Venetian merchant and traveller who undertook a remarkable twenty-five-year-long odyssey to southern Asia. His merchant family had built a robust business trading with Egypt, but young Niccolo wanted to see the world beyond Alexandria and Cairo. In 1419, he travelled to Syria, where he learnt Arabic, which allowed him to pass off as a Muslim. After Syria, he travelled to Baghdad and other cities in Persia, where he learnt Farsi (Persian). While in Persia, he was involved in the sea trade with India and sailed to the Gulf of Cambay in Gujarat. Trekking further inland, he reached the glorious city of Vijayanagara (modern Hampi) and Maliapur (now Mylapore, a suburb of Chennai) before proceeding to Southeast Asia. On his return journey, he stopped at ports like Cochin and Calicut in the pepper country, carefully observing the landscapes and local cultures and taking extensive notes during all his travels.

Niccolo married an Indian woman, who bore him four children. When he finally returned to Venice in 1444, his exotic-looking family drew much curiosity among the locals. He compiled his notes into a vivid travel account, where he described India as a land with an abundance of aloes wood, gold, silver, precious stones, pearls, pepper, lac, ginger, and other herbs and dried fruits. Even more seminal than his observations was his speculation that Asia could be reached by sailing around Africa, a speculation that would stir the imagination of future Venetian cartographers and Portuguese explorers.

THE AGE OF EUROPEAN EXPANSION

A small, impoverished and isolated nation located in the far southwest corner of Europe, Portugal was bounded by other Iberian countries on one side and on the other side, by the vast Atlantic Ocean that no one had crossed. Portugal had emerged as a country around the tenth century during the Christian Reconquista of the Iberian Peninsula from the Moors (Muslims), and by the twelfth century, it had declared independence from the kingdoms of León and Castile.

Portugal was distant from the busy shipping lanes of the Mediterranean Sea where the lucrative East-West trade in spices and silks was dominated by the powerful city-states of Venice and Genoa, both of which were known to be ruthless seekers of monopolies. In a story somewhat similar to that of sixteenth-century England, the Portuguese had to strengthen their small country financially and politically to survive amidst the dominant European and Islamic powers. Leveraging their brain and brawn, and their ingenuity and aggression, the Portuguese not only survived but emerged as unlikely winners and built the first of the great European global empires.

There's Victory after Fear

Venturing into the oceans back then was like venturing into space during the space race era of the 1960s. Portuguese seamen had reached the Canary Islands, 1300 kilometres southwest of the Iberian peninsula, and developed an unrivalled understanding of sailing conditions in the Atlantic Ocean, which was stormier compared to the mostly calm Mediterranean Sea. But they had no idea of what lay beyond the Canaries. A deep fear of the unknown kept them from venturing any further into the ocean. For astronomical navigation, the Portuguese used Arab-invented instruments such as the astrolabe and the quadrant, but any further exploration called for better instruments and ships and a deeper knowledge of astronomy, mathematics, and geography.

Things started to change for Portugal in the early fifteenth century when King John I of Portugal challenged his Moorish rivals, taking over their North African city of Ceuta (now part of Spain) in 1415. His son, Prince Henry, played a crucial role in the capture of Ceuta and came to realise the importance of sea power during the conquest. Henry developed a passion for seamanship and spent the remaining four decades of his life and his personal fortune on a zealous pursuit of this passion, earning the nickname of 'the Navigator' even though he himself never sailed on any of the voyages.[3] He gave up his aristocratic life for a hermit-like existence near the port of Lagos (in southern Portugal), where he founded a school of navigation and mapmaking, employing sailing experts and Jewish mapmakers, who had escaped from Spain after facing persecution there. Henry was interested in improving ship designs and was eager to test prototypes. His sustained efforts resulted in a major technological innovation—the caravel, a smaller ship with triangular sails that sailed windward and which was capable of attaining remarkable speeds. Knowledge of the caravel was kept secret by forbidding sales of these vessels to other nations.

There were several reasons behind Henry wanting to promote exploration. As a staunch Christian who believed strongly in the crusade against Islam, he hoped that by sailing south and then east along the coast of Africa, the Moorish power in North Africa could be attacked from the rear. He was also keen to identify profitable trading opportunities, while being driven at the same time by sheer curiosity about what lay further south. There was yet another reason—a medieval myth about a powerful Christian monarch called Prestor John, who was believed to be holding out against surrounding Muslim forces somewhere in Africa. It was hoped that the explorations would locate Prestor John, who would then join hands with the Portuguese armies against the Muslims.

Henry's sailors were well-trained and better informed, yet no one dared to go past Cape Bojador on the African coast, around 240 miles south of the Canaries, as the ocean beyond Bojador was believed to be boiling—a replica of hell on earth. Almost fifteen years would go by with no sailor taking the plunge and Henry's patience and funds starting to run out. He finally convinced one Gil Eannes to take up the mission, which Eannes accomplished in 1434, landing beyond Bojador and returning with a few plants that grew there. By itself, the voyage had accomplished little, but an age-old psychological barrier of fear had been breached. Eannes was deservingly knighted, and now many seamen showed an interest in going farther south. Advancing with their step-by-step exploration, the Portuguese sailors reached modern-day Mauritania and started trading European wheat and cloth for African gold and slaves. It was the first time African gold had reached Europe without Muslim mediation. The slaves were sent to the island of Madeira, which became the first European plantation colony. By 1447, the Portuguese had explored the coasts of Senegal, Gambia, and Guinea.

In the meantime, another development was taking place in the eastern Mediterranean region that would turn out to be one of the most epoch-making events in history.

The Fall of Constantinople

Originally settled by the Greeks as Byzantium, the new city of Constantinople (now Istanbul), located at the confluence of Europe and Asia, was built by Constantine the Great between 324 and 330 CE as the capital of the Eastern Roman Empire (also known as the Byzantine Empire). Over the next thousand years, the city suffered many attacks and prolonged sieges, although no one could get past its legendary defences. By 1400, Constantinople was on the decline while the star of the Muslim Ottoman Empire, founded by Osman I in the late thirteenth century, was rising. By 1452, the Ottomans had conquered most of the territory of the Byzantine Empire, reducing it to the city of Constantinople. Henceforth, Sultan Mehmed II began gearing up to conquer the famed city.

Destined for glory, Sultan Mehmed II, only twenty-one years old, had one advantage that previous besiegers of Constantinople lacked: cannons. He had paid enormous sums for giant cannons that could blow up the sturdiest of walls. After constructing a fortress at the Bosphorus (the narrow strait that passes through Istanbul and links the Mediterranean Sea to the Black Sea), Mehmed assembled a large and experienced army and began the siege of Constantinople in April 1453. The walled city was relentlessly bombarded from both land and sea, and was finally breached on 29 May 1453. Looting, pillaging, and destruction followed. The city that had been the jewel of Christendom for twelve centuries had fallen. A triumphant Mehmed entered Constantinople and ordered that the Hagia Sophia church be converted into a mosque. He now assumed the imperial title of *Kayser-i Rum* (Caesar of Rome).

Constantinople was soon transformed into a vibrant and cosmopolitan city. Along with a rapid growth in its population commenced an architectural boom with new palaces, mosques, *hamams* (bathhouses), and markets starting to spring up all over the city. Constantinople was not only the capital of the Ottomans now, but also the glorious capital of the Islamic world.

The Ottomans imposed heavy tolls on ships entering and leaving the Black Sea and seized many of the Venetian and Genoese ports and land possessions along the coast of the Black Sea. Meanwhile, the Mamluks of Egypt raised tariffs on spices passing through Alexandria. Now, cargo from Asia could only reach Europe if so allowed by the whims of the Ottomans and the Mamluks. Business got increasingly challenging for Venice and Genoa as costs escalated for their merchants, pushing the prosperous city-states into a downward spiral. Furthermore, the access to the Silk Road land routes to Asia virtually ended for the European merchants, while the demand for Asian goods in Europe stayed very much alive. Some radical alternative had to be found.

Crowdsourced Map of the World

The Renaissance was an intellectual and cultural movement that saw a 'rebirth' in arts, science, and European society. It is generally considered to have started in Florence, Italy, around 1400, from where it spread to the rest of Europe. The fall of Constantinople triggered a flood of refugees travelling to Europe that included Greek scholars, poets, printers, astronomers, architects, and philosophers who carried with them thousands of texts. Many of them settled in Venice and Florence, further contributing to the growing intellectual climate.

One area that witnessed broad interest and rapid growth during the Renaissance was mapmaking. Advances in mechanical devices such as the printing press allowed for the mass production of maps and the ability to make accurate reproductions.

In Venice, the home of Niccolo de Conti and Marco Polo, and an old hub of itinerant merchants and foreigners, lived a monk and mapmaker named Fra Mauro who had spent years meticulously documenting the accounts of travellers and using that information to construct maps. His fame as a mapmaker spread as far as Portugal, where the king commissioned Mauro to produce a world map. He created the most definitive map of the world that represented an encyclopedic storehouse of information with almost 3,000 annotations and not a single embellishment of dragons or monsters, common in the divinely inspired maps of the time.

The Iberian Race to the Indies

Back in Portugal, Henry's lifelong support for exploration and his commercially unsuccessful voyages had left him impoverished, and he died in debt in 1460. Little did he know, however, that his efforts would have profound consequences for his nation's future. By this time, Portuguese seamen had gone farther till the mouth of River Gambia in West Africa.

After Henry's death, Portuguese exploration slowed down for a decade but revived its momentum in 1471, when they reached modern Ghana, which had abundant gold, and hence the name Gold Coast. King John II, who took over the Portugese throne in 1481, generated great wealth from the cargoes of gold, ivory, and slaves that came in from Africa, and which financed further expeditions.

The undaunted explorer Bartolomeu Dias set out from Lisbon in August 1487 and reached the southern tip of Africa, demonstrating that the Atlantic and the Indian Ocean were connected. Due to the storms he witnessed at the cape during the outward voyage, Dias named it the Cape of Storms. According to one historical account, King John II was elated over Dias's accomplishment, but he changed the name of the cape to a more optimistic Cape of Good Hope, for it raised the possibility of reaching India by sea from Europe.[4]

When Dias's caravels were sailing into the Lisbon harbour from their successful voyage, among the onlookers was a Genoese man named Christopher Columbus, who had approached King John II in 1484 and proposed an alternate sea route to Indies—sailing west across the Atlantic instead of going around Africa. His idea was not entirely new. It was first put forward by the Greek geographer and astronomer Eratosthenes in the third century BCE. In the late thirteenth century, the Vivaldi brothers, who were Genoese merchants, had made the first attempt to reach Asia by sailing westward, never to be heard from again. In 1474, Paolo Toscanelli, one of the most respected astronomers and cosmographers of the day, also outlined the same theory that the fastest route from Europe to India was to sail west.

Born in 1451, Christopher Columbus had taken to seafaring at an early age as a trader and grew into a highly skilled sailor and a master of the winds. Like most educated men of the time, he believed that the Earth was round, which meant that the Atlantic Ocean could be traversed. His reasoning was correct, but his calculations not so much. Not realising that the Arab mile was longer than the European one, and cherry-picking a few other geographical facts to support his proposed adventure, he ended up grossly underestimating the circumference of the Earth and the distance to the Indies. King John's advisers had assessed Columbus's plan and dismissed it as impossible. In 1488, Columbus was visiting Lisbon to make another attempt at persuading the king, but Dias's achievement had already opened a pathway to Asia and made Columbus's proposal look redundant. Disappointed, Columbus left Portugal and decided to try his luck with other European monarchs.

Meanwhile, the kingdoms of Castile, León, and Aragon in Spain had united to face the threat of the expanding Ottoman Empire and other Muslim states. In the last months of 1491, the combined forces of Aragon and Castile laid siege to the city of Granada, the last Moorish outpost in Spain, which surrendered in January 1492.

The timing was just right for Columbus. The Spanish monarchs, King Ferdinand of Aragon and Queen Isabella of Castile, euphoric over their victory, agreed to sponsor his mission and granted him a generous contract. In an era when the Christian crusading spirit and the anti-Islamic fervour was at a peak, Ferdinand and Isabella saw the proposed mission as an opportunity to export Catholicism across the globe and build pro-Christian alliances. Columbus, a devout Catholic, was on the same page. Besides, there was a genuine demand in Europe for spices and other goods that called for establishing a direct sea route to the Indies.

In early August 1492 began one of the most audacious journeys in all of history. Columbus, carrying a heavily annotated copy of Marco Polo's book, and in command of three ships—the *Santa Maria*, the *Nina*, and the *Pinta* (all of caravel design)—departed from the harbour at Palos in southern Spain. Beyond a certain point, there were no familiar landmarks, maps or accumulated experience to rely upon. After ten long weeks in the ocean, Columbus sighted land, in what is now the Bahamas in the Caribbean. His years of effort and tenacity had borne fruit and his dream of reaching the Indies was fulfilled—or so he believed. Convinced with his achievement, Columbus addressed the natives he encountered as 'Indians', a moniker that has surprisingly stuck to date.

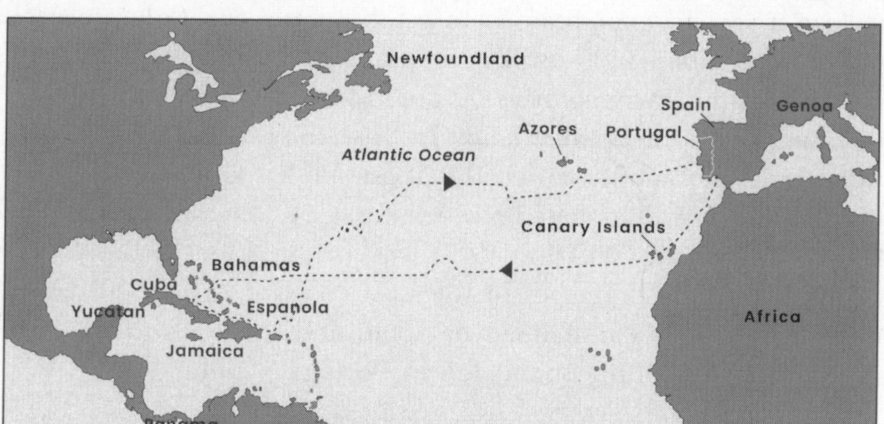

Columbus's landmark voyage

In one bold and successful attempt, Columbus had gained an unassailable lead over Portugal's decades-long systematic programme and commitment to oceanic exploration. On his return journey to Spain, unexpected storms forced Columbus to make a stopover at Lisbon, where King John invited him to his court. John regretted the lost opportunity to sponsor the mission though he did not hold back his admiration for Columbus's feat. The triumphant explorer, however, was not in a mood to display any humility and mocked the king. The king's men were infuriated and would have decapitated the Italian explorer had the king not restrained them. In March 1493, Columbus reached Spain and was generously honoured by the overjoyed Ferdinand and Isabella. In his official letter to the royal couple, Columbus wrote, 'there are very lofty and beautiful mountains, great farms, groves and fields, most fertile both for cultivation and for pasturage, and well adapted for constructing buildings... Hispana (an island so named by Columbus; modern Haiti and Dominican Republic) abounds in various kinds of spices, gold and metals'. His hyped account of the riches of the New World soon became a bestseller across Europe.

King John deeply resented Spain's entry into the field of exploration and discovery, which had been a forte of the Portuguese, and started planning to send his fleet across the Atlantic. When Ferdinand and Isabella heard of John's plans, they asked Columbus to lead a second expedition before John could act. Columbus set sail in September, 1493 on his second voyage with a large fleet of seventeen ships carrying over a thousand men, not only to explore but also to colonize the new lands. In 1494, the two nations, charged with global ambitions, signed the Treaty of Tordesillas that neatly divided the world in half between them. A line was drawn 370 leagues (around 2,000 kilometres) west of the Cape Verde islands (a few hundred kilometres to the west coast of Africa); all lands west of the line were claimed by Spain and the ones to the east of that line (including India) fell in Portugal's ambit.

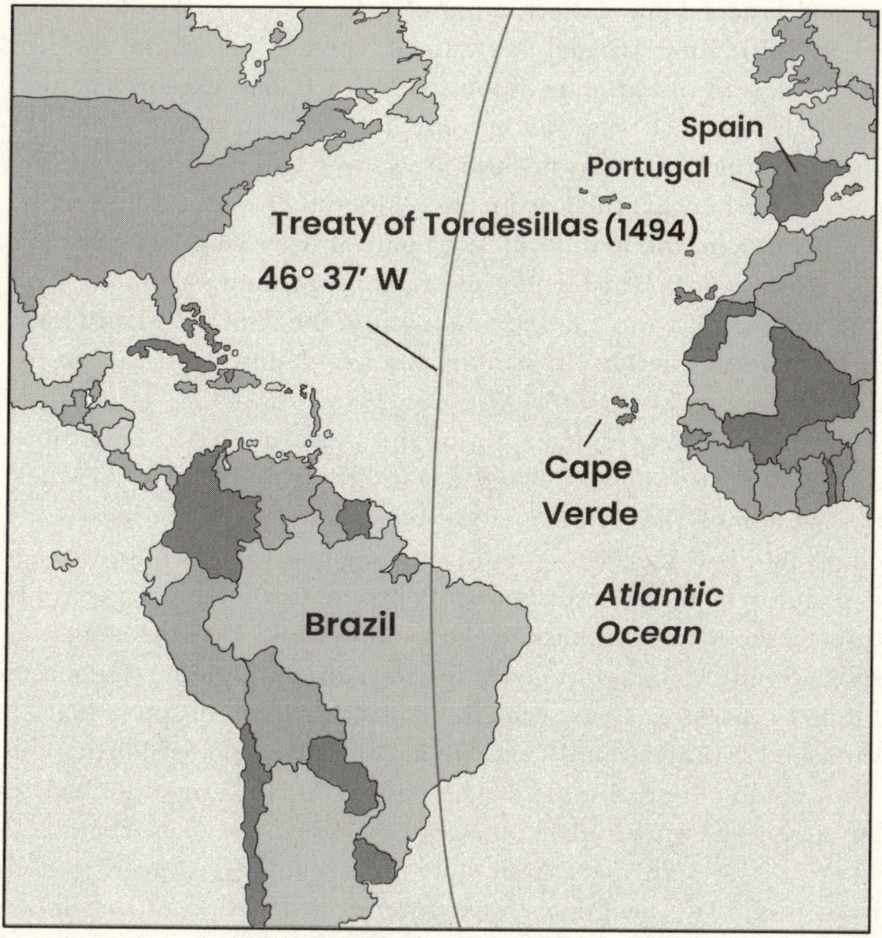

The demarcation line of the Treaty of Tordesillas

Back in Spain, people started to get suspicious when Columbus returned from subsequent voyages without any of the riches he had bragged about. At the end of his third voyage in 1500, he was arrested by a royal official appointed by the Spanish Crown to investigate charges of mismanagement and brutality towards the colonists. Columbus was sent back to Spain in shackles and was stripped of his rank as governor. After a fourth and final voyage, he died in 1506, still stubbornly holding on to the false claim that he had reached the eastern edge of Asia.

In 1501, King Manuel of Portugal, keen to determine the size of Brazil, sent out an expedition led by an Italian explorer named Amerigo Vespucci, who had become interested in seeing the world after meeting Columbus in 1496. It was only after Vespucci put the pieces together that the Europeans realised they were dealing with a whole new continent and not just a part of Asia. Vespucci's writings and extravagant claims made him famous, prompting the German cartographer Martin Waldseemüller to use the feminised Latin form of his name 'Amerigo' in naming the new lands 'America' on his map of the world in 1507.

Portugal's progress in exploring the area around Africa was slow; they had not advanced beyond the southern tip of Africa reached by Bartolomeu Dias in 1488. However, after seeing Columbus return empty-handed, the Portuguese camp regained momentum for an expedition to India. A spy named Pedro de Covilham was promptly dispatched on a reconnaissance mission to India. De Covilham, who spoke fluent Arabic, travelled through Cairo and Aden to Calicut in India. In his letter, he described the bustling trade in spices that he witnessed in Calicut and Goa. He also reported that if Portuguese ships could round the southern coast of Africa, they only had to advance a few hundred kilometres northward along its east coast, where they would meet Arab ships that regularly voyaged to and from India. De Covilham's letter offered positive proof that India could be reached by rounding Africa. Planning for what was perhaps the boldest and longest mission ever undertaken by Portugal was initiated, and a navigator named Vasco da Gama was appointed as the leader for the expedition.

On 8 July 1497, da Gama and the 170 men who were to sail with him, walked in procession through the streets of Lisbon to the docks where his four ships—the *St. Gabriel,* the *St. Raphael,* the *Berrio,* and a fourth store ship—lay at anchor. After a challenging journey, the fleet rounded Africa by Christmas and moved up the east coast, reaching Mozambique and Mombasa in April 1498. At both the places, they met with hostility when the local Muslims found out that they were Christians. At the next port of Malindi, da Gama found a guide who knew about the monsoon conditions at sea and helped da Gama sail north-east towards India, finally making landfall in Calicut on the Malabar Coast in May 1498.

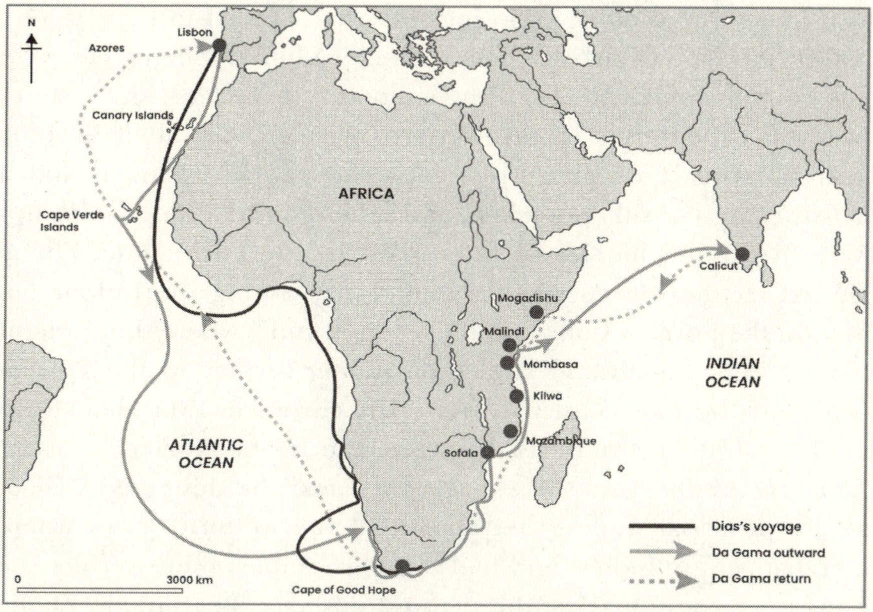

Vasco da Gama's route to Asia

As was the norm among seamen, da Gama sent ashore a *degredado*, a criminal deemed to be expendable, to initiate communication with the Indians. Neither of the sides, however, could understand each other's language until some visiting Tunisian merchants stepped in as translators. The Indians were astonished to learn how far the Portuguese had come from.

In the following days, the Portuguese were constantly surrounded by crowds who were intrigued by the newly arrived light-skinned foreigners. The Zamorin's (Samoothri, the Hindu ruler of the Malabar region) men burst into laughter when they saw the gifts that da Gama had brought for their master—casks of oil and honey, six hats, four strings of coral, a few pieces of striped cloth, and a few bells and bowls. Da Gama had to pretend that they were not meant for the Zamorin, rather they were things that he, a poor traveller, had brought for himself.

The Portuguese ships too, may not have impressed the Indians, as far bigger and more imposing ships had landed in Calicut long before da Gama's arrival. The Chinese admiral Zheng He, who was commissioned by the Ming emperor to embark on a series of naval expeditions to the western oceans, had sailed in 1405 with an armada of sixty-three ships carrying 27,000 men and a massive cargo of silk, porcelain, and other goods. Zheng He's ships were five times the size of those used by the Portuguese. Zheng He led six more such voyages until 1433, visiting the Indonesian islands, the ports of Calicut and Cochin in India where they bought pepper and sandalwood, and then sailing further to the Persian Gulf and the east coast of Africa. His chronicler Ma Huan gave vivid accounts of the ports they visited in his book *Ying-Yai Sheng-Lan* (*The Overall Survey of the Ocean's Shores*); he described Calicut as the principal trading destination of the western ocean where merchants were honest and had the remarkable ability to calculate numbers without making the slightest mistakes. Regrettably, Zheng He's achievements were not followed up with further exploratory voyages as the emperor's court saw a change of attitude towards the outside world and became isolationist, remaining so for the next few centuries.

Da Gama's return journey was full of mishaps; two ships were lost, and many men died of scurvy during the ordeal. Only 55 of the original crew of 170 made it back to Lisbon in August 1499. Despite the setbacks, da Gama had proved the feasibility of the route and had established that there were no maritime fleets in the Indian Ocean that could hinder Portuguese access to the spice trade. The then king of Portugal, Manuel I, was ecstatic and gave a magnificent reception for da Gama and his men for their triumphant homecoming. Mass celebrations took place in Lisbon, and da Gama was compared with Alexander the Great for opening up a new and unfamiliar world in the East. It is worth noting that in sharp contrast to that day of celebration in Portugal in August 1499 stands the day in December 1961 when 30,000 Indian troops liberated Goa and other possessions like Daman and Diu from Portuguese rule under Operation Vijay. Portugal went into a virtual mourning and Christmas celebrations were muted that year.

While Columbus had made vague and empty promises, da Gama had produced concrete evidence of the riches that lay in the East. King Manuel wrote a boastful letter to Ferdinand and Isabella of Spain, informing them of the Portuguese 'discovery' and telling them that his explorers had found large cities where extensive trade was carried out in spices and precious stones, which he was now going to take over. He even bestowed upon himself a new title: 'Lord of Guinea and of the conquest of the navigation and commerce of Ethiopia, Arabia, Persia and India'.[5]

The Spaniards were not the only ones feeling eclipsed. Even the Venetians, who had pioneered the art of commercial dominance, were shocked and saddened by the news of da Gama's feat. Akin to nimble modern-day start-ups disrupting the functioning of giant corporations and industries, Portugal had severely undermined, if not outright obsoleted Venice's business model. A Venetian merchant wrote in his diary: 'in this, I clearly see the ruin of the city of Venice'.[6]

The Portuguese soon made preparations for the next voyage, this one a much larger expedition commanded by a nobleman and navigator named Pedro Alvares Cabral, and accompanied by Bartolomeu Dias. The fleet had twelve well-armed ships, carrying a thousand men and ample bullion for trading. They departed in March 1500, and while sailing down the African coast, as they turned out into the Atlantic Ocean to gain the advantage of the south-east trade winds, their ships were carried further west than intended and accidentally ended up on the coast of South America. They'd landed in modern-day Brazil; one ship was sent back to Lisbon to announce their discovery. As the rest of the fleet proceeded to India, they ran into a fierce storm off the Cape of Good Hope, and four ships were lost. In a cruel twist of fate, one of the wrecked ships was captained by Bartolomeu Dias, the first European to have sighted the cape.

On reaching Calicut, Cabral had a more successful trading experience than da Gama as he was better supplied with trading goods. But short on diplomatic skills, Cabral ended up having an altercation with the local Muslim merchants, which turned into a violent conflict where he resorted to the bombardment of the unfortified town. His fleet then departed in a hurry and sailed 150 kilometres further down the coast to Cochin, where he was able to procure spices and establish a permanent trading post. Upon his return to Lisbon with five ships and a massive cargo of pepper, Cabral's expedition was considered a partial success given the loss of seven vessels and the violent incident in Calicut. The vast potential for profits had been unveiled, but that said, the sea route to India via the Cape of Good Hope would remain perilous and the list of shipwrecks would be painfully long for decades.

The First Circumnavigation of the Earth

In the list of greatest explorers in history, there was one more intrepid explorer from the same era who fearlessly went where no man had ever gone before. In fact, his feat eclipsed the voyages of Columbus and da Gama in both ambition and determination. It was the Portuguese navigator Ferdinand Magellan, who led the first expedition (1519–1522) to successfully circumnavigate the globe. His achievement could be repeated only after sixty years by Elizabethan hero, pirate, and navigator Francis Drake, whom readers would recall from the previous chapter.

In 1505, twenty-five-year-old Magellan was assigned to a Portuguese fleet headed for India. Over the next seven years, he was part of several naval expeditions and battles in places like Cannanore (now Kannur), Diu, and Malacca, where he was wounded a few times. At one point, Magellan was accused of trading with the enemy and fell out of favour with the Portuguese king, eventually losing his position. Hurt and disappointed, he began pondering over ways to win the honours that had eluded him. Poring over maps and charts of the latest geographical discoveries at the royal library in Lisbon, Magellan envisioned a unique voyage, an expedition far bolder than da Gama's journey to Asia. He would sail west from Europe all the way to the spice islands in Asia, crossing a strait that he believed existed below the southern end of America. He presented his idea to Spain's King Charles, explaining that the spice islands fell in the Spanish realm as per the Tordesillas line. The king accepted the idea with enthusiasm and agreed to sponsor the audacious expedition.

Embarking upon one of the greatest adventures in the history of navigation, Magellan departed from Spain in September 1519 in command of five ships carrying 260 men. Despite facing uncertainty, extreme cold, shipwreck, mutiny, treacherous passes, scurvy, starvation, and death, Magellan's men persevered under his steadfast leadership and expert seamanship. He discovered what is now known as the Strait of Magellan (at the bottom of South America) and became the first European to enter an unfamiliar but calm ocean that he named 'Pacific'. The Pacific Ocean, which covers nearly half of the world's total water surface and a third of the globe's total surface area, turned out to be much more vast as Magellan and his crew discovered painfully. Finally, Magellan sighted land in March 1521, claiming the islands and naming them the Philippines after King Philip II. A month later, the great explorer was killed in a skirmish on one of the islands where he was assisting a local king.

After a three-year-long marathon journey, only one ship made it back to Spain with eighteen surviving crew members in a battered and depleted condition. Magellan's monumental endeavour had revealed the true scale of our planet and proved that it was possible to sail around it. He had also paved the way for establishing a Spanish colony in Asia, while opening the doors to the lucrative spice trade for his sponsors.

ENGLAND MISSES THE BOAT

Around the year 1488, Christopher Columbus had sent his brother, Bartholomeu Columbus, to England to seek sponsorship from King Henry VII for their plan of sailing to Asia, but he was turned down. Four years later, the English king was jolted out of his complacency when Columbus returned from his landmark voyage under the banner of the Spanish Crown. Henry VII then commissioned a Venetian navigator named Giovanni Caboto (John Cabot), who claimed that it was possible to reach Asia via a more northerly route than the one Columbus had taken.

After an aborted attempt in 1496, Cabot sailed again in May 1497 from Bristol in a small vessel, the *Mathew,* with a crew of eighteen men. Few weeks later, he made landfall on the shores of what is now the Canadian province of Newfoundland, but which he, like Columbus, mistakenly believed to be the north-eastern coast of Asia. Howsoever, readers must note that Columbus and Cabot were not the earliest Europeans to have reached the New World. The Vikings had reached Canada's eastern seaboard five centuries before them and founded a settlement in Newfoundland that they called Vinland.

Cabot returned to England in August to an enthusiastic welcome and reported that the land and climate of the place where he reached were excellent, and the sea was full of so many fish that England need not depend on Iceland anymore. Raimondo de Soncino, the ambassador of the Duke of Milan in London, wrote in a letter to the duke that '(Henry VII) has acquired a portion of Asia, without a stroke of the sword' and that 'they hope to make London a greater place for spices than Alexandria.'

Cabot's voyage had certainly provided England with a claim to a new land and a great source of fishing, yet gold, silver, spices, or trade opportunities—for which the Bristol merchants had invested their money—were nowhere to be found. Planning began for a second expedition and Cabot set sail again in 1498 with five ships and about 200 men, but the fate of the voyage and Cabot remains a mystery. And a year later, he was given up for dead.

More voyages of exploration followed, including one led by Cabot's son Sebastian in 1508, in the hopes of discovering a quicker route to Asia, and each one found an enormous, cold and forested continent that was evidently not Asia. Nonetheless, the idea of reaching Asia through a north-western passage would remain entrenched in the English mind for decades.

When King Henry VII died in 1509, his son Henry VIII showed little interest in continuing with the expeditions for he was most concerned with protecting his realm from domestic disturbances as well as foreign threats. Also, the investors did not have an appetite for expensive oceanic ventures with limited upside potential anymore.

Concurrently, the Portuguese had followed up the initial expeditions of da Gama and Cabral with more voyages round the Cape of Good Hope that were fabulously profitable. In 1527, an English merchant named Robert Thorne, who had lived in Seville, Spain, for many years and had observed the Portuguese trade with Asia, compiled his notes with a map and shared them with Henry VIII. It was a comprehensive proposal for England to explore a north-western route to Asia and replicate the successful spice trade of the Portuguese. A voyage was attempted, but it ended in failure and the idea was shelved for decades.

In the meantime, the arrival of the Spaniards in the New World had been catastrophic for the flourishing Inca Empire, the largest empire in the world at the time extending from Colombia to Chile, and the Aztec Empire of Mexico. Gold and silver pillaged from the Incas and the Aztecs started to pour into Spain's coffers. However, the real windfall gains came in 1545, when the Spaniards discovered a prodigious source of silver at a mountainous place called Potosí, in modern Bolivia. A year later, silver was found in Zacatecas in Mexico, followed by other significant deposits across modern Peru, Bolivia, and Mexico. By the end of the sixteenth century, the Spanish treasure fleet was returning to the ports of Seville and Cadiz with a staggering 3 million kilos of silver annually. The Spaniards were also sending shipping vessels called Manila galleons, carrying silver and minted coins, from the west coast of Mexico across the Pacific to the Philippines to buy silks, spices, ivory, and porcelain. A large community of Chinese merchants had sprung up in the Philippines to cater to the Spanish demand for Asian luxuries.

Unlike the Spaniards, the Portuguese did not find silver or gold in the New World. But they did find an abundance of brazilwood trees, from where Brazil gets its name, that became the colony's chief export to Europe. They also introduced sugar plantations, deploying enslaved Africans to work on them, and turned the entire business into a profitable industry. Their real fortunes, however, lay in the Old World where they emerged as the dominant trading power.

ESTADO DA INDIA

New Rules of the Game

Unlike the Iberians, Indians did not have a tradition of seafaring or mapmaking. Historically, dominant-caste Hindus were restricted from going out to the seas, and trades like fishing and pearl-diving were left to those from the oppressed-castes. Tome Pires, a Portuguese pharmacist and traveller who wrote a landmark book on Asian business, *The Suma Oriental*, recorded that neither the Brahmins nor the Nayars of Malabar were going to the sea and that it was the Mappila Muslims who dominated the sea trade. Likewise, the Hindu and Jain merchants of Gujarat and the Saraswat Brahmins of Goa refrained from undertaking sea voyages or even operating the business of shipping, and stuck, instead, to retail trade, brokerage, and banking.

The mercantile world of the Indian Ocean operated according to long-established traditions where unarmed trade was the norm. Neither the Arabs nor the Indians had strong navies, other than a handful of small ships to control sporadic piracy. Ports like Calicut, Cambay, Cochin, Malacca, Aden, Hormuz, and Mombasa competed to attract the largest amounts of cargo by offering the lowest possible tariffs while ensuring that they were viewed as secure destinations.

The notion that any nation might want to forcefully control movement in the seas would have sounded absurd to the ruling elites of the time. Enter the Portuguese, who introduced to the Indian Ocean trade the practice of using state-controlled violence to control sea routes, a method that was common in Europe since the Greco-Roman times.[7] Besides, the Portuguese were motivated by religious fervour and a long-standing animosity towards the Muslims.

The Portuguese sailors noticed that the Indian and Arab ships and *dhows* (one- or two-masted Arab sailing vessels) sailed only at particular times of the year, harnessing the unique monsoon (from the Arabic *mawsim*) winds of the Indian Ocean, and were not strong enough to withstand cyclones or typhoons (from the Arabic *tufan*). In comparison, the Portuguese ships could withstand any weather condition, and having mastered the art of mounting cannons on their ships, they could blow apart the Indian and Arab ships with remarkable ease. They brutally enforced their spice monopoly, capturing or destroying ships of native merchants and rulers. In one instance where the Portuguese seized a few ships of Calicut merchants, they took the sailors prisoners and cut off their hands, noses, and ears, and burnt their mutilated bodies in one of their ships. The only way the native merchants could escape the Portuguese savagery was to buy from them *cartaz*, which were permits that granted safety to the native ports and to their ships. Simply put, it was a ruthless but well-organised protection racket.

The Portuguese resorted to such barbarism not just because of their desperate desire to survive in the global economy, but also because of a fanatic sense of nationalism, given how insignificant and weak their nation was perceived to be. Unlike Spain, which had a population of around 7.5 million in 1500, Portugal had barely 2 million people, which was simply not enough to build a land-based empire, but was enough to enforce their monopoly over oceanic routes. The spice trade formed a substantial part of their state revenue, which they could not afford to lose out to either the Arabs, the Egyptian Mamluks or other traders. Therefore, the Portuguese resorted to sensational violence, letting the terror resonate through the Indian Ocean as a warning until their next fleet arrived from Lisbon.

The Portuguese Establish a Foothold in the Indian Ocean

In 1505, a powerful armada of 22 ships carrying several thousand men (including Magellan) under the command of Francisco de Almeida, who was appointed Portugal's first viceroy, sailed to India. By now, Portugal was beginning to significantly impact the Asia-Europe spice trade dominated by the Muslims. As Portugal's fortunes soared, prospects got dimmer for the Venetian merchants who were still reeling from the fall of Constantinople. Several pragmatic traders started to transfer their capital from Venice to Lisbon. Two years later, a Portuguese fleet conquered Hormuz, the port city in the Persian Gulf, further denting the Muslim trade. The zamorin of Calicut, the Muslim rulers of Gujarat and Aden, and the Sharif of Mecca appealed to the Mamluk Sultan for assistance, who agreed and sent a large fleet. But Almeida's naval forces inflicted a decisive defeat on the Mamluk fleet off Diu in 1509, where a Portuguese base was then established.

In 1510, the Portuguese defeated the Bijapur sultans, anchoring their position in India. They established the permanent settlement of Goa, with one of the finest harbours in the world that was easily defensible and protected from storms. It served as the headquarters of Portuguese India, and as the seat of the Portuguese viceroy. With massive forts in places like Diu, Daman, Bassein, Chaul, and Cannanore, and with a formidable navy, Goa was able to enforce its domination over the seas and coastal India.

'Whoever is lord of Malacca', wrote Tom Pires, 'has his hand on the throat of Venice.' The Portuguese seized the port of Malacca in 1511, and that gave them control over the narrow strait from where the ships from Spice Islands passed on their way to India. Over the following decade, they spread their wings to Ceylon, Burma, and Madagascar, and built fortified trading posts at crucial ports and harbours from West Africa to Asia. By then, Asian imports contributed to nearly 40 per cent to the Portuguese crown's total revenue. Business continued to boom throughout the sixteenth century, and at its peak, Portuguese ships were returning with over 4,000 tons of cargo each year.

What is lesser known is that the Portuguese earned as much or even greater profits by trading commodities like spices, cotton, textiles, and sandalwood within Asia rather than carrying them to Lisbon. Then there was another highly lucrative business—the trading of horses, which were essential for the armies of the Indian rulers.Very few horses were bred in India, so they had to be procured from Central Asia. The New World bullion that made its way into the coffers of the Indian rulers was behind the boom in the horse trade and had brought another burst of splendour to the otherwise declining Central Asian cities. Through their command over the seas, the Portuguese came to dominate the business of shipping horses from the Persian ports to coastal India. The regional rulers of India tried to secure exclusive rights over the purchase of these Central Asian horses at Goa, where the Portuguese played them off against each other, earning spectacular profits.

The Portuguese, who now claimed to be 'lords of the sea', became so fearsome that ships from other countries dared not sail into the Indian Ocean without their written consent. It was the first time ever that an empire was built by controlling commercial maritime routes and networks that lay thousands of kilometres away from Portugal. In the long run, however, Portugal's strategy of aggression and violence in maritime trade would bring in increasingly diminished returns due to the ballooning military expenditure and a long list of enemies.

A Wave of Proselytisation

Initially, the Portuguese had shown little interest in religious conversions, but the relationship between the Portuguese Christians and the Indians was set to change in 1538 when the first bishop arrived in Goa. The Church expropriated the lands of the Hindu temples while many temples were destroyed entirely. To convert the natives, the Portuguese evangelists offered rice donations to the poor, many of whom accepted them opportunistically, becoming what were called 'rice Christians'.

A band of seven Spaniards had met in a chapel in Paris in 1534 and founded the Society of Jesus. From there on, the members of this organisation were called Jesuits, and they travelled all over Europe first and later around the world, spreading their message. One of these Jesuits was St. Francis Xavier (1506–1552) who went on to become the foremost Roman Catholic missionary of modern times, and who was instrumental in the establishment of Christianity in India and the Far East. Many prestigious schools and colleges named after him exist all over India.

St. Francis Xavier reached Goa in May 1542 and spent the next few years travelling from village to village. In one month, he is said to have converted over 10,000 villagers in southern Malabar. Horrified by what he regarded as the idolatrous practices of Goa's Hindus and doubting the religious sincerity of the new Christian converts in Goa, he wrote a letter to the king of Portugal in 1545, requesting an inquisition to be set up for the purification of Christian faith in Goa. The intolerant Portuguese administration imposed harsh measures on the Hindus, banning Christians from employing Hindus, making the public worship of Hinduism a punishable offence, and intimidating the natives with the threat of brutal torture. A wave of conversions followed, while many who did not want to convert to Christianity migrated further inland. An ambitious programme of constructing churches, monasteries, and convents was also launched.

Similarly in the islands of East Asia, the Portuguese missionary zeal and the increasing number of conversions left the Muslim sultans, who had greatly exploited their own people, feeling threatened. The friction over religion, along with their brutal trading practices made the Portuguese increasingly unpopular in the region, as the Dutchman Linschoten would later record in his diary and Francis Drake would find out in the Moluccas.

THE CITY OF VICTORY

Vijayanagara, meaning the 'city of victory', was the imperial capital of the great Vijayanagara empire (named after the capital city itself) that existed centuries ago. A part of the city's ruins is located at Hampi (about 350 kilometres north of Bengaluru), which is now a UNESCO World Heritage Site.

By the fifteen and sixteenth centuries, Vijayanagara was one of the greatest cities in the world, the second-most populous after Beijing, attracting explorers and traders from faraway nations. In his travel account, Niccolo de Conti had described it thus: 'The great city of Bizenegalia (Vijayanagara) is situated near very steep mountains. The circumference of the city is sixty miles; its walls are carried up to the mountains and enclose the valleys at their foot, so that its extent is thereby increased. In this city, there are estimated to be ninety thousand men fit to bear arms.... Their king is more powerful than all the other kings of India.'

While Vijayanagara hasn't found the prominence in Indian history books that it deserves, one must note that it had altogether disappeared from all historical records and public memory until the year 1900 when Robert Sewell, a British civil servant, wrote *A Forgotten Empire*, an aptly titled translation of the account of Vijayanagara by Portuguese travellers Domingo Paes and Fernao Nuniz.

The Vijayanagara Empire was founded in 1336 by two brothers, Harihara and Bukka, who appear to have voluntarily given their allegiance to the Delhi sultan Muhammad bin Tughlaq when he was based at Daulatabad (near Aurangabad, Maharashtra). Besides providing a barrier against the southward expansion of the Muslim Delhi Sultanate, Vijayanagara gave royal patronage to Hindu culture, although contact with Muslims was routine, as was reflected in their architecture. It was the illustrious emperor Krishnadeva Raya who, during his reign from 1509 to 1529, turned Vijayanagara into the paramount power in the peninsula. He was known for his hospitality towards foreign visitors and was equally admired by them. Domingo Paes wrote that Vijayanagara was 'as large as Rome and very beautiful to the sight', and that Krishnadeva Raya was 'a great ruler and a man of much justice'.[8]

Afonso de Albuquerque, the governor of Portuguese India from 1509 to 1515, sent his ambassador to Krishnadeva's court desperately seeking help against the ruler of Calicut. The governor asserted that the king of Portugal had ordered him to wage war against the Moors (Muslims) but not against the Hindus, and that they could have a reciprocal understanding. That marked the beginning of diplomatic relations between the Portuguese and Vijayanagara kingdom.

After over two centuries of glorious run came the drastic fall of Vijayanagara at the Battle of Talikota (1565), where its army was routed by the combined forces of the Deccani Muslim states (Bijapur, Ahmadnagar and Golconda). For the next five months, the city was plundered, its temples and palaces destroyed, and residents massacred. The great city never rose again.

THE GUNPOWDER EMPIRES

In 1505, as the Portuguese armada under the command of Francisco de Almeida was approaching India, another conqueror was leading his horse-riding warriors through treacherous mountain passes of the Hindu Kush range on his first raid on Hindustan. His name was Zahir-ud-Din Muhammad (1483–1530). Popularly known as Babur, he was born in the city of Andijan in the Ferghana valley in Uzbekistan and was a direct descendant of both Timur (also known as Tamerlane) as well as Genghis Khan. Babur had briefly held Samarkand, the city that every one of Timur's descendants coveted, but was driven out at a young age by fierce opponents. He escaped along with a small band of loyal followers to Afghanistan, where he gradually built a strong army. In 1504, Babur seized Kabul, which became his home for the next two decades. After several failed attempts at reclaiming Samarkand, Babur decided to look eastwards at India.

In 1526, Babur descended upon the plains of northern India with a force of around 10,000 men and met with the massive, ten-times larger army of Ibrahim Lodhi, the Delhi Sultan, at Panipat, 90 kilometres north of Delhi. Despite being outnumbered, Babur held a notable advantage over his daunting opponent—powerful artillery that he had obtained from the Ottoman Turks. He routed the sultan's army and marched into Delhi, thus founding the Mughal Empire in India.

Babur wrote his memoir, called the *Baburnama*, which was the first autobiography in Islamic literature, and where he presented a vivid picture of life in Central Asia, Afghanistan, and India:

> Hindustan is a place of little charm. There is no beauty in its people, no graceful intercourse, no poetic talent or understanding, no etiquette, nobility, or manliness. The arts and crafts have no harmony or symmetry. There are no good horses, meat, grapes, melons, or other fruit. There is no ice, cold water, good food or bread in the markets. There are no baths and no madrasas... The one nice aspect of Hindustan is that it is a large country with lots of gold and money. The weather turns very nice during the monsoon... Another nice thing is the unlimited numbers of craftsmen and practitioners of every trade.[9]

Like the Portuguese who had used firepower to dominate the waters, the Mughals used canons and gunpowder to establish their supremacy over land. Their peers, the Safavids in Iran and the Ottomans in the Middle East and eastern Europe, both land-oriented Islamic empires with similar Turkic-Mongol roots, followed the same path and all three came to be known as the Gunpowder Empires.

The Mughals

While the Portuguese were firming up their position on the west coast of India, Babur's descendants were consolidating their territorial conquests and creating an empire that would dominate the whole subcontinent for two centuries and also far supersede the Safavids and even the Ottomans in wealth. Unlike the Safavids and the Ottomans, the Mughals governed an overwhelmingly non-Muslim population, creating a distinctive culture that was a hybrid of both Central Asian and Indian heritage and traditions. Babur's grandson Akbar, the greatest of all the Mughal emperors, was exceptionally tolerant of the different religions of his subjects, which put him in stark contrast to his Iberian peers who brutally imposed Catholicism on the people they conquered.

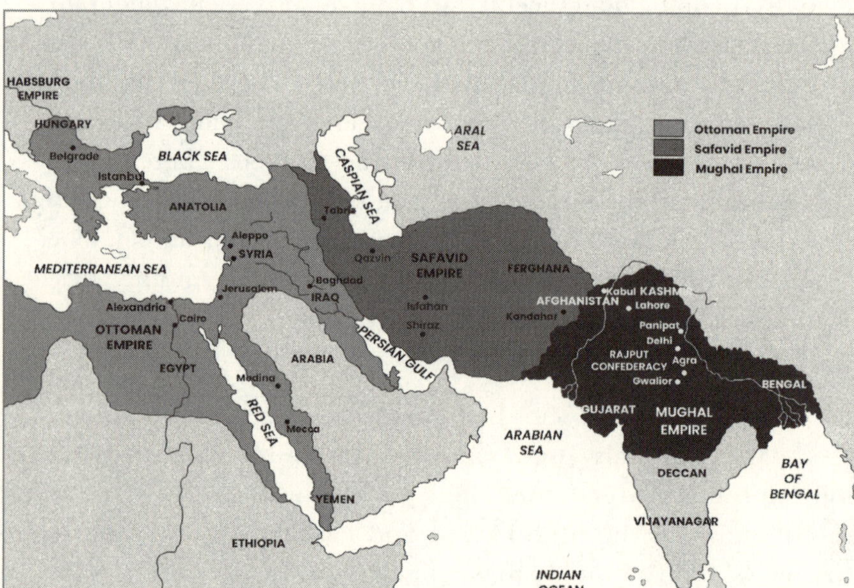

The Gunpowder Empires

While the Portuguese dominated the Indian Ocean, their influence on India remained restricted to the narrow coastal strip between the sea and the Western Ghats, a mountain range that acted as a natural barrier. The Portuguese expansion was also constrained by their population, which had reached a mere 2 million by 1600, compared to the over hundred million subjects of the Mughal Empire.

The Mughals associated prestige and glory with winning campaigns on land and were not really drawn to the sea. Babur never saw the sea in his lifetime, while Akbar glimpsed it for the first time when he visited coastal Gujarat. The Mughals were not alarmed by the Portuguese and therefore did not see any reason to track their maritime activities. After all, no invader had ever arrived in India by sea. Nevertheless, they did care about one thing—the access to Mecca that the ports of Western India provided to pilgrims.[10] Conversely, the Portuguese factories (trading ports) needed Mughal support as they were dependent on products from towns that lay that lay deep inland, and were, therefore, vulnerable to raids. A strategic balance thus prevailed between the two newly arrived powers in India.[11]

The Ottomans

The Ottoman Empire became one of the most powerful and long lasting empires in the world, reaching its peak during the reign of Suleiman the Magnificent, Babur's peer, from 1520 to 1566. Centred in modern Turkey, the empire was enormously wealthy and included eastern Europe, western Asia, the north coast of Africa, and parts of Arabia. The empire's military strength, steady expansion into Europe and a strong naval presence in the Mediterranean Sea remained a cause of worry for the Europeans.

The Ottomans had a series of armed conflicts with the Portuguese in the Indian Ocean, the Persian Gulf, and the Red Sea. In 1538, when the Ottoman fleet allied with a naval force of the Muslim ruler of Gujarat and laid siege to the Portuguese fort in Diu, the Portuguese managed to thwart the attack. Another attempt was made in 1546 to besiege the fortress of Diu, but the

Portuguese prevailed again. Not being able to cause any significant damage to Portuguese shipping, the Ottomans discontinued further action and turned their attention westwards towards Europe.

The Safavids

The Safavids, who had roots in Azerbaijan, came to the forefront in 1502 when Shah Ismail I, an exact contemporary of Babur, united the various provinces of Persia and claimed the throne. The Safavid Empire, although militarily muscular, was not a match for the Ottomans, but as the empire grew in territory, the Safavids came into conflict with the Ottomans, who became their perennial enemies. They fought over the region of modern Iraq for over a century, with the control of Baghdad going back and forth between them. The Ottoman and the Safavid conquests of the Armenian highlands in the sixteenth century drove many Armenians across the Ottoman and Persian empires. Some settled in cities like Istanbul and Isfahan while others migrated to the Mughal hubs of Lahore, Delhi, Agra, and Surat. The Safavids strategically allied with the Portuguese as a defence measure against the Ottomans.

The empire reached its pinnacle under Shah Abbas the Great, who ruled from 1588 to 1629. Art, especially painting and calligraphy, and architecture blossomed in the Safavid era, and their sophisticated buildings and cities like Isfahan became an inspiration for the Mughals. In the seventeenth century, the Safavids fought against the Mughal emperor Shah Jahan's army and seized Kandahar, further adding to the humiliation of the failed Mughal campaign to win Samarkand from the Uzbek Turks.

GLOBAL IMPACT OF THE EXPANSIONS

It's hard to imagine any grocery store across India not selling tomatoes, potatoes, chillies, capsicum, pumpkins, corn, sweet potatoes, papayas, pineapples, plums, guava, *chikoo* (sapota), *rajmah* (kidney beans), peanuts, cashews, and cocoa or a *paanwallah* (roadside vendor who sells betel leaves and related condiments) not selling tobacco products. Taken for granted today, these products were not around in India prior to the sixteenth century. Some of them were brought to India by the Portuguese directly from Brazil whereas others arrived from South and Central America via Europe. The *genda* (marigold) flower, which forms an integral part of Hindu rituals and adorns deities in temples, is also not native to India, but Mexico.[12]

When Columbus landed in the New World, he inadvertently triggered a world-changing megatrend. Two distinct ecosystems, separated tens of millions of years ago by the continental drift, were rejoined, as were two branches of humanity that separated 12,000 years ago. It would have dramatic and lasting effects on human history as well as our planet's history. The animals, plants, and diseases of these two worlds began to cross over in a process that American historian Alfred Crosby has called the Columbian Exchange. Never before in Earth's history had species jumped continents at such a scale and pace as they did now.

Europeans brought domesticated livestock like horses, cows, sheep, goats, and pigs to the Americas along with crops like wheat, barley, rye, sugarcane, rice, and cotton that flourished over time, becoming staple crops and the basis for transatlantic trade.

In the Old World, the increase in the diversity of crops vastly improved yields and brought drier lands under irrigation. Maize (corn) had the greatest success as it spread across Europe, North Africa, China, and South Africa before finally reaching India. The potato was the other success story. It thrived in northern Europe, especially Ireland. The food supply improved exponentially, and the improved diets resulted in healthier people, boosting both population and trade levels across Eurasia and Africa.

On the other hand, the reunion of the long-separated human siblings was not a happy one for they met on unequal terms. Europeans were armed with guns and brought diseases like influenza, measles, smallpox, cholera, malaria, and chickenpox, against which the native populations of the new world had no defence or immunity. Driven by an insatiable greed for gold, silver, and land, the Europeans mercilessly slaughtered the natives by the droves. Simultaneously, wave after wave of epidemics struck, wiping out entire tribes. There are no clear estimates of the population of the Americas prior to the arrival of Columbus, but it could have been as high as 110 million. By 1650, however, the native population had dropped to less than 6 million, which was the deadliest carnage in human history.

The American gold and silver that flooded Europe allowed merchants and trading companies to buy vast quantities of merchandise from Asia. Between 1600 and 1800, around a fifth of the precious metals produced throughout the world reached India. The Mughals minted the silver into rupees, which became their primary currency. The booming demand for goods brought about large-scale employment; Bengal, for instance, created an extra 1,00,000 jobs in the textile industry.[13] Indian villages and communities were monetised, and the Mughals saw their tax and land revenues rising, which they could now use to wage wars and further enlarge their empire.

Loaded with bullion, the Spanish kings became the most powerful rulers in Europe and used their newfound wealth to build opulent cathedrals and palaces, and to finance wars against their rivals—the English, the Dutch, the French, and the Ottomans. But the habit of buying everything instead of growing or building it, and discouraging all intellectual activity that might threaten Catholicism led to a deterioration of skills and knowledge over time. All this while, the massive inflation resulting from the windfall gains sent Spain's economy into a tailspin, hastening the downfall of the Spanish empire.

With the European expansion came the transatlantic slave trade. The Portuguese king Henry who originally sponsored the voyages of exploration along the coast of West Africa also has the dubious distinction of being a founder of the African slave trade, the biggest forced migration in history. Between 1525 and 1866, in what became a highly lucrative business, Europeans transported around 12.5 million Africans to the Americas as slaves, of which approximately 10 million survived the harrowing journey, only to toil under the hot sun in sugar, cotton, and tobacco plantations at the mercy of their owners.

How widespread was the trade along the Silk Road from Asia to Europe before it was disrupted by da Gama's landfall in Calicut? In the thirteenth and the fourteenth centuries, many European friars, missionaries, and travellers like Marco Polo had undertaken perilous overland journeys to Asia. What prompted them to do so? What kind of exchanges took place between the East and the West back then?

6

TORNADO FROM THE EAST

1200s–1400s

If you had not committed great sins, God would not have sent a punishment like me upon you.

—Genghis Khan

As of the early thirteenth century, Europeans had a fanciful and vague image of the faraway lands of Asia, from where came exotic goods like silks, spices, and porcelain along with fantastic tales, myths, and legends after changing many hands while traversing thousands of kilometres across Eurasia.

Around the 1240s, alarm bells were ringing in Europe as an unexpected, unknown, and rather dreadful threat erupted in the East and rapidly advanced westwards. Ruthless horse-riding raiders, said to drink the blood of their enemies, were laying cities to waste and annihilating entire populations. But no one knew who these fast and furious marauders were, what tongue they spoke, and what their homeland was like.

As we saw in the previous chapters, global empires had emerged from unlikely places like Portugal and Britain, located at the fringes of Eurasia. The thirteenth century, too, saw the rise of a dark horse: the empire of the Mongols, which originated in the harsh steppe lands at the opposite end of Eurasia and took the sedentary civilisations by storm. The Mongols achieved on horseback what the Europeans later accomplished with sailing ships in the oceans. At their peak, the Mongols controlled around 23 million square kilometres, which made them the largest contiguous land empire in history. Nonetheless, this achievement came at a staggering cost of around 30 million deaths, which earned them the title of the most savage empire of all time.

THE SILK ROAD

'Silk Road' is a relatively recent term, coined by the German geographer Ferdinand von Richthofen in the mid-nineteenth century. It wasn't a single road, rather a vast trade network that linked the East and the West since ancient times, covering land as well as sea routes. At its height, the Silk Road stretched from Japan and China to Italy, passing through a dazzling array of peoples, languages, and cultures across Central Asia, India, and the Middle East.

Goods like silk, paper, gunpowder, tea, and porcelain came from China; pepper, cotton textiles, indigo, sandalwood, ivory, and precious stones from India; spices like cloves, nutmeg, and cinnamon from Indonesia and Ceylon; and myrrh and frankincense from Somalia. Travelling in the other direction were goods produced in Europe, like glassware, grapes, wine, animal furs and skins, honey, weapons, and armour.

The land routes typically started at Chang'an (Xi'an), the capital of several ruling dynasties in China, crossed the vast Taklamakan Desert with stops at various oasis towns, and continued through Central Asia and Persia before reaching the ports on the Black Sea and the Mediterranean Sea. Some ancient routes traversed through Indian cities like Pataliputra (Patna), Multan and Taxila, before exiting from the Khyber Pass towards Afghanistan and Central Asia. Caravans of merchants with their horses and camels laden with goods trudged along the trade routes, stopping over at caravanserais, which were large roadside inns where travellers could rest, socialise, and prepare for their onward journey.

Almost no one travelled the entire route. The middlemen at multiple stations and ports handled and redirected the goods. Merchants had to learn the languages and customs of the regions they traversed through to be able to negotiate successfully. The trade-related exchange inevitably led to a sharing of ideas and beliefs. Knowledge of the arts, literature, science, and religion spread along the Silk Road network, spawning interlinked hubs of culture and learning. It was along the same trade routes that Buddhism had spread from India to Afghanistan, Central Asia, China, and Southeast Asia.

THE MONGOLS

At the centre of the vast Eurasian landmass lies an 8,000-kilometre long belt of semi-arid grassland called the steppe, stretching from Hungary in the west through Ukraine, Central Asia, Mongolia, to northern China in the east. The steppe, particularly the eastern half, is not conducive to agriculture as it is too dry or too cold, but the grasses make it suitable for herding animals like horses or sheep.

Large swathes of the steppe lands were populated by nomadic herders living in scattered tribes that were tied to each other in elaborate protocols of tribal kinship, language, and culture. Besides being master horse riders, the tribesmen could wield the bow and arrow to devastating effect. For ages, the horse-riding nomadic warriors—referred to as the Scythians, the Xiongnu, the Huns, and the Tatars at various times—came in waves and wreaked havoc on the surrounding agriculture- and commerce-based ancient civilisations of China, India, Persia, and Anatolia.

In the twelfth century, among the many nomadic tribes living around modern-day Mongolia, one particular group gained prominence—the Mongols. They claimed to be direct descendants of the Huns, who had conquered lands from India to Rome in the fourth and the fifth centuries.

The Mongols were never engaged in agriculture, nor were they involved in any trade like metal casting or pottery or weaving. They did not build any monuments, or found any new religion.[1] They were used to procuring goods from the Silk Road network, which lay south of their homeland, and had thus had a brief view of the riches of the southern civilisations. Early accounts describe the Mongols as brutes who wore skins of dogs and mice, followed no religion or law, and wandered from one place to another. No one could have imagined what these uncivilized brutes were about to achieve in the twelfth and the thirteenth centuries.

The Great Khan

In 1162, a boy named Temüjin was born near the border between modern Mongolia and Siberia. Legend has it that he arrived into the world clutching a blood clot in his tiny right hand, a divine indication that he was destined to do great things. Temüjin received no formal education and grew up in a world that was marked with violence among rival clans and tribes. His father was poisoned to death before Temüjin had turned ten, and his clan left his mother and her seven children, including Temüjin, to die on the unforgiving steppes. During his early years, Temüjin killed his older half-brother in an altercation over sharing hunting spoils and became the head of the poverty-stricken household.

At age sixteen, he married a girl named Borte, who bore him four sons and an unknown number of daughters. At one point, Borte was kidnapped by a rival clan, and Temüjin launched a daring rescue operation, earning a reputation as a fierce warrior. With his incredible charisma, he began to attract a growing number of followers and soon started making alliances with other nomadic tribes. Breaking away from tradition, Temüjin started building a meritocratic system where he assigned key positions based on individual ability rather than bloodlines. Total discipline and obedience were the norm at all levels in his chain of command. He built an inner circle of devoted warriors, known as *nokurs*, upon whom he could rely unquestioningly. The lightning mobility of his horse-borne archers, the unfamiliarity of their tactics, and their well-orchestrated attacks quickly turned them into a fearsome military machine.

By 1206, Temüjin had eliminated all his rivals and established himself as the undisputed master of the Mongolian steppe. He was proclaimed by a federation of tribes as Chinggis Khan, which roughly translates to 'Universal Ruler'. In the West, he came to be known as Genghis Khan. His proclamation is seen as the beginning of the Mongol Empire.

The name Genghis Khan may imply that he was a Muslim, but that was not the case. Temüjin was a follower of Mongol animist beliefs, while many of his loyal followers were Muslims as well as Buddhists and Christians. We don't know how Genghis Khan looked as no contemporary portraits or sculptures of him have been found, leaving each culture to project its own imagined picture of him.

Genghis Khan's first campaign (1205–09) outside of Mongolia was directed against the Hsi Hsia (Xi Xia) kingdom in north-western China, and it ended in their ruler surrendering and paying tribute to the Mongols. This was followed by an attack on the Jin Dynasty of northern China, and by 1215, Genghis Khan had taken over the capital of Zhongdu (modern-day Beijing).

Meanwhile, when Ala al-Din Muhammad, the shah of the Muslim Khwarizm Empire (which covered present-day Turkmenistan, Uzbekistan, Afghanistan, and Iran), ignorantly executed a few Mongol ambassadors, Genghis Khan was so enraged that he put his Chinese foray on hold and took his war campaign into Central Asia (1219–1225). He sacked Urgench, the shah's base, and other Khwarizm cities like Bukhara and Samarkand, followed by Merv, Nishapur, and Herat. The Khwarizm campaign was unprecedented in scale and ferocity, with entire populations put to the sword. Muhammad looked to escape the fury of Genghis Khan, but he didn't have many options. He reached out to Iltutmish, the sultan of the recently established Delhi Sultanate, who refused to harbour him in India. He finally escaped to a small island in the Caspian Sea where he died in 1220.

The shah's son, Jalal al-Din, recouped the remnants of the Khwarizmid army in Afghanistan, and in 1221, inflicted a defeat upon the Mongol army near Kabul. Incensed, Genghis Khan advanced southward through Afghanistan and laid siege to Bamiyan, the site of two massive Buddha statues carved out of sandstone cliffs, and destroyed the city. Advancing further to Ghazni, Genghis Khan defeated the forces of Jalal al-Din, who then escaped from the mountains of Afghanistan to the plains of India. Genghis Khan chased him and handed him another decisive defeat on the banks of the Indus. Jalal al-Din escaped capture by swimming across the river and sought refuge with Iltutmish, and got the same response that his father had received. Had Iltutmish harboured him, Delhi and other cities of India would have likely met the same fate as the Khwarizmid cities, given the ferocious run Genghis was having.

The Mongol conquest in India stopped at the city of Multan in 1222. Genghis had earlier considered conquering all of northern India, but it was the terrain and climate of India that came to its rescue. The torrid heat and humidity of India's plains sapped the energy of the Mongol warriors and their horses. Even their bows, which worked just fine in the steppe region, started to lose their accuracy and effectiveness.[2] Genghis finally retreated into the mountains towards Afghanistan, leaving behind two *tumens* (regiments) of 10,000 men each. However, a short while later, these two regiments also departed from India after struggling with persistent health issues.

Genghis used violence selectively and started the practice of obliterating a fortress or a city with theatrical slaughtering, piling up skulls and corpses that served as a warning to the rulers of surrounding kingdoms, prompting them into instant submission. In 1227, during a final war against the western Xia kingdom, which had refused to contribute troops to the Khwarizm invasion, Genghis fell while riding his horse and sustained internal injuries. Though he continued with the campaign, he never recovered from the fall and died in August that year.

With a touch of genius, Genghis Khan, the illiterate nomad, had written entirely new rules of warfare that involved meticulous planning, a relatively small but highly disciplined army, unprecedented mobility, and a mastery of logistics. In doing so, he conquered more than twice as much land as any other person in history, in terms of the total area occupied or the number of people subjugated.

After Genghis Khan

In his lifetime, Genghis Khan had broadly divided his empire into four *khanates* (territories ruled by the Khans) among his sons and grandsons—the Mongol homeland (comprising Mongolia and northern China), Il-Khanate (comprising Iran, Iraq, and Syria), Chagatai Khanate (comprising Central Asia), and the Golden Horde (comprising southwest Siberia and west Turkistan).

Ogodei, the third son of Genghis, was appointed as the Great Khan. He launched spectacular campaigns and massively expanded his father's empire. As the Mongols advanced in China, the Chin Dynasty was overthrown in 1234. On the western frontier, the city of Vladimir (in modern Russia) fell in 1238 and Kyiv (capital of modern Ukraine) in 1240, and the whole region came under their sway by 1241. Petrified refugees fleeing from Kyiv and the surrounding area ran towards Central Europe, further spreading panic with their horror stories of the Mongol blitz.

Mongol general Subedei, regarded as one of the greatest military strategists in history, led his forces on campaigns during bitterly cold winters, making them march over frozen lakes and rivers to great success. He charged further west into Poland and eastern Germany, destroying the forces of Poland and the duke of Silesia, whose severed head was paraded on the end of a lance. Subedei then turned south towards Hungary and Austria.

The sheer speed of the Mongol cavalry units riding their smaller horses and using armour-piercing arrows had rendered the heavily armoured knights of Europe and their larger horses completely ineffective. Mongol armies could ride up to 150 kilometres a day, an unimaginable speed in those times, and that enabled them to fight campaigns far away from their home base. They would conduct extensive reconnaissance before hitting a target, and their movements were coordinated by signals and a well-organised messenger service. One of their signature tactics was to enact a false flight from the battlefield, only to lure and trap their opponents into a surprise slaughter in a more strategically advantageous site.

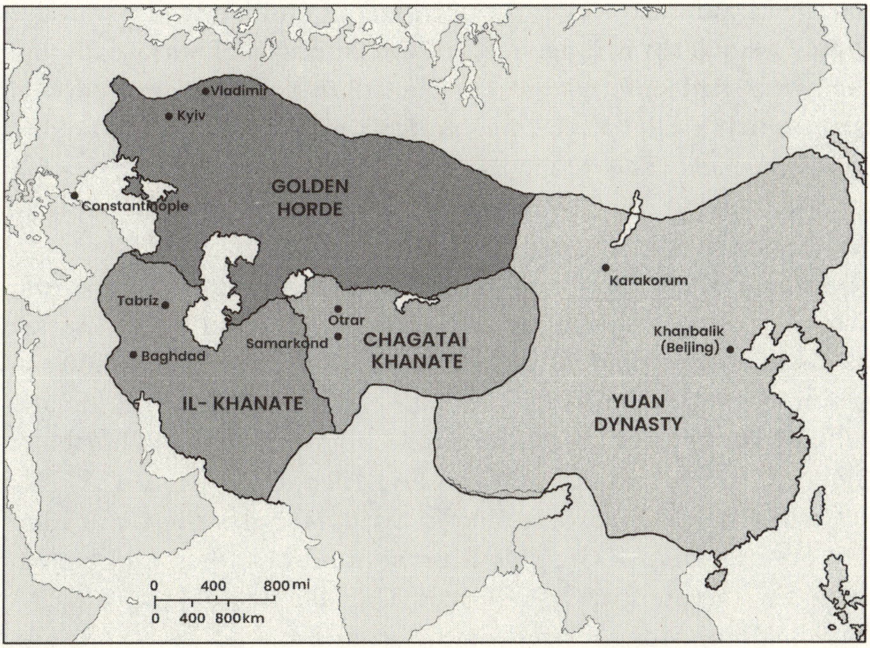

The Mongol Empire after Genghis Khan

Hysteria had taken over Europe by then. Pope Gregory IX called on the European rulers to help defend Hungary, but none came forward. The Europeans were saved by a stroke of luck as the Great Khan Ogodei died in December 1241 in the Mongol capital of Karakorum and his forces withdrew after that.

Similar to their experience in India, the Mongol advance into Europe was also constrained by the terrain. The grass steppes ended at Hungary, turning into a natural barrier for the Mongol soldiers, who had up to five horses each and needed the pastures. And as they hit European forests, rivers, and farmlands, which were not a firm ground for the horses, their advantage of agility was lost. Besides, western Europe was not a prime target for the Mongols given its relative paucity of wealth and resources when compared to the Chinese and Muslim kingdoms.

By the 1250s, the Mongols again turned towards India and started making incursions, becoming the most potent threat to the Delhi Sultanate. The Turkic rulers of India and the Mongols shared a similarity in language, culture, and style of warfare, though the Turks had entered the Persian cultural sphere and adopted Islam much earlier while the Mongols were still nomads holding animist beliefs. The Mongols too, would embrace Islam later as they assimilated into the Turkic populations of Iran, Afghanistan, and southern Russia.

Hulegu Khan, who was Genghis Khan's grandson and the ruler of Iran, started advancing towards Iraq in 1257 and in 1258 sacked Baghdad, the capital of the Abbasid caliphate. The caliph was captured and subjected to a brutal death along with an estimated 2,00,000 residents of the city. The following year, Hulegu's horsemen rode into Syria, taking Damascus and Aleppo.

While they were progressing in Syria, Mongke, the Great Khan and another one of Genghis Khan's grandsons, died and Hulegu withdrew a greater part of his forces. The Mamluks of Egypt attacked the remaining Mongol forces on the ground and inflicted a crushing defeat on them near the Sea of Galilee in September 1260. This was the first defeat for the Mongols in southwestern Asia, and it blocked their advance into Egypt.

In China, Kublai Khan, who was the Great Khan from 1260–1294, triumphed over the Song Empire in 1279, thereby unifying the whole nation. He founded the Yuan Dynasty and turned out to be one of China's greatest emperors.

While the Yuan Empire in China and the Il-Khanate in Persia were steady states that were not pursuing further territorial expansion, the Chagatai Khanate made continuous attempts to raid the plains of India in the 1290s and the 1300s, sending its armies through the mountain passes of Afghanistan. Alauddin Khilji, the pugnacious sultan of Delhi, managed to keep the Mongol threat at bay, defeating them several times, a feat that made him assume the moniker of *Sikandar-I sani* (the second Alexander). The subsequent sultans, including the Tughlaqs, were less successful and ended up paying tributes to the Mongols.

Towards the end of the thirteenth century, the Mongol empire had become too vast and cracks had started to appear among its four main branches. After Kublai Khan died in 1294, the heirs were unable to agree upon one Great Khan, and the Mongol Empire became permanently fragmented.

In China, floods on the Yellow River, famine, the spread of bubonic plague, and revolts throughout the countryside brought an end to the Mongol rule in 1368, and the Mongol Yuan dynasty was replaced by the ethnic Ming dynasty. By 1369, the Golden Horde was tottering and lost Belarus and Ukraine to the West. The Chagatai Khanate too, started disintegrating and came to be increasingly dominated by local warlords. Lastly, the Il-Khanate was also ravaged by the plague and split among several successors.

Though the Mongol Empire crumbled in the fourteenth century, its vestiges never disappeared entirely and continue to reflect in the cultures and traditions of modern China, Russia, India, Iran, Central Asia, and Turkey. Turkic-Mongol words like *ba'urchi/bawarchi* (cook)[3], *ba'atur/bahadur* (brave), *defter* (registers and ledgers), *ordo/urdu* (camp), and *sipahi* (cavalry officer) found their way into the modern Indian vocabulary.

Pax Mongolica

The Mongols have been portrayed as merciless savages and the very term 'Mongol' has become a synonym for barbarian. This characterisation can be attributed to the fact that the history of the Mongols was written by the people they conquered. But there is another side to the story, as there always is. Despite the large-scale slaughter, the Mongols had brought political unification, rule of law, and culture to their domains and had also opened communication lines between the East and the West. In every country that they conquered, the initial devastation and paranoia gave way to long periods of peace and stability. The war routes thus became trade arteries. In cities like Samarkand, the Mongols invested generously, deploying skilled craftsmen and workers from China and Persia in construction projects. The Silk Road trade was revived and turned into the largest free-trade zone that ever existed in the world.

If Genghis Khan's rule evoked fear and panic, it was also a source of innovative practices like the first international postal system, diplomatic immunity to envoys from rival nations, and a regular census of Mongol subjects. The Mongol Empire showed exceptional tolerance towards the diverse religious beliefs of its subjects, unlike Europe, where religion was a matter of life and death, although some commentators attribute the Mongol openness to astute politics.

EARLY WESTERN TRAVELLERS TO THE EAST

Around the 1240s–50s, Pope Innocent IV and several European monarchs dispatched a series of envoys to Asia to explore the homeland of the Mongols and what their culture was like. They were hoping to ultimately convert the Mongols to Christianity, which could tip the scale against their Muslim rivals, in addition to enabling access to the Silk Road for Christian merchants.

In one of the earliest inter-civilisational encounters, John of Plano Carpini, an Italian Franciscan monk, was sent by the pope in 1245 to meet with the Great Khan Mongke. His goal was to probe what triggered the Mongol incursion into Europe, gather reliable information about their numbers, and uncover their future plans. Braving the rigours of a long and arduous journey, John reached Mongolia and met with the Great Khan, who gave him a letter demanding that the pope and all European princes appear in his court to offer their submission. John's travel account was the first authentic and detailed description of Asia and the 'mysterious' world of the Mongols. The account aroused great interest in Europe.

In a similar mission, King Louis IX of France sent a Flemish Franciscan monk named William of Rubruck to Mongolia. William's roundtrip journey lasted three years (1253–56), and upon returning, he wrote an account of this journey, calling it *Itinerarium.*[4] William described the cosmopolitan nature of the Mongol capital Karakorum, where he saw Muslim and Chinese craftsmen and met with a French silversmith, several Germans, and the nephew of an English bishop. Outside the Mongol court, William saw a startling number of dignitaries from countries that recognised Mongol overlordship. He wrote about the strange lifestyle of the Mongols—that they did not eat any vegetables and drank fermented mare's milk.

By the second half of the thirteenth century, as the Silk Road became safe and secure, many European merchants and travellers began heading to the East. In 1264, two merchant brothers from Venice, Niccolo and Maffeo Polo, joined an embassy departing to meet the Great Khan Kublai. Two years later, they reached Khanbaliq or Dadu (modern-day Beijing), where the Mongol capital had recently been shifted from Karakorum. The Polo brothers were well received by Kublai Khan, who was impressed with their intelligence and knowledge of the world. Besides, Kublai was known to welcome foreigners and hire them into his service for he was suspicious of the old and entrenched Mandarin bureaucracy. The Polo brothers returned home after spending three years at Kublai's court.

Within a few years, the Polos were itching for another journey to China, in search of further profit and adventure. This time, they took Niccolo's seventeen-year-old son Marco with them. The trio sailed from Venice and after a long odyssey lasting four years, reached Kublai's summer palace in Xanadu in May 1275. Niccolo presented Marco in service to Kublai, who had recently completed his conquest of the whole of China and needed administrators. Impressed with Marco's linguistic skills, the Great Khan offered him employment in an administrative and diplomatic role which required him to travel extensively in China.

The Polos ended up staying in China for sixteen long years, after which they were allowed to leave as part of an official naval expedition accompanying a Mongol princess on her way to Persia. The journey took them through the Strait of Malacca, across the Indian Ocean to the southern tip of India, and then up the west coast of India to Hormuz. From Hormuz, they crossed Persia and Anatolia and arrived in Venice in 1295, having been away for twenty-four years.

After returning home, Marco took command of a Venetian ship, and during a war with Genoa, he was captured and thrown into a Genoese prison. As Marco entertained everyone in the prison with his tales of travel and adventure, a fellow prisoner named Rusticello, who wrote romantic novels, noted them down. The end result was an enthralling travel account titled *Book of the Marvels of the World*, also known as *The Travels of Marco Polo*, or simply *The Travels*, which was published around the year 1300 and became an instant sensation in Europe. Marco became a household name, earning the sobriquet 'Il Milione', the man with a million stories (or lies).

Marco's detailed descriptions of ports in the Indian Ocean indicate a flourishing maritime trade. He wrote about a variety of things such as Chinese ships regularly sailing to India, the highly profitable business of merchant ships carrying Arab horses to India, the islands of Java being rich in pepper, nutmeg, and cloves, and the Coromandel coast of India that produced the finest cottons. Marco narrated the ingenious technique that Indians deployed for retrieving diamonds from the bottom of steep ravines: throwing animal flesh to the bottom to attract eagles who would then bring up the pieces of meat with diamonds impressed into them.

The Polos weren't the first Europeans to visit China, but Marco Polo was the first European to publish a detailed account of it. European readers were amazed to learn how populous, wealthy, and sophisticated the East was. Many thought of the book as a work of fiction and fantasy, only to realise much later that it was a real travel account.

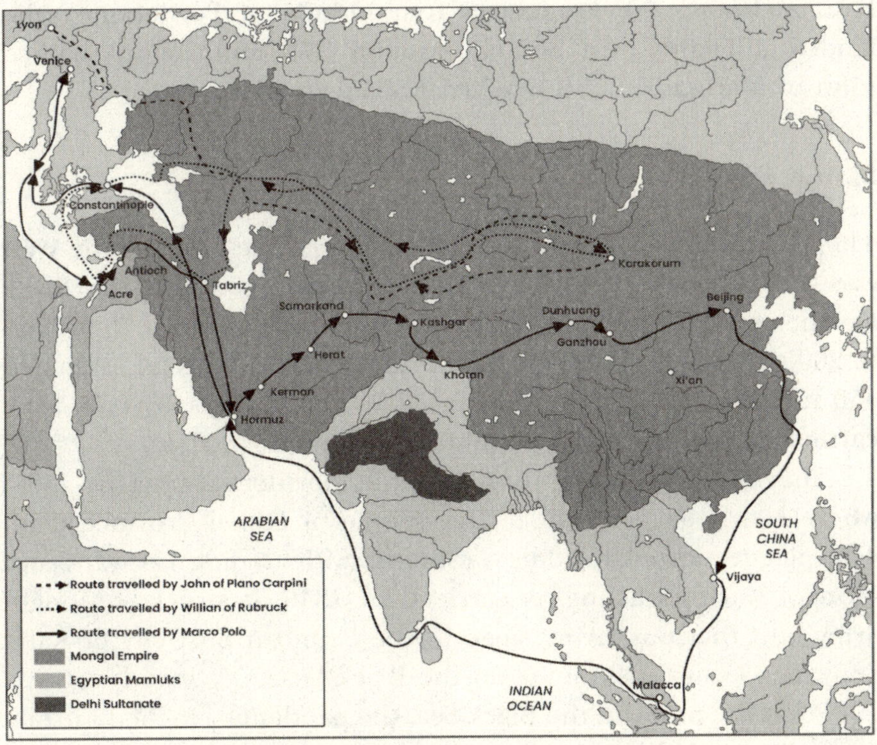

Travel routes of the early Western travellers to Asia

Around 1320, a French Dominican missionary named Jourdain de Severac, who was living in Persia, was on his way to China. He had planned a brief stopover in India, but events turned out such that he ended up spending more than a decade in India. The pope declared him the bishop of Columbum (modern-day Kollam in Kerala) on the coast of southern India. Jourdain wrote about his observations of the East in two letters and a book called *Mirabilia Descripta* (*Description of Marvels*), describing Armenia, Persia, and India. 'Every thing indeed is a marvel in this India!' he remarked. 'Verily it is quite another world!' For several centuries, the *Mirabilia* remained a valuable source of information for European missionaries who made the strenuous journey to India.

In the following years, many more Europeans travelled to the

East, including the Franciscan friar Odoric of Pordenone, who landed at Thane, near Bombay, around 1321 and a monk named John of Marignolli, who reached Kollam in 1346.

BLACK DEATH

The increasing interaction and trade between the East and the West had a cataclysmic outcome in the fourteenth century—the Black Death, a plague pandemic that killed anywhere between 75 million to 200 million people when the world population was an estimated 450 million. The plague was caused by the bacillus *Yersinia pestis*, carried by rodents and transmitted to humans by fleas.

The initial outbreak took place in northern China in 1331, where nearly 90 per cent of the people of Hopei Province died. The plague started hurtling westwards with trading caravans and Mongol warriors acting as carriers. In 1346, it struck a Mongol army unit that was laying siege to the Crimean port city of Kaffa (now Feodosia in Ukraine) on the Black Sea.

From the ports on the Black Sea, the pandemic reached Europe via Sicily, carried by infected sailors and rats on Genoese trading ships. And within five years, from 1347–52, nearly half of Europe's population was wiped out. Some places were affected more than others and lost up to 90 per cent of their populations; London and Paris, each saw a half of their residents perish during the pandemic. Dead bodies lay rotting everywhere, leaving a constant stench; it seemed like the world was coming to an end. Europe would not recover its pre-plague population for the next 200 years.

The origins of the bacillus causing the plague are not clear. They are believed to be somewhere in Central Asia or the Siberian and Mongolian steppe. Historian William McNeill, who wrote *Plagues and Peoples,* has argued that the plague was endemic among the burrowing rodents and their fleas found in the foothills of the Himalayas between India, China, and Burma. And it was the Mongol campaigns in the same region that brought the bacillus to the Eurasian steppes. The Indian subcontinent itself was fortunate to have been spared by the plague; at least there are no recorded chronicles of any such epidemic outbreak. India's population base thus remained intact as compared to China and Europe, which faced a drastic population correction.

Intriguingly, the catastrophe had a positive impact too. In Europe, the severe reduction of the working population led to increased wages and availability of land, which prompted the farmers to call for an end to serfdom. The population's diet, sense of hygiene, and health protocols improved. The pandemic had brought death at a massive scale, but it had caused no damage to either infrastructure or property, which meant that the survivors inherited far more possessions than their original share.

As millions of pieces of clothing were suddenly rendered useless, a new utility was found for them by the end of the fourteenth century—manufacturing rag paper (a high-quality paper made from cotton rags). The oversupply of rag paper brought its price down drastically, which then fueled the growth of the printing press that was invented by Gutenberg.[5] Book production exploded, making them affordable to the masses and marking the dawn of the first information revolution.

Having gone through untold misery during the plague pandemic, people gave up on the blind faith they had in the Church and began to challenge their beliefs. They adopted a more rational outlook of the world, reorienting their purpose from divine matters to human beings and real life. Population migrations shifted the centres of power and wealth in Europe, where several city-states like Florence and Milan gained from the trend. For the ruling elite in these city-states, who had acquired power through political conquest, one of the ways of legitimising their rule was by extending lavish patronage to painters, artists, and other talented people. All these developments came together and contributed to the unleashing of creative and intellectual energies across Europe during the Renaissance.

THE FURY OF TIMUR

In Central Asia, after the collapse of the Chagatai Khanate, a brilliant commander of mixed Turkic and Mongol ancestry named Timur emerged in the late fourteenth century. Born in 1336 near Samarkand to a minor chieftain, Timur had suffered an arrow wound to his leg at an early age which left him with a limp. This earned him the sobriquet *Timur-i-Lenk* in Persian, or Timur the Lame, which became Tamerlane, as he is known in the West. Timur grew up to become an able and successful mercenary commander in Persia and soon gathered a large following.

By 1370, he had taken over Balkh (in modern Afghanistan) and the region around it. Over the next decade, he captured the rest of Central Asia, thereby founding the Timurid Empire, which would go on to become the largest empire in the world at the time. Since Timur was not a direct descendant of Genghis Khan, he could not be a khan, but he did not let that constrain his aspirations and ruled instead as an *amir* (the Arabic word for prince). He married a Chagatai princess and shrewdly designated himself as *Gurkan*, a Turkicised version of the Mongol word meaning 'son-in-law', and his dynasty as Gurkani, thereby drawing Mongol relevance and prestige.

Though Timur claimed to be a good Muslim, he had no qualms about destroying Islamic cities and kingdoms. By 1395, he had taken over all of Persia and conquered lands as far as Moscow. He now turned his gaze to India, and in 1398, his cavalry crossed the Hindukush mountains and descended into the plains of India. The Delhi sultan Firuz Shah Tughluq had died in 1388, and since then the sultanate's power and military capabilities had diminished significantly. In the absence of any meaningful opposition, Timur brutally sacked Delhi, killing thousands of the city's inhabitants. His forces seized ninety war elephants and loaded them with treasures before stomping back to Samarkand. Timur had delivered a crippling blow to the sultanate, though it managed to limp for another hundred years.

In the meantime, the Ottomans had expanded their domains and built a centralised, well-administered, militarily strong state by the 1390s. Sultan Bayezid I, the 'Thunderbolt', had conquered modern Bulgaria, Greece, and Serbia, leaving the rest of Europe feeling nervous and threatened. Bayezid was met with a jolt in 1402 when his army was crushed by Timur's smaller but ferocious force at Angora (now Ankara). Timur took Bayezid prisoner and dragged him to Samarkand, where he died in captivity but only after being paraded in a cage like an animal.

The European rulers, including the kings of France and England, rejoiced over the Ottoman defeat at the hands of Timur, some calling him a European ally. But then it dawned upon them that Timur was now standing at the gates of Europe, well within striking distance. The kings of Spain, France, and other countries quickly dispatched envoys congratulating him over his victories, hoping to stave off a potential invasion.

Timur was, however, looking towards the East, planning his boldest campaign: the conquest of the Chinese Ming dynasty, which had overthrown the Mongol Yuan regime. Under Timur's command, his army set out in the unusually cold month of December in the year 1404, but Timur fell ill enroute and died in 1405 in Otrar (Kazakhstan). He was buried in the beautiful mausoleum in Samarkand known as Gur-e-Emir, which is considered to have been an inspiration for the future Mughal monuments, leading to the Taj Mahal.

Despite being a barbaric conqueror, Timur was a man of art and culture. He transformed Samarkand into a glorious city with beautiful palaces, mausoleums, gardens, book workshops, and religious buildings by deploying the best architects and craftsmen of his day.

Timur would remain a legendary figure in European imagination for centuries. In England, the play *Tamburlaine,* produced around 1590, was a super-hit and inspired one of the greatest travellers, an Oxford-educated Englishman named Tom Coryate, to make an overland journey to Asia to see Timur's tomb in Samarkand. Coryate reached India where he met with Jahangir, but could never make it to Samarkand as he died in Surat, Gujarat.[6]

After Timur's death, his sons and grandsons were embroiled in a conflict over the throne, and the empire withered away gradually. Over a century later, his descendant Babur founded the great Mughal Empire in India, reviving the Timurid ambition for empire-building, military achievements, and excellence in art and architecture. All the subsequent Mughal emperors took pride in their Timurid lineage and dreamed of conquering their ancestral homeland in Central Asia. It wasn't until the mid-seventeenth century that the Mughal emperor Shah Jahan, hoping to establish himself as the true successor to Timur, sent his army into Central Asia to capture Samarkand and Bukhara from the ruling Uzbek Turks. But the campaign failed miserably, owing to the harsh landscape, extreme cold, and food shortages, and caused a huge drain on the exchequer, not to mention the loss of prestige. The Mughal dream would forever remain unfulfilled.

The brutal sack of Baghdad and the ruthless murder of the Abbasid caliph in 1258 by the Mongols was a blow to the Islamic world. It is said that the golden age of Islam ended at that point. What was the Islamic world like before the Mongols arrived on the scene? How did the Islamic golden age come about? How did Islam spread from Spain to India?

7

THE ISLAMIC AGE

610s–1200s

From India to Spain, the brilliant civilisation of Islam flourished. What was lost to Christendom at this time was not lost to civilisation, but quite the contrary.

—Bertrand Russel

500 years before Christopher Columbus had miscalculated the distance to Asia and stumbled upon America, there lived a Muslim man in modern-day Uzbekistan who had calculated Earth's circumference with remarkable accuracy. He had also scientifically concluded that an undiscovered landmass existed in the ocean between Europe and Asia, which some have claimed as being the American landmass. His name was Abu al-Rayhan Mohammed ibn Ahmad al-Biruni, a polymath born in the year 973. Al-Biruni had built an observatory at a place called Nandana Fort (Punjab, Pakistan) and argued that the sun might be the centre of the solar system, centuries before Copernicus was born. NASA even named a crater on the moon after Al-Biruni. Besides being an astronomer and geographer, he was a historian, botanist, pharmacologist, geologist, poet, philosopher, and a mathematician.

Al-Biruni wasn't a one-off wonder of his time, rather he was one of the many such men from modern-day Central Asia whose writings remained the most authoritative texts for centuries. These men lived during the glory days of Islam, from the eighth to the thirteenth centuries, when visitors were dazzled by the opulence and cultural sophistication of cities like Baghdad, Damascus, Cairo, Cordoba, Merv, Samarkhand, Bukhara, Mosul, Balkh, Kabul, Ghazni, Nishapur, Tus, and Reyy. Sadly, many of these cities have turned either into dusty towns or permanent warzones and deserted ruins, while others have been entirely forgotten.

The rise of Islam was one of the most pivotal developments in world history. Similar to the emergence of the Mongols, the Portuguese, and the British from the remote corners of Eurasia, the story of Islam began in yet another unlikely place in the world—the deserts of Arabia.

EARLY DAYS AND EXPANSION OF ISLAM

Roughly the size of India, the Arabian peninsula is dominated by vast expanses of deserts with rocky and craggy mountains along the peninsula's northwestern, southern, and eastern borders, and a few isolated oases. Despite the harsh landscape, for ages, the region supported both nomadic and urban populations that depended on agriculture, shipping, and trade in spices, incense, myrrh, and textiles.

In the sixth century, several trading towns dotted the Red Sea coast in western Arabia, where merchants procured goods from ports in the Indian Ocean and transported them in camel caravans across the desert. One such prominent trading town was Mecca, which was also a cosmopolitan pilgrimage centre with temples dedicated to various pagan deities.

To the north of the Arabian peninsula lay the two superpowers of the time—the Byzantine or the Eastern Roman Empire with Constantinople as its capital and the Persian Empire of the Sassanians, whose capital was Ctesiphon (near Baghdad). Embroiled in a conflict that had already spanned centuries, the two empires were drawn into a major war that began in the year 602 and lasted for twenty-five years. The Arabs knew both the empires well, having engaged with them as traders, soldiers, and mercenaries. Several religions—Christianity, Judaism, and Zoroastrianism—had been founded in the region of the Byzantine and Sassanid empires and had co-existed for centuries; Buddhism had arrived in the eastern part of the region from the Indian subcontinent since the first century CE.

Prophet Muhammad, the founder of Islam, was born in the year 570 in Mecca. Orphaned by the age of six, he was passed into the care of his paternal uncle Abu Talib, a respected merchant. Muhammad travelled with him in caravans to other trading towns and started to get recognised for being trustworthy. In his early twenties, he joined the services of a wealthy widow named Khadija. Muhammad's honesty and character left her impressed, and despite the age difference—she was nearly forty while he was twenty-five—she proposed to him, and they got married. Their years together brought them both affluence and happiness.

As he approached the age of forty, Muhammad started to feel a rising sense of discontentment over the rapid spread of a new-found materialism around Mecca even as the less fortunate struggled to make ends meet. He began to retreat to a cave in the mountains outside the town where he started to receive a series of revelations from God. Muhammad finally shared his experience with his tribe, and his recitations were written down in a single text called the *Quran*.

Muhammad delivered his message with immense passion and belief, drawing many followers. However, the elites of Mecca, for whom religion and pilgrims brought wealth, were enraged by his criticism of polytheism. They started intimidating Muhammad and his followers, forcing them to flee to the town of Yathrib (later named Medina) in 622, an event which is known as Hijra, and which marks the start of the Islamic calendar. After several skirmishes with the Meccans, the Muslims, led by Muhammad, got a boost to their confidence when they decisively defeated a much larger force sent by the Meccans. Their unbeaten run continued, and in 630, Muhammad and his followers finally entered Mecca, unopposed.

By the time he passed away in 632, Muhammad had united the many Arabic tribes under the aegis of the new religion.

Over the next three decades, four *khalifas* (caliphs), meaning 'deputy', succeeded the Prophet—his wise and modest friend Abu Bakr (632–34), his senior companion Umar (634–44), his son-in-law and the first convert from an elite background Uthman (644–656), and his cousin and son-in-law Ali (656–661).

It was under the leadership of Caliph Umar that mounted Arab armies roared out of the deserts of Arabia and challenged the Byzantines and the Persians. They shattered a Byzantine army in 634 near Gaza, which sent their morale soaring. Two years later, they took over Damascus and defeated a force led by the Byzantine emperor's brother at the Battle of Yarmouk, confirming their control of Syria. Around the same time, in a historic battle, the Muslims prevailed over a much larger Persian army at a place called al-Qadisiyyah (located to the south of Baghdad), after which they captured the Persian capital of Ctesiphon. The Muslim zeal for conquest brought victories in all directions. City after city buckled under the onslaught. Within ten years of Muhammad's death, the political map of the region had changed permanently—the Persian Empire crumbled, and the Byzantine Empire lost two-thirds of its territory, recoiling into a defensive shell.

Caliph Uthman looked eastwards with a keen desire to find out if the Sindh region was worth conquering. A scout was dispatched on a reconnaissance mission who reached the inhospitable Makran desert that leads to Sindh and reported: 'The water supply is scanty, the dates are inferior, and the robbers are bold; a small army would be lost there and a large army would starve', thereby stalling any plans of an invasion. Expansion in other regions, however, continued, and by 652, the Muslims had conquered most of what is now the Middle East.[1]

While the Muslim defeat of the powerful Persian and Byzantines empires was stunning, there were numerous factors that contributed to this unlikely victory. A plague pandemic had broken out in the sixth century and devastated the Middle East and the Mediterranean regions. Probably originating in either China or India, the Plague of Justinian, named after the Byzantine emperor Justinian I, was first reported in Egypt around 541 CE and from there it spread to Constantinople. An estimated 25–50 million people were dead by the end of the century.

The sustained twenty-five-year war between the Byzantine and the Persian empires that ended in the year 628 further drained them out. Economic turmoil, internal dissent, and corruption had become endemic in both the camps while attacks by the Central Asian Turkic people made matters worse. On the other hand, the Muslims were united under one banner and fought fervently for their faith. They also had another winning factor on their side: Khalid ibn al-Walid, the great general and military strategist who routed the Byzantine and Persian armies.

The highly successful caliphate phase was also marked with assassinations, succession challenges, and a permanent divide among the followers of Islam. Caliph Umar was murdered by a Persian slave, while Caliph Uthman was besieged and killed by a group of rebels. Ali, whose followers believed he was the rightful successor to Muhammad, was passed over until he finally became the fourth caliph. A member of Uthman's Umayyad clan and the governor of Syria, Muawiyah ibn Abi Sufyan accused Caliph Ali of failing to pursue the murderers of Caliph Uthman. Muawiyah became Ali's principal opponent and fought several battles against him. Caliph Ali died after he was struck in the back of his head with a poisoned sword by a member of a group of puritanical Muslims called the Kharijites. His death ended the first era of Islamic history and led to a permanent schism in Islam—his followers became the Shia sect, while the followers of all four caliphs became the majority Sunni sect.

The Umayyads (661–750)

After Ali's assassination, Muawiyah subdued other rival claimants to the position of caliph, and transformed the caliphate into a hereditary office, thus founding the Umayyad dynasty. The capital was relocated from Mecca to Damascus, and the prevalent tribal traditions were replaced by a sophisticated bureaucracy. The caliphate grew rapidly under the Umayyads, advancing further into Persia and Central Asia in the east, and into modern Tunisia and Morocco in the west. The Umayyads transformed Islam from a religious entity to a political empire, setting in motion a glorious era in Islamic history. The Umayyad treasuries were awash with wealth that was spent on building grand mosques and market squares in Damascus, transforming the formerly Christian Roman metropolis into a splendid Islamic city. Similar projects were commissioned in cities like Aleppo and Palmyra (Syria), Jerash (Jordan), Jerusalem and Scythopolis (Israel), and Kairouan (Tunisia). The new Islamic architecture was influenced by the Byzantine and Persian Sassanid building techniques that had been honed over centuries.

In 711, the Umayyad general Tariq ibn Ziyad led the Muslim conquest of Spain, crossing what is now the Strait of Gibraltar (derived from Jabal al-Tariq or the Mount of Tariq, named after him) from the North African coast into the Spanish mainland, which they eventually came to control. The same year, the Umayyads launched an invasion at the other end of the empire. With the caliph's permission, al-Hajjaj, the governor of Iraq, sent a seventeen-year-old commander named Muhammad bin Qasim with a massive army, comprising a 6,000-strong cavalry and a 3,000-strong camel corps, to invade Sindh. What triggered the offensive is not clear—the capture of an Arab ship by pirates off the port city of Deybal (near modern Karachi) is often cited as a reason for the invasion. The story goes that the pirates not only plundered the ship's cargo but also seized several Arab girls who were aboard. Al-Hajjaj wrote a stern letter to Raja Dahir, the king of Sindh, who claimed he couldn't do anything to help the Arabs on the ship.[2]

Upon reaching Deybal, Qasim ruthlessly slaughtered all adult men, enslaved their women and children, and plundered the town. He met with little resistance as his army advanced north. Finally, Qasim crossed the Indus River with his forces and seized the fortress of Brahmanabad, the base of Raja Dahir, who was killed in the raid. Qasim continued his march, capturing Alor (Rohri in Sindh province, Pakistan) and finally the city of Multan. He then embarked upon his return journey, the details of which are not clear. One account states that he was ordered back to Iraq as a captive by the new caliph and executed to settle political scores.

The subsequent history of Arabs in India is obscure. Although their foothold endured in Sindh for the next three centuries, they did not expand their territory any further, possibly due to the firm opposition by the native Gurjara-Pratihara and Chalukya kingdoms. In his book *The Age of Wrath*, historian Abraham Eraly observes that it is perplexing why there weren't more efforts made by the Arabs to advance further into India, given its immense riches.

Somewhere between the eighth and tenth centuries, a Persian community of Zoroastrians, settled in Hormuz on the Persian Gulf, started facing persecution by the Muslims and decided to leave their homeland. They set sail for India and landed in Diu, subsequently moving to Gujarat. As legend has it, they convinced the local ruler that they would be 'like sugar in a full cup of milk, adding sweetness but not causing it to overflow'.[3] The Parsis, as they came to be known, took to agriculture and made Gujarat their home for the next several centuries. The Islamic invasions may have caused the exodus of another ethnic group—the Roma or Romany people. Based on recent genetic and linguistic research, it is believed that the Roma were nomadic people from northern India who migrated westwards in multiple waves towards Europe between the eighth and tenth centuries.

Meanwhile, the Umayyads had waged a series of wars against the Byzantines. They were brimming with confidence until the Byzantines handed them a crushing defeat in 717, when they laid siege to Constantinople, the most impregnable city the world had ever known.

In Europe, the Muslim advance from Al-Andalus (Spain) into France was halted when Charles Martel, the ruler of the Frankish kingdom (the predecessor state to modern France and Germany), defeated the Umayyad forces in 732 at the Battle of Poitiers, 300 kilometres south of Paris. Martel's victory has been documented in European records as a pivotal victory that checked Islam's conquest of Christian Europe. Intriguingly, Muslim records from the same period don't seem to mention the battle.[4] After all, western Europe was not quite known for its riches, and its long, cold winters could have barely enticed the Muslims. Instead, Muslim chroniclers have recognised the defeat at Constantinople (717) as a major setback that enabled eastern and western Christendom to survive.

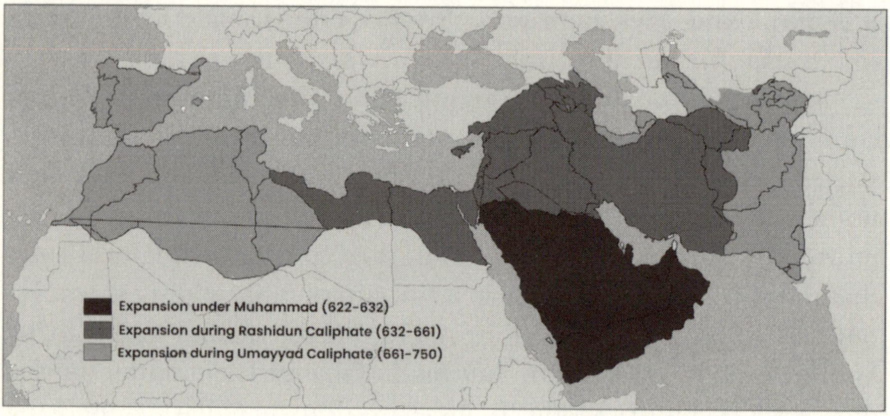

Early spread of Islam

The Abbasids (750–961)

Though the Umayyads had brought prosperity and civilisation to the lands they conquered, and built one of the largest empires in history, they had not delivered on a fundamental tenet of Islam—equality for all Muslims. Arabs were clearly favoured over the Mawali (non-Arab Muslims) and enjoyed a superior social and administrative status. Another aspect where the Umayyads seemed to be deviating from the core essence of Islam was their imperial magnificence and grandeur compared to the humble and austere lifestyle of the founders of Islam.

It was because of these misses that the Abbasids, another family of Meccan origins and descendants of the Prophet's youngest uncle, Abbas, began to campaign against the Umayyads, attacking their moral character and administration. They started fomenting a secret rebellion in the city of Merv (in modern Turkmenistan). The unrest reached a climax in 747 when a rebel force marched towards Damascus and routed the Umayyads, executing the entire clan except the grandson of a former caliph, who managed to escape to Al-Andalus and went on to establish an independent caliphate that became a distinctive hybrid of Islamic, Christian, and Jewish cultures. Cordoba, the capital of this new caliphate, was transformed from a decaying city to one of the greatest and wealthiest cities in Europe; Toledo and Seville grew into renowned centres of culture. Today, we see only a few remnants of that golden era as the later Spanish rulers made an active effort to erase it.

Though Persia had been conquered by the Arabs and its populace had accepted Islam, the rich culture and language of the Persians could not be subdued in entirety. Some historians have called the victory of the Abbasids and the subsequent reinstatement of the Persian language and culture a 'reconquest' by Persia.

In 751, the Abbasid army saw action at the eastern frontier of their empire when they met the army of the Tang Empire of China at the Battle of Talas River (near the modern Kyrgystan–Kazakhstan border). The Arab forces triumphed over the Tang forces, marking Talas as the farthest eastern frontier of the Caliphate. Until the arrival of Islam, Buddhism had been prominent in Central Asia with principal monasteries in cities like Balkh and Bukhara, a city which got its name from the Sanskrit word *vihara*, meaning 'monastery'. Over the next three centuries, most of the formerly Buddhist, Zoroastrian, and Nestorian Christian tribes of Central Asia became Muslim, and the Uyghur people (Turkic-speaking ethnic group) became the pre-eminent Islamic force on the eastern frontier.

There was another notable consequence of the battle of Talas that would change the world. The Chinese prisoners of war captured by the Arabs transmitted to them information about a key invention—the art of papermaking—which then spread all over the Islamic world and from there to Europe.

In 765, the Abbasids moved their capital from Damascus to their splendid new capital of Baghdad which they had built on the banks of Tigris River, in the heart of the ancient land of Mesopotamia, from where had sprung the earliest of cities and empires. The new city, called Madinat al-Salam or 'City of Peace', had a unique circular design which was based on that of Ctesiphon and the Nawbahar (New Monastery) Buddhist monastery at Balkh. The city's planning was directed by Khalid ibn Barmak, who was born in Balkh to the last Buddhist abbot of Nawbahar and who had converted to Islam. His family, called the Barmakids (from the Sanskrit word *pramukha*, meaning 'chief administrator'), hailed from Kashmir and had gone on to gain prominence in centres like Balkh and Merv. For generations, they had facilitated a cultural exchange between India and Central Asia, and Nawbahar had been a hub for the translation of Buddhist texts from India before they were redirected to China.[5]

Baghdad became the wealthiest and the most populous city in the world, outside of China, and it left its visitors spellbound with its opulent palaces, bazaars, mosques, libraries, and gardens. Merchants, construction workers, craftsmen, scribes, and scholars were attracted to the cosmopolitan city like bees to honey. A constant stream of cargo ships from Africa, India, and China entered through the port of Basra, known as *al-bahr al Hindi*, meaning the gateway to the Indian Ocean, and sailed up the Tigris to Baghdad. Even Viking traders from Scandinavia are known to have reached Baghdad and Central Asia, trading goods like fur, swords, and slaves for the much-coveted silver dirhams, spices, and silk. In a remarkable archaeological discovery, a statue of Buddha has been discovered on the Swedish island of Helgo, a prominent Viking trading centre from the sixth to the eleventh century. One Indian king is known to have sent a well-equipped war elephant in the late eighth century as a gift to the Abbasid caliph, who passed it on to the European king Charlemagne. Probably the first living being from India to reach northern Europe, the pachyderm was deployed in a battle in Denmark.

After shining for over two centuries, the dominance and power of the Abbasids started to fade due to civil wars and agrarian disorder, even though the caliphate survived. Around the same time, a dynasty of Shia Muslims called Fatimids, who claimed to be descendants of the Prophet's daughter Fatima (hence the name), rose from Tunisia and came to control North Africa. They built a new city along the Nile River called Qahira, meaning 'victory' in Arabic, that came to be called Cairo in the West. By the eleventh century, Cairo had marched ahead of Baghdad and Cordoba, although all three caliphates continued to exist side by side.

Mahmud Of Ghazni

The Islamic world was an amalgam of diverse groups of people and cultures from Arabia, Persia, and North Africa. By the tenth century, another group of rugged, horse-riding warriors were entering their domains and making their mark. These new entrants on the scene were the Turkic people. The Abbasid caliphs had begun the practice of inducting young Turkic slaves from lands north of Persia and grooming them as soldiers and bodyguards. They were considered to be exceptionally loyal and came to be known as ghulams or mamluks (both the terms meaning slaves or slave soldiers). Some of the ghulams rose to the level of a commander while some even became rulers of provinces.[6]

In the year 962, one such ghulam named Alptigin, who had risen to the rank of a general under the Persian Samanid dynasty, managed to carve a kingdom for himself in Ghazni in eastern Afghanistan. It was his grandson Mahmud of Ghazni who turned it into an empire by conquering lands stretching from eastern Persia to northern India. His name evokes strong emotions in India to date as the ruthless conqueror and *but-shikan* (the destroyer of idols) who raided India no fewer than seventeen times between

1001 and 1026, carrying off vast quantities of booty that included gold, silver, precious jewels, slaves, and elephants.

THE CRUSADES

A group of Turkic people called the Seljuqs came to prominence in the eleventh century as they conquered vast lands across Central Asia and Persia. In the historic battle of Manzikert (1071), they demolished a massive Byzantine army, and their victory was followed by a Turkic influx in the region. The Seljuqs started wresting Byzantine cities, and by 1087, they had taken over Jerusalem as well. Seeing matters slip out of his hands, the Byzantine emperor Alexios was unnerved and reached out to his Christian counterparts in continental Europe for support.

The Byzantines and the Christian peers in the West had, however, seen a worsening of their ties through the previous centuries over religious matters. The deepening gulf had caused Christianity to formally split into two branches in 1054—Orthodox Church the east and Roman Catholic Church in the west, with leaders on both the sides excommunicating each other.

Upon receiving Alexios's request for help, Pope Urban (1088–1099) astutely decided to support him, hoping to reunite the Catholic and the Orthodox churches, and in the process elevate the prestige of the papacy in Europe for taking on the threat of Islam. In the town of Clermont in central France, in November 1095, Pope Urban delivered a rousing speech laced with exaggerated accounts of the persecution of Christians. He urged all Christians to launch a crusade for defending Christendom and reclaiming Jerusalem from the Muslims. His call to arms reverberated all over Europe and around 90,000 people—from poor peasants to knights and noblemen, driven either by piety, chivalric glory, hope for booty, or adventure—came forward to take part in a religious war campaign that became the First Crusade. It was followed by a series of crusades over the following two centuries, with thousands of Europeans heading east to fight the holy wars.

The long-lasting clash between the crescent and the cross brought wins and losses for both sides. While the ultimate objective of keeping Jerusalem in Christian hands could not be achieved, the Crusades brought people across Europe together and helped shape a collective identity, while at the same time, the Church gained prestige and authority. The campaigns to the east had created a need for supplies to feed and arm the crusaders, which brought wealth to ports like Venice and towns that fell along the routes followed by them. For Muslims, the impact of the Crusades was mostly limited to cities on the eastern Mediterranean coast, and not so much in Persia, Central Asia, or Arabia.

In Al-Andalus, the Cordoba Caliphate had started to decline since the beginning of the eleventh century. The caliphate ended in 1031, leaving Al-Andalus fragmented into smaller states that faced attacks from Christian armies as part of the Reconquista, a series of campaigns launched by the Christian kingdoms to recapture the Iberial peninsula from the Moors. The Christian armies conquered Cordoba in 1236, Valencia in 1238, and Seville in 1248. Granada remained the only place where the Moors held on for another two centuries, until its fall in 1492, completing the Christian reconquest of the Iberian peninsula.

Even as the Crusades raged on, there was a greater threat that was troubling the Islamic world—the Mongols. Baghdad, the capital of the declining Abbasid caliphate, bore the full brunt of Mongol fury in 1258. After 500 years of glory, the city was completely destroyed, and the Abbasid era was over. To add to the people's misery, the Black Death arrived in the fourteenth century. Much of the Islamic world suffered from the pandemic, and for some parts, the damage was permanent. Despite this calamity, Islam made a comeback as the Mongol khans, the Turkic leaders, and their Turco-Mongol successors embraced the Islamic faith. Their empires went on to cover even greater territories, marking a second glorious inning for Islam.

The religious war between the Christian West and the Islamic East might have subsided by the end of the thirteenth century, but the confrontation between the two worlds was far from abating. Over the following centuries, as Europe continued its trajectory of intellectual, economic, and military progress, their zeal for expansion and domination took the Christian states deeper into Islamic territories. The British, French, and the Russians deposed many Muslim nawabs, sultans, kings, emperors, emirs, shahs and the Western armies marched into cities like Seringapatam, Shahjahanabad, Cairo, Kabul, Ghazni, Kandahar, Samarkand, Istanbul, Beirut, Damascus, Aleppo, Jerusalem, and Baghdad.

THE ISLAMIC ENLIGHTENMENT

The Umayyads had initiated a tradition of promoting art, scholarship, and culture that was continued by the Abbasids, who went a step further and removed the political barriers imposed by tribe and ethnicity. The Abbasid domains turned into a cosmopolitan world open to new streams of knowledge where curious minds could travel freely and interchange ideas. In the first two centuries of their rule, the Islamic civilisation reached its pinnacle, and this period is referred to as the Golden Age of Islam.

The spread of the art of papermaking, brought to the Arabs by the Chinese after the Talas victory, had a far-reaching impact as it now became much cheaper and efficient to create books, letters, and records of transactions. In a trend similar to the revolution sparked off by Gutenberg's invention of the printing press in fifteenth-century Europe, book production started to boom in the major centres of the Abbasid empire.

Many scholars were drawn to the private libraries of Abbasid nobles, who not only displayed their book collections as a status symbol, but also promoted academic discourse. Caliph Harun al-Rashid (763–809) built a magnificent library in Baghdad called the Khizanat al-Hikma (the Library of Wisdom), which his son, Caliph Al-Ma'mun (786–833), further transformed into an unrivalled centre of scholarship called the Bayt al-Hikma (the House of Wisdom). A wide range of languages, including Arabic, Farsi, Aramaic, Hebrew,

Syriac, Greek, and Latin, were spoken and read at the Bayt al-Hikma, which housed a multitude of writers, scribes, translators, and librarians. In an extensive translation movement during the Abbasid period, classical Greek and Roman works in philosophy, astronomy, geography, and anatomy were translated into Arabic.

The sophisticated Barmakids of Baghdad understood the value of the cross-pollination of knowledge. They appointed a Hindu physician named Dhanya or Dhanin to head their hospital in Baghdad[7] and sent scouts to places like Varanasi and Ujjain in India to bring back texts on subjects such as medicine, astronomy, and mathematics. A delegation from Sindh to the caliph's court included an astronomer, named Kanaka, who is believed to have carried with him the seventh-century treatises *Brahmasphuta-Siddhanta* and *Khandakhadyaka* written by the astronomer Brahmagupta. On the caliph's orders, the works were translated from Sanskrit to Arabic in a book called *Zij Sindhind*.[8]

The Islamic world became a hub and a conduit of culture and ideas from distant lands. A merchant named Sulayman Tajir travelled to India and China around the year 851 and wrote a diary called *Akhbar al-Sin wa'l-Hind* (*An Account of China and India*), which is one of the earliest records of Muslim travellers. The *Panchatantra,* a collection of ancient Indian animal fables, which historian Upinder Singh has called 'the one Indian text that has probably travelled most widely than any other texts', reached Persia in the sixth century and was translated into Arabic in the eighth century. The story of Sindbad the Sailor, one of the most famous heroes of Middle Eastern literature, probably originated around the Sindh region or the Sindh (Indus) River.

Besides Baghdad, other centres of interaction and intellectual inquiry emerged in a vast realm stretching from Persia and Central Asia to Al-Andalus and Sicily. These centres boasted of libraries and a flourishing trade in books. The University of Karaouine in Fez, Morocco, was founded in the year 859 and is recognised as the oldest continuously running, degree-granting university in the world. In 975, the Fatimids established the Al-Azhar University in

Cairo, which continues to be a large and prestigious institution to date and counts among its alumni Maulana Abul Kalam Azad, an erudite leader of India's freedom struggle.

This age of enlightenment produced many brilliant minds, whose works inspired future generations of scientists and thinkers around the world.

Born in Khwarizm (now Khiva, Uzbekistan), Al-Khwarizmi (780–850) was a mathematician, astronomer, and geographer, who wrote the pioneering book *Hisab al-Jabr wa-l-Muqabala* from which we get the term algebra; similarly, the word algorithm stems from the Latinisation of his name. Al-Khwarizmi headed scientific missions to India, studied the Hindu numerical system, and popularised it in the wider Islamic world and beyond.

Another outstanding astronomer was Al-Farghani (797–860), who was born in the Ferghana Valley in modern Uzbekistan. Al-Farghani, also known as Alfragnus in Europe, was quite popular a name in the continent and the Latin editions of his major work in astronomy, *Elements,* were widely read in Europe until centuries later. Columbus was also one of his readers, although he had mistaken Al-Farghani's 7,091-foot Arabic mile to be the 4,856-foot Roman mile, which made him grossly underestimate the Earth's circumference.

There were many other mathematicians, astronomers, pharmacologists, and philosophers like Ibn al-Haytham or Alhazen, Abu Musa Jabir ibn Hayyan or Geber, Al-Kindi or Alkindus, and Al-Farabi, who won an illustrious place in history for their intellectual endeavours.

Geniuses continued to emerge even after the peak of the Abbasid era was over. Mahmud of Ghazni, otherwise known for his brutal campaigns, was a great patron of poetry, literature, and scholarship, which also helped elevate his prestige and establish Ghazni in the same league as Baghdad. He announced handsome rewards that drew around 900 poets, astronomers, historians, and philosophers to his court. The ones who did not respond to his lucrative terms faced his wrath and were coerced into joining his court.

Al-Biruni (973–1052), born in Khwarizm, had long held a fascination for Indian science and culture. In his writings, he had lamented that there was no reliable source on Indian history and astronomy. When Mahmud came to control the entire Indus Valley, Al-Biruni sensed an opportunity to access the knowledge capital of India. At the age of forty-five, he began to learn Sanskrit and devoted the next twelve years to exploring India, its people, culture, and customs, while pursuing his interest in astronomy. He studied the works of ancient Indian astronomers like Aryabhatta, Varāhamihira, and Brahmagupta and notable commentators on ancient texts like Balabhadra and Utpala. Al-Biruni leveraged the concepts of zero and negative numbers from India and came up with an amazingly simple formula for calculating the Earth's circumference.

He wrote nearly 150 works on a range of subjects like astronomy, geography, engineering, and history, including his encyclopedic work *Tahqiq ma Ii'l-Hind* (*Al-Biruni's India*). He did not hold back his criticism of the people of India: 'Their haughtiness is such that, if you tell them of any science or scholar in Khurasan and Persis, they will think you to be both an ignoramus and a liar … The religious books of the Hindus and their codes of tradition, the Puranas, contain sentences about the shape of the world which stand in direct opposition to scientific truth as known to their astronomers.'[9]

A younger peer of Al-Biruni was the Bukhara-born scholar Ibn Sina (980–1037), known as Avicenna in the West. Regarded as one of the greatest scientific minds, his work *Canon of Medicine* remained for many centuries the classical medical text throughout the Islamic world and Europe. He further refined and enriched the field of Unani (meaning Greek) medicine that had origins in ancient Greece. Over time, the Unani system gained wide acceptance in India where physicians fused it with traditional knowledge of healing. Several colleges of Unani medicine are operational in India to date.[10]

Unfortunately, this phase of intellectual and creative flowering eluded India, in spite of its geographical proximity to the Islamic world, as Pandit Nehru lamentably expressed in *The Discovery of India*:

> Though the Arabs learned much from India, the Indians did not learn much from the Arabs. The Indians remained aloof, wrapped up in their own conceits, and keeping as far as possible within their own shells. This was unfortunate, for the intellectual ferment of Baghdad and the Arab renaissance movement would have shaken up the Indian mind just when it was losing much of its creative vigour.

Fading Glory

By the thirteenth century, the Islamic world had started to lose its spirit of inquiry and became unaccepting of discourse and innovation. There's much debate among historians and academics regarding the timeline and the root cause of this downward spiral.

The Mu'tazila school of Islamic theology that was deeply influenced by Greek reason and rationalism was witnessing growing discontent and was seen as being excessively rationalist. In comparison, the Ash'ari school of theology, founded by the Arab theologian Abu al-Hasan al-Ash'ari in the tenth century, insisted that reason must be subordinate to revelation and that the Quran was unchallengeable. Interestingly, many of the conservative ideas and writings on the Hadiths (records of the Islamic traditions or sayings of the Prophet Muhammad) came from the same Central Asian cities that had produced revolutionary scientific ideas.

Nizam al-Mulk (1018–1092), a Persian scholar born in Tus (in modern day Iran), rose to the influential position of vizier under the Seljuq sultans. He had created a system of education known as 'Nizamiyah' that focused on religious studies. Within a few years, several Nizamiyah madrasas were operational at places like Nishapur, Shiraz, and Khargird with thousands of students enrolled, making them the largest institutions in the world at the time. These madrasas had fundamentally altered the goal of Muslim education from critical analysis to revelation and indoctrination.

This approach would get replicated throughout the Muslim world in the coming decades.

In the late eleventh century arrived another intellectual giant named Al-Ghazali (1058–1111), who was also born in Tus. In his younger years, he had established himself as one of the foremost Muslim theologians of his age. When Al-Ghazali showed up at Nizam al-Mulk's court, the vizier was deeply impressed and appointed him the head of the Nizamiyah madrasa in Baghdad.

Al-Ghazali was a prominent Ash'arite and challenged the philosophy of Ibn Sina and others, pushing for a restraint on the exercise of logic and reason. He believed that wherever mathematics and logic conflicted with the revelations, they were wrong. His rejection and incessant attacks would have a long-lasting impact on the Islamic world. The fact that Al-Ghazali had mastered logic and intensively studied the philosophies of Al-Farabi and Ibn Sina, besides the works of other Greek philosophers, lent credibility to his criticism. In his book *The Aim of Philosophers,* he first explained what the philosophy of Aristotle was, before arguing how it was wrong. As a follow up to his first book, Al-Ghazali wrote a seminal work called *Tahafut al-falasifa* (*The Incoherence of Philosophers*), where he defended Islam against the philosophers, arguing that God was the only force causing everything.

Al-Ghazali's arguments were contested by the Cordoba-born polymath Ibn Rushd (Latinised as Averroes) in his book *Tahâfut al-tahâfut* (*The Incoherence of the Incoherence*), though it was already too late by then. As Ibn Rushd's book was written in Spain, it ended up influencing European thought, but hardly made any difference in the Islamic world. By the twelfth century, the rationalist factions were almost completely marginalised. The conservatives won, and the spirit of free-thinking and scientific inquiry gradually diminished in the Islamic world, creating a template for subsequent generations.[11]

The final blow to Islam's golden age came in 1258 when the Mongols sacked Baghdad. They burnt libraries, including the House of Wisdom, and threw thousands of books and literary treasures into the Tigris River. The assault by the Mongols pushed the Islamic theologians into an ideological crisis as the Islamic world had not faced any significant defeats or suffered from large-scale deaths since the seventh century. Many wondered if it was some form of divine punishment for deviating from God's message, and resolved to tread the path of religious conservatism.

INTELLECTUAL AWAKENING IN EUROPE

In the tenth century, European thinkers and scholars visiting cities in the Islamic world were astounded by the thriving intellectual climate they witnessed there, as compared to the levels of ignorance in Europe, that they called *Latinorum penuria* or 'the poverty of the Latins'. The royal library of Cordoba, for instance, had a massive collection of 4,00,000 books, compared to only a few hundred in the largest library in Christian Europe. The Muslim learning centres had not only maintained the classical Greek and Roman texts but had further built upon them and synthesised the knowledge contained within these texts with knowledge from India, Persia, and Egypt.

French scholar Gerbert of Aurillac (946–1003), who later became Pope Sylvester II (999–1003), was an educational reformer as well as a leading mathematician and astronomer of his time. He spent three years studying in Al-Andalus[12] and endorsed the study of Muslim and Greco-Roman texts. Gerbert introduced to Europe the Hindu-Arabic numeral system and the concept of *sunya* (zero), which was initially not accepted by the Europeans as they associated it with demonic qualities. Using these new numerals, Gerbert, known as 'the Scientific Pope', devised an abacus that has been called 'the first computer'. During his lifetime, the first science book was translated from Arabic into Latin through the combined efforts of Muslim, Jewish, and Christian scholars.

In the eleventh century emerged an influential figure who would take Greco-Arabic science to the West. Constantine the African (1020–1087) was a Muslim merchant born in Carthage (modern Tunis) who spent forty years travelling through Egypt, Syria, Persia,

Ethiopia, and India collecting scientific texts. He later embraced Christianity and joined the Benedictine community, finally settling in the monastery of Monte Cassino (120 kilometres southeast of Rome) where he translated thirty-seven books from Arabic to Latin.

Towards the end of the eleventh century, as the Islamic cities in Al-Andalus began to fall to the Christian armies, their libraries, filled with books and manuscripts, slipped into Christian hands. All this while, the crusaders brought back more and more classical texts from the East that attracted scholars from England, France, and Germany, who began to feverishly translate these texts into Latin. Toledo became a knowledge hub where Arabic works and Arabic translations of ancient Greek texts and Indian works such as the *Zij Sindhind* were translated into Latin.

An itinerant English scholar named Adelard of Bath (1080–1152), who taught in France, travelled to Sicily, North Africa, Syria, and Palestine, scouring libraries for Arab and Greek texts. He returned with a copy of Al-Khwarizmi's book on mathematics along with a shortened version of his astronomical tables, and translated the two works. Both translations became instant classics in England and in mainland Europe. Another prolific translator was Robert of Chester, an English mathematician and astronomer, who lived in the twelfth century and studied in Barcelona. He is known for introducing Arabic algebra and alchemy to Europe.

The most productive translator of Arab and Greek works to Latin was the Italian scholar Gerard of Cremona (1114–1187). Gerard had moved to Toledo to learn Arabic so he could read the works of Ptolemy, which were not available in Latin. He ended up spending the rest of his life there with around eighty translations to his credit. His work distinctly contributed to the growth of medieval European science.[13]

For 200 years after Hindu-Arabic numerals had been introduced in Europe by Gerbert of Aurillac, their usage had remained restricted to a few mathematicians and scholars. It was in 1202 when the Italian mathematician Leonardo of Pisa (1170–1240), more popularly known as Fibonacci, published the massive tome

Liber Abaci (*The Book of Calculation*) that Hindu-Arabic numerals were popularised throughout Europe. Born to a Pisan merchant who was based at the port of Bugia (Bejaia, Algeria), Fibonacci studied under an Arab master and later travelled to Egypt, Syria, Constantinople, Greece, and Sicily, where he encountered the numerals. His immensely popular book explained the basics of reading and using the Hindu-Arabic numerals, followed by complex calculations and applications in geometry. The merchant community found them far more efficient and logical than the cumbersome Roman numerals when handling large numbers or converting weights and measures.

Another revolutionary idea that presumably came from India was the concept of double-entry bookkeeping, which Indian traders had been using for centuries. It was introduced to Europe by the Italian mathematician Luca Pacioli (1447–1517) and is said to have been a driving force behind the economic success of the West.[14]

It has been suggested that romance literature and the themes of chivalry, love, loyalty, and betrayal that evolved in Europe during the Crusades had parallels in Persian poetry; works like Daniel Defoe's *Robinson Crusoe* and Jonathan Swift's *Gulliver's Travels* are said to have taken cues from Sindbad's tales of adventure. Likewise, the architectural styles of many iconic structures in Europe, like the famed Notre-Dame Cathedral in Paris, can be traced back to the Islamic style of architecture that once flowered in Syria, Egypt, Iran, and Iraq.[15] The domes of the Cathedral of Santa Maria del Fiore in Florence, St. Paul's Cathedral in London, and even the Capitol Dome in Washington, D.C., are said to have been inspired by the fourteenth-century Dome of Soltaniyeh in Iran, which American scholar A.U. Pope has described as 'anticipating the Taj Mahal'.[16]

In the eleventh century, Christian Europe and the Islamic world were witnessing a reversal of fortunes. As Ash'arism was taking root in Muslim societies, Europeans were undergoing a religious and intellectual reformation, escaping the Church's firm grip over knowledge. Some scholars have considered this development in Europe as a forerunner of the Renaissance.

While the cathedral schools, the dominant centres of learning in Europe for centuries, were on the wane, Pope Gregory VII (1073–1085) initiated reforms, laying the framework for independent universities. A few years before the Nizamiyah madrasa was opened in Baghdad, the first European university was established at Bologna in Italy in 1088, followed by the University of Salamanca (1134) in Spain. The University of Paris was founded in 1150 and became the model for later universities in northern Europe. The University of Oxford was founded in 1167 when King Henry II banned English students from attending the University of Paris. In 1180, a wealthy English merchant named Jocius of London returned from Jerusalem and founded the College des Dix-huit in Paris, which eventually merged with the University of Paris.[17] The university boom continued. In the town of Oxford, ongoing hostilities between the townsfolk and the scholars led to an outbreak of violence in 1209. A group of scholars fled to Cambridge where they founded the University of Cambridge. The University of Montpellier, France (1220), and the University of Padua, Italy (1222) followed.

Why did the European universities evolve into centres of learning and inquiry while the Islamic madrasas remained static?

One peculiar difference between the two was that the European universities were legally autonomous and could therefore develop their own rules, methods, and curricula. Though they had started as monastic schools, over time, the monarchs had allowed them to be independent of the Catholic Church. The madrasas, in contrast, were established by a *waqf* (an endowment made to a religious, charitable, or educational cause by a Muslim) and had to conform to the spiritual goals and commitments of their influential patrons. Islamic law granted legal standing to physical persons only and not to institutions or corporations.

The autonomy of universities in Europe was part of a broader legal revolution in the twelfth and thirteenth centuries where cities, towns, merchant guilds, and other charitable organisations were granted the same corporate structure. Another landmark development during this time was the signing of the Magna Carta in England in 1215. Recognised as one of the most authoritative documents in the history of democracy, the Magna Carta established many of the principles, like freedom and justice, that govern modern Western constitutional thought to date.

European scholars, however, continued to look to the works of Islamic astronomers and philosophers. Like the thirteenth-century English polymath Roger Bacon, famous for his work in optics and being an early proponent of the scientific method, was influenced by the writings of the pioneering Arab thinker Ibn al-Haytham or Alhazen, who is referred to as 'the father of modern optics'. In the ensuing centuries, Europe witnessed the flowering of the Renaissance, followed by the Scientific Revolution, thereby stepping into a virtuous loop. The invention of the printing press led to the explosion and democratisation of knowledge in Christian Europe, while the Muslim leaders either ignored it or refused to adopt it, leading to an ever-widening divergence between the followers of the two great faiths.

Over time, as the Europeans knowledge grew exponentially, they became proud of their intellectual superiority, seeing themselves as the vanguard of progress and civilisation. The achievements of the Islamic world began to fade from their collective memory, reaching a point where the Europeans adopted a dismissive attitude towards the Orient. In the nineteenth century, Lord Macaulay, the English politician and historian, arrogantly stated: 'a single shelf of a good European library was worth the whole native literature of India and Arabia'.

CONTEMPORANEOUS EVENTS IN INDIA AND BEYOND

After Muhammad bin Qasim's invasion in 711, Islam had remained confined to the Sindh region for almost three centuries, while the rest of India—primarily the northern and southern areas—saw numerous regional dynasties and kingdoms compete with each other over territory and influence. In northern India, the Gurjara-Pratihara dynasty dominated the western regions and checked any further eastward advance of the Arabs. The Palas controlled Bengal and Bihar till the eleventh century, after which another family called the Senas took over the region. In southern India, the Chalukyas, ruling from their capital city of Badami, dominated the Deccan region for a century, restraining any Arab advance towards central and southern India. After their reign ended in 760, their descendants founded another dynasty called the Rashtrakutas whose kingdom was described as one of the greatest in the world by the Arab traveller Sulayman Tajir in his account.

However, the most successful and dynamic of all the dynasties was the Chola dynasty of southern India. The rise of Chola power began with the accession of Rajaraja in 985 and his victorious campaigns against the Pandyas of Madurai and the Cheras of Kerala in South India. In a never-before-seen overseas conquest by any Indian king, Rajaraja invaded Buddhist Sri Lanka, sacking its ancient capital of Anuradhapura, and the Maldive Islands. His son Rajendra succeeded him in 1014 and added parts of Burma and Malaya to the Chola empire. Around 1025, Rajendra launched a grand naval campaign against the Srivijaya kingdom based in Sumatra, conquering more than a dozen harbour cities, as retaliation for Srivijayan interference in the direct trade between the Cholas and the Song dynasty of China. Historian Hermann Kulke has interpreted the naval campaign as a Chola quest to dominate the trade in the Indian Ocean where the emerging powers of the Fatimids in Egypt and the Song dynasty of China had started to wield influence.[18]

Gems of Hindu and Buddhist Architecture

The period between the seventh to the thirteenth centuries witnessed a great flowering of temple architecture with tens of thousands of craftsmen being deployed on grand projects funded by royal patrons. The Chalukyas merged the architectural forms of northern and southern India and built exquisite temples at Pattadakal, Aihole, and their capital Badami. The Pallavas, the great temple builders, built the famous rock-carved temples at Mahabalipuram. Many other awe-inspiring masterpieces emerged—the Brihadisvara Temple at Thanjavur (Chola dynasty), the Ellora Caves, a group of thirty-four temples and monasteries (Rashtrakuta dynasty), the Khajuraho Temples famous for their erotic sculptures (Chandela dynasty), the Hoysaleswara Temple at Halebidu (Hoysala dynasty), the Jagannath Temple at Puri and the giant chariot-shaped Sun Temple at Konark (Eastern Ganga dynasty). Many of these temple complexes are richly adorned with intricate carvings and sculptures.

The Hindu and Buddhist architectural styles in fact extended beyond India's boundaries to modern Myanmar (Buddhist temples and stupas at Bagan), Thailand (the historic city of Ayutthaya renowned for its temples), Indonesia (the Borobudur Buddhist stupa and the Prambanan temple complex), Cambodia (the temple complex of Angkor Wat), and Vietnam (the temples of Champa). The entire Southeast Asian region has been called Greater India, where Indian culture had permeated since the first century.

Strangely enough, these splendid Hindu temples of Southeast Asia remain largely unknown and beyond the sacred horizons of the vast Hindu population of India, including the most devout.

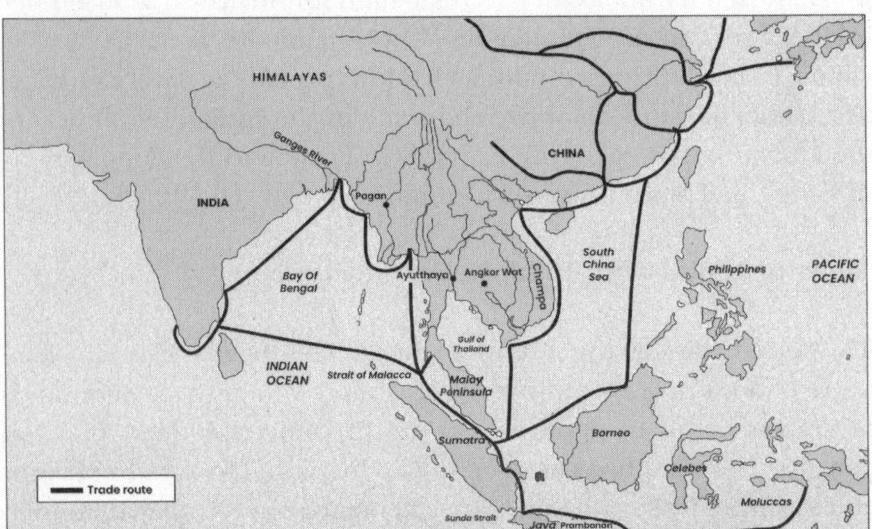

The spread of Hindu and Buddhist cultures to Southeast Asia

THE DELHI SULTANATE

In 1150, Ala-ud-Din Hussain, a chieftain of the Ghur (or Ghor) province in central Afghanistan, sacked Ghazni. The city was plundered for seven days and libraries, palaces, and mosques were razed, earning Alauddin the title of *Jahan-soz* (world burner). Ghazni never recovered from this assault.

Ala-ud-Din's nephews Ghiyas-ud-Din and Mu'izz-ud-Din (known as Muhammad Ghuri) took Ghurid power to new heights. While Ghiyas ended up controlling Afghanistan and eastern Iran, Muhammad Ghuri charged into the plains of the Indus Valley in 1175. Within a year, he had taken control of Multan, Peshawar, and the strategic Khyber Pass. In 1187, he captured Lahore, the last stronghold of the Ghaznavids, thereby ending their dynasty.

In 1191, Ghuri met with the chivalrous Rajput king Prithviraj Chauhan on the battlefield in Tarain, 120 kilometres north of Delhi. Prithviraj Chauhan defeated Ghuri, who then retreated to Ghazni. After spending a year regrouping with his commanders, Ghuri returned the next year to the plains of India. In the Second Battle of Tarain (1192), which is considered a watershed in the history of the Indian subcontinent, Ghuri won and Prithviraj was captured and executed.

Historians have attributed several reasons to why Prithviraj and other Indian kings lost to the Ghurids. Located at the crossroads of civilisations, the Ghurid kingdom had access to the latest military equipment, technological innovations, and high-quality horses. Their mounted archers could wield a bow while riding, which made them invincible at cavalry warfare. The Indian rulers had to spend fortunes on importing war horses as the Indian subcontinent, given its humidity and shortage of extensive pastures, was ill-suited for horse breeding. The war elephants deployed by Indian commanders also proved to be less effective against the swift horses of the Ghurids. Whereas the Ghurids had a sophisticated military system with a permanent core of professional soldiers who had fought many battles together, the Indian armies were composed of an assortment of fighting forces under individual lords who were called for duty when needed. Another drawback was the fact that the Indian rulers did not have much incentive to unite, nor did they see India as a nation the way we do in modern times. And from a cultural perspective, the Indian warriors placed notions of valour and honour above pragmatism and strategy.

After 1192, Ghuri excluded leaders belonging to his elite clan from commanding positions and instead appointed slaves of nomadic Turkic origin (similar to the Mamluks), like Qutb al-Din Aibak and Muhammad bin Bakhtiyar Khalji, who were absolutely loyal to him. Soon Ghuri had to return to Ghazni to deal with unrest on the western frontier, but he placed Delhi and Lahore under Aibak's governorship. In Delhi, Aibak constructed the Quwwat al-Islam (the Might of Islam) mosque in 1198 and in the following year started the construction of the Qutb Minar, which was modelled after the Minaret of Jam (today a UNESCO World Heritage Site) in the Ghurid capital in Afghanistan.

In the years that followed, Ghuri's slave generals began raiding towns across north and central India, reaching Bengal in the east. Any resistance by the Hindu kingdoms was met with brutal suppression and destruction of the temples that housed their patron deities. Bakhtiar Khalji raided ancient Buddhist universities like Nalanda and Vikramshila at a time when the universities like Oxford were being founded in Europe. According to a contemporary Persian historian, Minhaj Siraj, Khalji burnt libraries, destroying extensive collections of books and manuscripts, and hastening the decline of Buddhism.

In 1206, Ghuri was assassinated, and a succession struggle followed among his slave generals with Aibak taking control of Delhi and thereby founding the Delhi Sultanate. Over the following years, as the Delhi Sultanate was gaining strength, Islam's golden age was coming to an end. The Mongol invasions in Central Asia and Persia kept pushing streams of soldiers, slaves, and scholars of various ethnicities into India. At the same time, the Mongol invasions isolated the Delhi Sultanate, making it politically independent.

Over the next 300 years, the Delhi Sultanate had a series of sultans and dynasties—the Slave Dynasty (1206–90), the Khaljis (1290–1316), the Tughluqs (1320–1412), the Sayyids (1414–51), and the Lodis (1451–1526). Their stories were, more often than not, similar—despotic, ruthless, and power-crazed sultans with Turkic or Afghan roots who would either be toppled by the next spirited warlord or succeeded by one of the heirs who emerged victorious in a struggle for succession. Several prominent sultans built a newer city or citadel in Delhi, relegating their predecessor's capital to the list of ruins that made up the architectural past of the city.

It was in 1333, during the reign of the eccentric sultan Muhammad bin Tughlaq, that Ibn Battuta, the famous Moroccan explorer, arrived in India. The sultan granted Battuta the position of grand *qazi* (judge) in Delhi, a position he held for several years. In his famous travel account, *Tuhfat al-Nuzzar fi Ghara'ib al-Amsar wa-'Aja'ib al-Asfar (A Gift to Those Who Contemplate the Wonders of Cities and the Marvels of Travelling)*, Battuta described Delhi:

> The city of Dihli is of vast extent and population and made up now of four neighbouring and contiguous towns. One of them is the city called by this name, Dihli; it is the old city built by the infidels and captured in the year 1188. The second is called Siri. The third is called Tughlaq Abad, after its founder, the Sultan Tughlaq, the father of the sultan of India to whose court we came... The fourth is called Jahan Panah, and is set apart for the residence of the Sultan Muhammad Shah, the reigning king of India.

Though the Delhi Sultanate era recorded impressive achievements in art and architecture, it never saw a blossoming of science and intellectual curiosity that was a mainstay of the Islamic world from the eighth to the thirteenth centuries.

THE WORLD OF MYSTICS

While Sufism is a well-known term associated with singing and dancing mystics, what is not clear is its relation to Islam. Is it a more liberal version of Islam that draws even the non-Muslims? Or is it a rebellious movement against orthodox Islamic customs? Professor Nile Green, author of *Sufism: A Global History*, defines Sufism as a 'powerful tradition of Muslim knowledge and practices' that shaped societies and cultures across the world.

The exact origin of Sufism, known as *tasawwuf* in Arabic, is much debated, although many do agree that the word *sufi* is derived from the Arabic word *suf* (wool). Sufi was used as a nickname for hermits dressed in woollen garments in and around Baghdad as early as the eighth century. These wandering hermits, or Sufis, reflected the early stages of Islamic asceticism that developed, probably as a counterweight to the growing materialism in Islamic society. A woman from Basra named Rabiah is said to have introduced the element of love for God, which changed this early asceticism into mysticism.

In the beginning, the movement involved small groups with followers gathered around their spiritual masters in circles. From the tenth century onwards, the movement started to spread eastwards into Central Asia and Persia, which became home to many Sufi monastic orders. The Sufi institutions came to be called *khanaqahs* (spiritual retreats), and their doctrines held significant clout. The prominent public intellectual Al-Ghazali made Sufism an acceptable part of orthodox Islam and built a khanaqah in Nishapur, where he taught for several years.

By the thirteenth century, Sufism had spread in all directions, reaching Spain, parts of Africa, Syria, Anatolia, North India, and the island of Sumatra, through the movement of travellers, merchants, and Sufi saints who were uprooted by the Mongol invasions. Sufism offered solace and a spiritual direction to the Muslim populations who were in a state of shock caused by the mayhem wrought by the Mongols and who faced an uncertain future. Later, when the Mongols themselves converted to Islam, they also looked to eminent Sufis as their spiritual teachers.

The Sufis founded brotherhoods and cults of saints and adapted elements of local cultures and vernacular languages to convey their teachings to the masses. Followers were drawn to charismatic Sufi saints who were believed to possess *baraka* (spiritual power) and an ability to perform *karamat* (miracles). The Sufi mystics were known as *wali* (friend of God), with *auliya* being the plural form of *wali.* Some Sufi saints were given the title of *qalandar,* while the same term also referred to groups of Sufi vagabonds.

Sufism reached India in the 1190s when Persia-born Mu'in al-Din Chishti (1142–1236), regarded as India's supreme Sufi saint, followed Muhammad Ghuri's army and settled in Ajmer, where he established the Chishtiyya order (named after the town of Chisht in Afghanistan). Over the thirteenth and fourteenth centuries, his spiritual heirs, like Nizam al-Din Auliya (1238–1325), who became the leading Sufi mystic of Delhi, spread the Chishtiyya order to large parts of India, alongside the expansion of the Delhi Sultanate.

Sufism continued to gain strength well into the fifteenth and the sixteenth centuries. Sufi saints were now described through the terminology of kingship, such as *shah* (emperor), their shrines *dargah* (royal courts), and their headgear *taj* (crown).[19] The Safavid Empire of Iran was founded in 1501 when a teenaged leader of a tribal Sufi group, descended from Sufi Sheykh Safi al-Din, conquered the city of Tabriz and subsequently the rest of Iran. The Ottoman foray into southeast Europe and the Levant was helped by Sufi settlers. The Mughal emperors had a long-drawn association with Sufism. When Babur entered Delhi after his historic victory at Panipat in 1526, the first thing he did was to pay a visit to the Sufi dargahs of Delhi, thereby acknowledging their political stature.[20] Similarly, Akbar decided to build his new capital of Fatehpur Sikri around the home of Sufi saint Salim Chishti and made annual pilgrimages to the Chishti shrine in Ajmer. Over the following centuries, Sufism spread further east, reaching as far as the southern Philippines.

While Islam was prominent in urban areas like Delhi and Lahore, it was the Sufis who made sizeable inroads into the hinterlands of India, serving as a bridge between the Muslim rulers and their large non-Muslim subject populations. They merged famous local legends with Islamic teachings and introduced religious poetry in Punjabi, Sindhi, Urdu, and Bengali. State-supported Sufi shrines and khanaqahs dotted the banks of the Indus River and provided a host of religious and socio-economic services like settling disputes or teaching moral behaviour. In Bengal, the Sufis received generous land grants (mostly forests and swamps) from the Muslim rulers and employed indigenous people to clear and reclaim the land for rice cultivation, thereby creating a means of livelihood for them.[21] This missionary practice of introducing the indigenous people, many of whom were not under the Hindu fold at the time either, to Islamic institutions in their Sufi form has been called 'conversion by the plough'.[22]

In urban areas where Muslim elites were concentrated, the Sufis provided teachings as scholars of the Quran, inspiring the court poets and scribes to record and popularise their words.

The rise of Islam had blocked Europe's interaction with Asia. But what was the nature of that East–West exchange in the preceding centuries? What was the Middle East and the wider world like before the advent of Islam? How and when did Buddhism spread from India to Central Asia and China? Historians have described the fourth and fifth centuries in India as a golden age. How did it come to an end?

8

GLOBALISATION 1.0: FROM ROME TO CHINA

100 BCE–640s CE

There is no year in which India does not drain the Roman empire of fifty million sesterces. So dearly do we pay for our luxury and our women.

—Pliny the Elder, Roman author

India conquered and dominated China culturally for twenty centuries without ever having to send a single soldier across her border.

—Hu Shih (1891–1962), Chinese diplomat and scholar

The early centuries of the first millennium saw the beginnings of a world trade system dominated broadly by three major empires or population centres—the Roman Empire, the Han Empire of China, and the Indian subcontinent—with around 50 million people each. Their economic systems were so closely integrated that one of them faltering could trigger a worldwide slump.

Besides the interconnected trade, there was a diffusion of cultures all over Eurasia. As Rome was introducing its political and administrative institutions, architecture, the Latin language, and Christianity across Europe, North Africa, and the Near East (region around the eastern shores of the Mediterranean Sea), a similar process was underway in Asia. Buddhism, which has been described as 'India's greatest export to the world',[1] travelled from India to Central Asia, China, Sri Lanka, and Southeast Asia along the trading routes. In a similar vein, China brought its Confucian philosophy and culture to East Asia and Southeast Asia. Several geographical terms have been used at various times by scholars and travellers to broadly describe parts of Asia that were under the sway of the ancient civilisations of India and China—Indies, East Indies, Indo-China, Greater China, Greater India, or what Harvard Professor Sheldon Pollock has called Sanskrit Cosmopolis.[2]

THE GLORY OF ROME

Rome is said to have been founded on the banks of the Tiber River in 753 BCE by two brothers, Romulus (hence Rome) and Remus. To the south of Rome were the Greek colonies from where the Romans inherited Greek culture and further built upon it. With the early centuries shrouded in legend, it was around the third century BCE that Rome began to advance itself from a provincial backwater into a regional power, expanding beyond the Italian peninsula.

By the first century BCE, glorious victories over new regions had become a way of life for the Romans. Every ambitious Roman general dreamed of winning battles in faraway lands and returning home to celebrate the triumph and be recognised by the Senate, the supreme governing body of the Roman Republic. Around 63 BCE, three great statesmen and generals emerged in Roman politics—Pompey the Great, Julius Caesar, and Marcus Crassus—and in 60 BCE, they entered into an uneasy alliance known as the First Triumvirate. The three titans would soon turn into rivals.

Pompey had made a mark for his bravery while fighting in Sicily and Africa, thus earning the title of Pompey the Great. Julius Caesar became a rising star as he conquered the vast region of Gaul (roughly modern-day France), led the first military expedition to Britain, and brought Egypt under Rome's sphere of influence. It was Caesar who gave the name *Germani* to the barbarians who lived beyond the Rhine. Crassus, hoping to match the victories of Caesar and Pompey, commanded the eastern legions to Persia in 55 BCE, where the Parthians had established their capital at Ctesiphon. Plutarch, the celebrated Greek biographer, described Crassus as emulating Alexander's march on India nearly three centuries earlier.[3] With a fighting force of about 40,000 men, Crassus was anticipating a comfortable victory that would extend the empire's boundaries further east. However, the battle near Carrhae (in southern Turkey) in 53 BCE turned out to be a calamity, where the mounted Parthian archers rained arrows on a confused and shocked Roman army, wiping out three-fourths of its men. It was a major psychological blow for Rome.

Meanwhile, the growing power of Julius Caesar had ignited a civil war in the Roman world, from which he emerged as the victorious dictator of Rome. Caesar sought to avenge Crassus's disastrous defeat in Persia, but his plans never materialised as he was brutally assassinated by his opponents in 44 BCE.

In his will, Caesar had named his adopted son Octavian as his successor, but this was not received well by Mark Antony, a general who had served under Caesar. Thus began a fierce rivalry between Antony and Octavian. With both the camps being formidable, they realised that it was best to split Rome's provinces into two—Antony got the east while Octavian controlled the west.

In the east lay the fabulously wealthy kingdom of Egypt, blessed with fertile lands along the Nile River, that had turned it into the granary of the Mediterranean. It was ruled by the legendary queen Cleopatra, a descendant of the Ptolemaic dynasty that had been in power for 300 years since the death of Alexander the Great. Described by the Roman historian Dio Cassius as 'a woman of surpassing beauty',[4] Cleopatra was a former lover of Julius Caesar, with whom she had a son named Caesarion. Subsequently, through her charm and intellect, Cleopatra managed to seduce Antony, and their affair began in 41 BCE. Five years later, Antony carried out Caesar's planned invasion of Persia but ended up losing half his men in the mountains of north-west Iran and was forced to retreat through Armenia in the dead of winter. Cleopatra helped Antony cope with the setback and provided him with financial and political support to stabilise his position.

The two lovers and allies now devised an ambitious plan to defeat Octavian and take over Rome. But destiny had other plans. After fighting a war against Octavian for two years, Antony and Cleopatra ended up losing the decisive battle at Actium in western Greece in 31 BCE. They had supposedly planned to take refuge in India, but that never came about as both of them ended up killing themselves the following year. Before her death, Cleopatra had sent Caesarion to India by way of Ethiopia, with a hoard of treasures. He was either caught midway or lured back to Egypt under false promises of safety and then executed by Octavian. Circa 27 BCE, Octavian assumed the title of Augustus Caesar, becoming the first emperor of Rome. With the prestigious acquisition of Egypt and further expansion into modern Germany, Austria, Hungary, Northern Spain, and Central Turkey, Augustus transformed the Roman world, which covered many lands, cultures, and languages, into a highly organised empire over the next four decades.

The period between 27 BCE and 180 CE, known as Pax Romana (meaning Roman Peace), was marked by remarkable stability and relative peace, where the Roman Empire protected and governed its provinces while they, in turn, accepted Roman taxation and control. The empire reached its zenith in the early years of the second century CE when one in every four people on earth was a Roman subject. With over a million inhabitants, Rome became the greatest city in the world. No European city would surpass that population mark until nineteenth-century London. Other than occasional revolts and violence, the empire was a vast, multicultural melting pot where Latin was the lingua franca and where its citizens could travel and trade unhindered. Alexandria in Egypt was the second-most important city in the empire, as well as a hub of culture and scholarship; Antioch (now Antakya in Turkey) became the third-largest city by population and size.

Besides excelling at the art of war, the Romans were ingenious engineers and architects, incorporating an array of skills from the regions they conquered. The arch became a signature feature of their architecture and was applied to a wide range of structures—bridges, aqueducts, and buildings. The construction of the Colosseum, the largest amphitheatre in the world, was completed in 80 CE and could hold up to 80,000 spectators. They built the most sophisticated network of paved roads covering more than 4,00,000 kilometres.

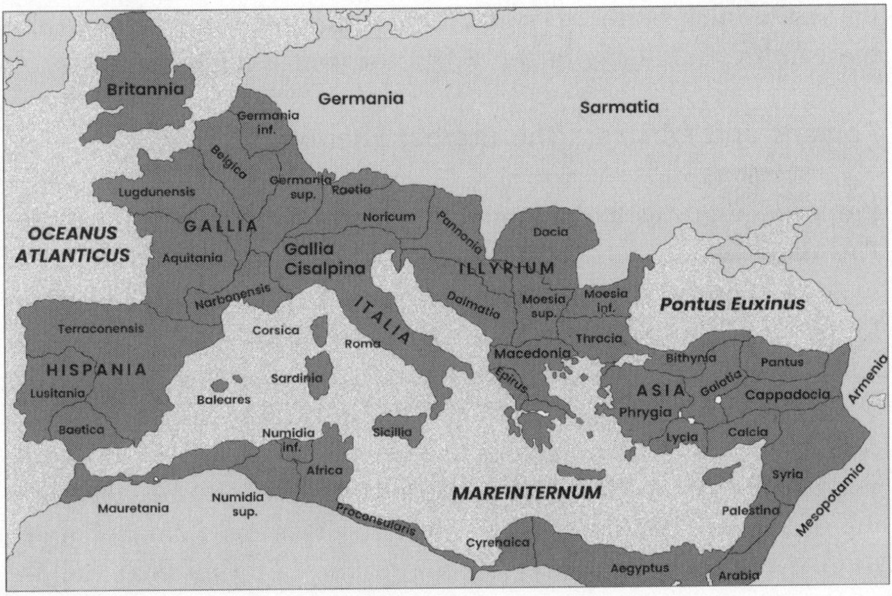

The Roman Empire in 117 CE

It was during the reign of Augustus that Jesus of Nazareth was born, probably in 4 BCE, in Judaea. Christianity remained a small messianic sect until Emperor Constantine converted in 313 CE, an event which became a turning point in Christian history. With its message of equality, Christianity had the ability to unite the multiracial and multicultural empire of the Romans. In 380 CE, it was declared the state religion of the Roman Empire, replacing the traditional Roman spirits and gods.

Another lasting legacy of Constantine was the building of the new imperial capital between 324 and 330 CE at the site of ancient Byzantium, which he named Nova Roma (New Rome). Signifying the erosion of Rome as the nerve centre of the empire and an eastward shift of power, Nova Roma, that later came to be called Constantinople (now Istanbul), was located at the crossroads of Europe and Asia. The magnificent city had wide avenues lined with statues of Alexander the Great, Caesar, Augustus, and of course, Constantine. Surrounded almost entirely by water, and with unusually thick boundary walls, Constantinople would remain the most impregnable city in the world for over a millennium.

Romans and Persians: The Eternal Enemies

Emperor Augustus had adopted a policy of diplomacy towards the Parthians, and peace had prevailed between the two empires for nearly a century. The hostilities, however, reopened in 113 CE when Emperor Trajan launched an unprovoked invasion of the Parthian lands. Rome and Persia fought many vicious wars in what turned out to be the most prolonged conflict in history, lasting over five centuries, despite the changes in political conditions on both the sides. In Persia, the Parthians (238 BCE–227 CE) were replaced by the Sassanids (227 CE–651 CE) while the Western Roman Empire (ended in 476 CE) handed over power to the Eastern Roman Empire or the Byzantine Empire. The pendulum swung both ways during the vicious struggle. The Romans captured the Parthian capital of Ctesiphon on multiple occasions but could not hold on to the city. In 260 CE, the Sassanian *shahenshah* ('king of kings') Shapur defeated and captured the Roman emperor Valerian, who died a prisoner after suffering many indignities, such as being used by Shapur as a mounting block before riding. The Roman-Persian conflict was finally ended by the Muslim Arab conquests in the seventh century that led to the fall of the Sassanids and a substantial loss of territory for the Byzantines.

ROMAN BRITAIN VERSUS BRITISH INDIA

To the Romans, Britain had remained terra incognita, existing only in fables as a mysterious and exotic land covered with forests, marshes, and mist. The island was neither a threat to Rome nor a source of any meaningful revenues and was, ergo, left a free territory. It was in 55 BCE that Julius Caesar launched the first military expedition to Britain. The ambitious Roman general, who was inspired by Alexander the Great, claimed that he needed to punish the native British tribes for providing support to the Gauls. The real reason, however, might have been his desire for glory and popularity in Rome. After defeating the British tribes and imposing a tribute, he rushed to Gaul to suppress a rebellion. In his account *De Bello Gallico* (*The Battle for Gaul*), Caesar described the landscape, coasts, harbours, landing places, and inhabitants of the island in what is the first coherent sketch of Britain.

Nearly a century went by before the Romans looked at the island again. In 43 CE, Emperor Claudius decided to invade Britain, not for any strategic gains but as a publicity stunt to secure his throne. Over the following years, Britain was claimed as part of the Roman Empire. Modern Scotland became Caledonia while southern Britain became the province of Britannia, described as a 'dreary land' in the letters sent home by Roman soldiers. A small area on the banks of the Thames River named Londinium became the Romans' administrative centre, and over time, it grew into the most prominent town of Britannia.

In the year 60 CE, when King Prasutagus of the Iceni (now Norfolk) tribe died, leaving behind two daughters and no male heir, the Romans took over his lands. His wife Boudicca spearheaded a rebellion against the Roman occupation, and managed to win the support of several other tribes. Together, they destroyed Camulodunum (Colchester) and Londinium, massacring thousands of Romans and their supporters. But given the military power of the Roman Empire, the Roman governor Paulinus was able to stamp out the flames of revolt. The story goes that Boudicca killed herself by consuming poison rather than falling into Roman hands. To date, she is seen as a folk hero that British children learn about in school.

Londinium was rebuilt, and the Romanisation of Britain continued at a brisk pace. New towns were founded with Roman architectural features like street grids, theatres, bathhouses, amphitheatres, and basilicas dominating the urban landscape. Many of these new towns have survived, like Bath, York, Leicester, Manchester, Gloucester, and of course Londinium, which became London. The Romans introduced to the island the Latin language, Roman law, and Christianity, making Britain a part of the Classic Age civilisations. They groomed native Britons into Romanised gentlemen who ran the administration and collected taxes on Rome's behalf as loyal servants.

After over a millennium and a half, Britain's star was ascendant and it built one of the greatest empires in the world. London became the new Rome. Many of the British political leaders, architects, and scholars in the eighteenth century were infatuated with the Roman Empire. Historian Edward Gibbon wrote his magnum opus, *The Decline and Fall of the Roman Empire,* that is considered the most celebrated history book in English language. Buildings like the Royal Crescent in the city of Bath, constructed between 1767 and 1775, drew inspiration from the Colosseum in Rome.

The emergence of British India followed a trajectory that was uncannily similar to that of Roman Britain, as if the British were re-enacting the part played by their erstwhile colonial masters. For a long time, India had existed in British imagination as an enigmatic, faraway land where they had introduced such progressive things as the English language, English common law, civil services, modern education, modern transport, or simply 'civilisation' as many imperialists believed. They conducted extensive population censuses and land surveys—practices that the Romans had brought to Britain—that were nothing but tools of conquest and control within the colonial state machinery. They also built, cities, bridges, canals, railway lines, hill stations, clubs, gymkhanas, and cantonments all over India. As could be expected, the inspiration behind the circular design of Connaught Place in New Delhi was the Royal Crescent in Bath. The British also groomed 'a class of persons, Indian in blood and colour, but English in taste, in opinions, in morals, and in intellect' to function as collaborators and facilitators of their regime in India as envisaged by Lord Macaulay.[5] They even adopted Rome's divide and rule tactics. The Indian rebellion of 1857 has striking similarities with the British revolt of 61 CE against the Romans, with Rani Lakshmi Bai playing the part of Queen Boudicca. Several British historians have argued that it was the British subjugation of India that engendered a unified national identity in the subcontinent. So was the case in Britain where early signs of British identity developed among the scattered tribes on the island due to the Roman invasion.

In 410 CE, Britain was facing attacks from a coalition of Picts (a group of tribes living in what is now Scotland) and Saxons (migrants from northern Europe who settled in England) from the north, and its citizens appealed to the Roman emperor Honorius for help, who then famously told them to 'look to their own defences'.[6] The empire was falling apart and the Roman legions in Britain were ordered to withdraw and return to Rome, that was under attack from other European tribes. After lasting for over 350 years (43 CE–410 CE), it was the end of Roman Britain, and within a few decades, the end of the Roman Empire. So it was in August 1947, when India was facing the worst communal riots in history, that homeward-bound British soldiers were boarding ships in Bombay. After a nearly 350-year-long association (1608–1947), it was the last chapter of British India, followed by the sunset of the British Empire.

INDO-ROMAN TRADE

Around 100 BCE, a direct maritime trading route from Egypt to India was discovered, which harnessed the monsoon winds to cross the Arabian Sea. The volume of cargo on this shorter route soon eclipsed the older coast-hugging route. Goods were dispatched from ports in India like Barygaza (modern-day Bharuch) in Gujarat, Kalligeris (present-day Kanhagiri) near Mumbai, and Muziris (near Kochi) in Kerala to such Egyptian ports as Myos Hormos and Berenice on the Red Sea. They were then transported through the desert in camel caravans to a river port on the Nile called Coptos, and from there sent upstream to Alexandria, the prime hub of international commerce, and finally, over to Europe via the Mediterranean.

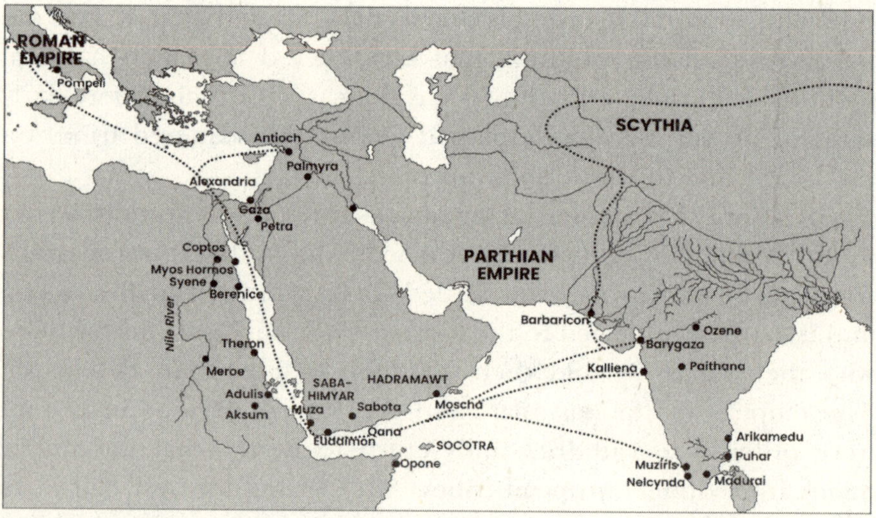

Indo-Roman trade route

Rome's annexation of Egypt in 31 BCE was a transformational event that gave the Romans access to Egypt's enormous wealth and resources. The overabundance of grains in Egypt caused their prices to tumble in Rome, thereby boosting the disposable incomes of its residents. With the vital sea routes to India, Arabia, and East Africa under the control of a single regime, the climate had turned ideal for long-distance commerce.

Roman trade with India started booming, and within a decade up to 120 vessels were sailing each year to India. The monopoly of the Arab merchants was broken, and the Mediterranean markets were flooded with goods from Asia. The Roman government imposed a 25 per cent import tax called *tetarte* that provided nearly one-third of the funds needed to finance their empire.[7]

Rome's wealthy citizens came to acquire the most exotic and extravagant of tastes, creating an insatiable demand for Indian products like spices, cotton textiles, perfumes, ivory, gems, and pearls. Pepper became so essential that the import duty on it had to be waived as a concession to the people, while ivory was used to embellish weapons, furniture, jewellery, and musical instruments. In the opposite direction, Roman vessels carried tin, lead, drugs, fine ointments, glassware, wine, and silverware to India although their exports were far lower than what the Indians were selling them. The trade imbalance meant a drain of precious bullion from Rome, which writers like Pliny the Elder often lamented.

Like the American dollar that commands trust around the world today, Roman coins were an accepted medium of exchange far beyond the empire's boundaries. Several hoards of Roman coins have been unearthed at places like Madurai, Kolhapur, and the ancient ports of Puhar (also known as Poompuhar) and Arikamedu (near Pondicherry) in coastal Tamil Nadu, which bears testimony to the extensive trade relations between Rome and India. Besides coins, several other items of Roman origin have been discovered in South India, including glassware and large narrow-necked jars used for transporting wine and olive oil. In 1938, an intriguing discovery was made in the ancient trading town of Pompeii (Italy), which had been entirely buried under volcanic ash when Mount Vesuvius erupted in 79 CE: among the numerous artefacts unearthed was an ancient ivory statuette of a feminine figure that was heavily adorned with jewellery and which, given its resemblance to the Hindu goddess Lakshmi, came to be known as the Pompeii Lakshmi.

Ancient Tamil and Sanskrit texts refer to the Roman traders, who were in fact Egyptian Jews and Greeks from Alexandria, eastern Mediterranean, and North Africa (all part of the Roman Empire), as

Yavanas, a term derived from the Persian word *Yona* which referred to the Ionian Greeks. They describe the Yavanas's large ships that came with gold and 'cool and fragrant wine' and returned laden with pepper, which they referred to as *Yavanapriya* meaning 'dear to the Yavanas'.

Sanskrit texts describe the vivid colour and supposed magical properties of the red coral that came from *Alakandaka* (Alexandria) or *Romaka* (the Roman Empire), and categorised them as *ratna* (jewels). Indian words for articles of trade entered Greek and Latin vocabulary—Sanskrit *srngavera* for ginger, *pippali* for pepper, *sarkara* for sugar, *karpasa* for cotton, and Tamil *arisi* for rice.[8]

Besides commodities, there was a vibrant demand in the Roman Empire for exotic live animals—lions, tigers, and rhinoceroses for use in circuses, along with peacocks, monkeys, and parrots that could be trained to speak Latin. Indian rulers sent elaborate gifts to the Roman emperors that included precious gems, elephants along with *mahouts* (elephant drivers), and skilled gymnasts.[9] Owning servants and slaves, particularly ones from the exotic East, was a marker of a person's wealth and cultural sophistication in the status-conscious Roman society. Indian eunuchs fetched extraordinarily high prices for being rare. Roman women were great spenders and sought Indian male servants as personal attendants to escort them on the streets and female servants to help them with their fashion and clothing needs. Indian fortune-tellers and astrologers could also be seen offering their services on the streets of Rome.[10]

There was a movement of people in the other direction too. Roman craftsmen and carpenters were highly sought after in southern India and were behind the design and construction of wooden statues and pavilions and the decoration of royal buildings. The Pandyan kings hired Roman mercenaries and military veterans as guards and tasked them with securing the gates of Madurai, a role they performed well given their intimidating looks and posture.

India's location in the Indian Ocean had worked to its advantage as Rome's access to China was hindered by the Parthians, who were located midway, not to mention the massive expanses of steppelands and the inhospitable deserts that dominated the land route. Chinese silk, porcelain, and other goods were, therefore, shipped to ports in Gujarat and Malabar from where they were redirected to Egypt. Roman vessels could have sailed directly from Egypt to ports in southern China or Southeast Asia, but that voyage was too long and risky. India thus became a central node in a vast global trade network.

We know about the details of this Indo-Roman trade through the writings of various scholars, like the Roman author and natural philosopher Pliny the Elder, the Greek geographer and historian Strabo, and the Greek astronomer and geographer Ptolemy, who wrote the famous work *Geographia.* Another invaluable source of information is an anonymous work by an Egyptian Greek merchant, titled *Periplus Maris Erythraei* (*Sailing Guide to the Indian Ocean*). Written in the first century CE, the *Periplus* is a merchants' handbook to trade in the Indian Ocean. The author provided objective details about various routes, ports, commodities, and prosperous inland cities like Ozene (Ujjain), along with first-hand observations on tides and sailing hazards to inform fellow merchants exploring international trade.

The *Muziris Papyrus,* a Roman document from the second century CE discovered in Egypt, contains cargo details of a ship called the *Hermapollon* that had returned from the port of Muziris in southern India. It was carrying over 220 tons of Indian merchandise worth 9 million sesterces that allowed the Roman customs agents at the Egyptian ports of Berenice and Myos Hormos to collect about 2.2 million sesterces worth of import tax.[11]

THE AGE OF INVASIONS

In the second century BCE, the Han dynasty of China began extending and strengthening the Great Wall to protect their lands from marauding nomadic tribes like the Xiongnu. Matters became worse for the nomadic populations with the onset of excessively cold weather that brought along famines, forcing them to migrate south-westwards. This set in motion a domino effect, displacing other tribes like the Yueh-chi (Kushans) and the Scythians (Sakas) out of their homelands, and pushing them across Central Asia towards Afghanistan and north-west India. Historians have called this era in India 'the Age of Invasions' as hordes of nomadic tribes entered from the north-west, one after another.

The Indo-Parthians, a branch of the Parthians, who had already established themselves in north-west India, were pushed southward by the Sakas, who charged into India from Afghanistan. Besides lands with unparalleled fertility, India offered opportunities in trade across the subcontinent as well as the seas. The Sakas spread to Punjab, the lower Indus Valley, Gujarat, and Central India, reaching commercial centres like Barygaza (Bharuch), Mathura, and Ujjain. The Romans traded with the Sakas, offering them fine wines, silverware, concubines, and slave musicians in return for precious stones. There are records of an embassy sent by the Saka king Azes II to Emperor Augustus.

The Sakas and the Indo-Parthians were further dispossessed when a chieftain named Kujula Kadphises led his Kushan tribe from Afghanistan into north-western India in the second half of the first century CE. The domains of the Indo-Parthians were substantially reduced, while the Sakas remained powerful in central and western India. It is possible that the Pallava kingdom in the Tamil country was founded by the Indo-Parthians, also known as the Pahlavas.

Kujula and his successor, Wima Kadphises, added to their Afghan dominions those of Punjab, Kashmir, and the Gangetic Plains. They gave up their nomadic lifestyle and absorbed the cultures of the Chinese, Parthians, Romans, and Indians with whom they came in contact. The next king, Kanishka, ascended the throne in 78 CE, and during his twenty-five years of rule, the Kushan Empire reached its peak, stretching from northern India to Central Asia, Iran, and western China. He ruled from two regions—one around north-west India and Afghanistan with Purushapura (Peshawar) as the capital and another around the fertile Gangetic plains, with Mathura as the capital.

With the Silk Road running through their dominions, the Kushans became prosperous through trade, particularly trade with Rome. Chinese caravans proceeded southwards through the Kushan regions to ports in Gujarat and the Indus delta from where they could send their shipments to Roman Egypt. It appears that the Kushans melted large quantities of Roman gold coins to restrike them as their own coins stamped with images of deities from diverse cultures—Greek, Roman, Iranian, Hindu, and Buddhist—a sign of their tolerance and cosmopolitan nature.

It was during the Kushan era that the Gandhara and Mathura schools of art flourished. The Gandhara school drew upon the Greco-Roman traditions and represented the Buddha in human form with a youthful face, dressed in garments as seen in Roman imperial statues. In comparison, the Mathura school was indigenous in style and incorporated images from Hinduism and Jainism in addition to Buddhism.

The Kushans reached a stature almost at par with Parthia, China, and Rome, and inspired by Persian, Chinese, and Roman themes, their leaders began assuming lofty titles such as *maharajadhiraja* (king of kings), *devaputra* (son of heaven), *soter* (saviour) and *kaisara* (caesar).[12] Kanishka would even go on to seek the hand of a Han princess. When a Kushan embassy reached Rome, it was graciously welcomed by Emperor Trajan, and the envoys were given the rare privilege of sitting in the senatorial gallery at the Colosseum. Not much is known of Kanishka's successors, but it is believed that the Kushan Empire started declining after Kanishka, ending in the third century CE.

On the one hand, the age of invasions had brought anarchy, lawlessness, and incessant conflict between multiple tribes and dynasties in India, while on the other, it was marked by a cultural enrichment of the land and its people, bringing in new ideas and traditions, besides creating new opportunities for enterprising merchants.

WHEN CHINA MET INDIA

The oft-quoted reference to China and India as 'the two Asian neighbours' ignores the fact that the core populations of the two ancient civilisations were, and continue to be, thousands of kilometres apart, separated by the most inhospitable deserts and the highest mountain ranges on the planet. Since the earliest times, India saw invaders, merchants, and migrants arrive from the west (Persia, Greece, and Central Asia) whereas there was hardly any contact with China.

The earliest contact between India and China took place in the second century BCE when Zhang Qian (167–114 BCE), a diplomat from Han China, opened trade routes that formed the early Silk Road, linking Chinese markets to Central Asia and beyond to Rome. In his travels to the Han western periphery around 125 BCE, Zhang learned about the possible paths to 'Shendu' (the regions around River Sindhu or Indus). His accounts were compiled by Sima Qian, the Han historian who wrote *Shiji*, or the *Records of the Grand Historian*, a monumental work on the history of ancient China and the world. He described Shendu thus:

> [Shendu] lies several thousand li southeast of Daxia. The people cultivate the land and live much like the people of Daxia. The region is said to be hot and damp. The inhabitants ride elephants when they go into battle. The kingdom is situated on a great river.[13]

The collapse of the Xiongnu confederacy in 55 BCE opened more doors for the Han Empire to make inroads into Central Asia. During the first century CE, the Chinese came to know about *xibu* (fine cotton cloth) that was produced in Shendu. They needed it in large volumes for the uniforms of their soldiers who were serving in hotter regions. China thus became one of the earliest foreign markets for Indian cotton. At the same time, Indians began to see the Chinese commodities arrive in their markets. Contemporary Indian texts mention several commodities with a prefix of 'cina', as in *cinapatta* (silk), *cinapista* (vermillion), and *cinaka* (camphor).

Buddhism Reaches China

Legend has it that one night the Han emperor Ming, who ruled from 57–75 CE, dreamt of a golden deity flying in front of the imperial palace. One of his ministers interpreted the deity in his dream as the Indian sage Buddha, who could fly and whose body was said to have a golden hue. The emperor immediately dispatched envoys to India who later returned with two Indian Buddhist monks, Dharmaraksa and Kasyapamatanga, and white horses carrying Buddhist texts and relics.

Historical records indicate that the earliest Buddhists to reach China came from the Kushan territories of north-west India and Central Asia in the first century CE and brought with them Buddhist texts written in Sanskrit. Curiously, it was around the same time that Christianity reached India. After evangelising Parthia, Saint Thomas, one of the twelve apostles chosen by Jesus Christ, arrived in the court of King Gondophernes (probably in Taxila) in 40 CE. The story of the subsequent years is obscure but Saint Thomas is said to have landed in the town of Kodungallur on the Malabar coast of India in 52 CE and established the first Christian church in India. He then proceeded overland to the east coast of the Tamil country, where he is said to have been martyred at Mylapore (now part of Chennai).

When Kanishka rose to power, he became a great patron of Buddhism and encouraged missionary activity. He built a colossal stupa at his capital of Purushapura, which travellers spoke of as the grandest monument in India. As the first century CE drew to a close, Buddhist communities had sprung up in the western outposts in China such as Yarkand, Khotan, Turfan, Kucha, and Dunhuang. Paintings, relics, and manuscripts began arriving from India, but the challenge was to translate these texts and make them intelligible to a Chinese audience.

One of the most outstanding translators of Buddhist *sutras* (scriptures) was a scholar named Kumarajiva (343–413 CE), who was born in Qiuci (now Kucha), then the largest and most prosperous town on the Silk Road along the northern edge of the Taklamakan Desert. His father was a Brahmin from India, and his mother came from the royal family of Kucha. At the age of nine, Kumarajiva went to Kashmir with his mother to study under an Indian Buddhist master, Bandhudatta. After a few years, he moved from Kashmir to Kashgar, a prosperous town in the Xinjiang region, where he continued his Buddhist education and also studied ancient Hindu scriptures and texts.

By the time he reached his thirties, Kumarajiva was recognised as an accomplished Buddhist scholar throughout China, and was equally fluent in both Sanskrit and Chinese. In 401 CE, the Qin emperor invited him to Chang'an (located near the present-day city of Xi'an in central China) and gave him the honorific title of *Kuo-shih* (teacher of the state) along with a garden retreat and financial support to set up a translation workshop. Kumarajiva went on to translate more than 300 volumes of sutras and preached Buddhist texts daily to over 3,000 followers. On occasions, the emperor himself would attend Kumarajiva's sessions.

Another exemplary figure and a peer of Kumarajiva was the Buddhist monk Faxian (337–422 CE). Distressed by the imperfect state of Buddhist teachings in China, he decided to make a journey from Chang'an through Central Asia to India, home of the original teachings of the Buddha. He set out in 399 CE. Trekking through the forbidding deserts of western China, crossing treacherous Himalayan mountain passes, and fording several rivers, he reached Purushapura. From there he continued to Buddhist sites like Sarnath, Bodhgaya, Kapilavastu, and Sravasti, before finally reaching Pataliputra, where he stayed at a monastery for three years. Gathering Buddhist manuscripts and making sketches of Buddhist images, he continued his pilgrimage to Simhaladvipa (ancient name for Sri Lanka meaning dwelling-place-of-lions island). His return journey through the sea proved to be as perilous as the overland route to India. After surviving a shipwreck, he finally reached China after being away for fifteen years.

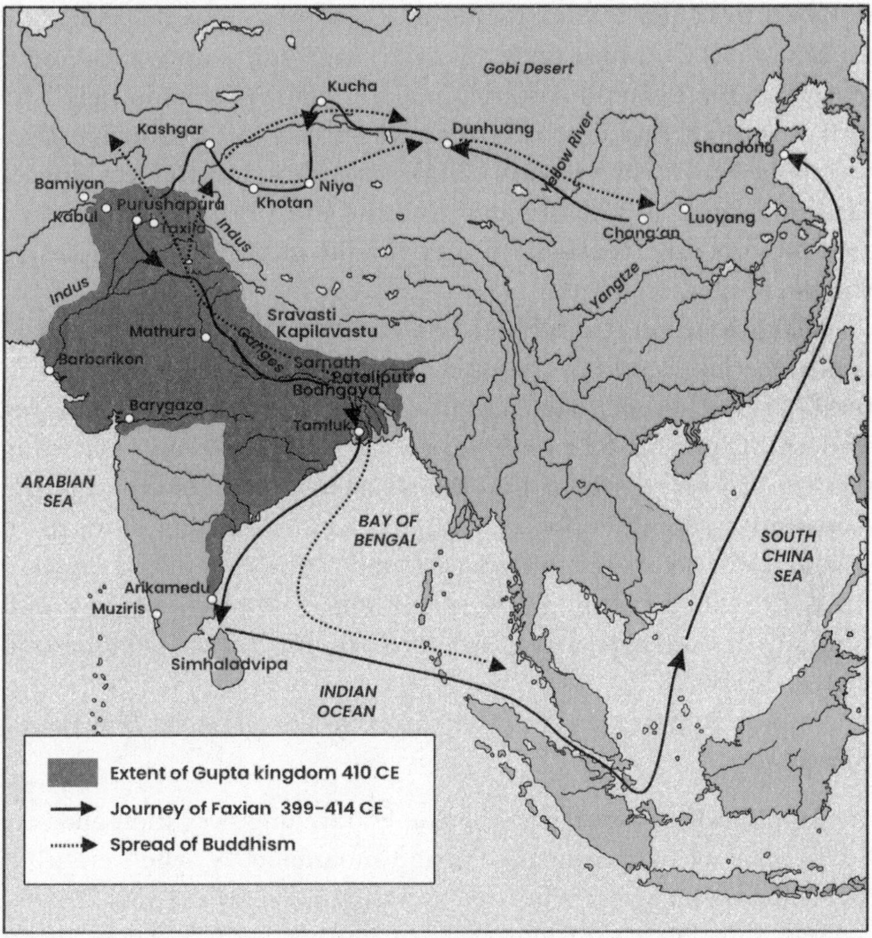

Faxian's pilgrimage to India

In 416 CE, Faxian wrote his memoir *Foguoji* (*A Record of Buddhist Kingdoms*), which provided many geographical details that were not available in Buddhist texts, like descriptions of mountain ranges, rivers, and towns, and the distances between them. His account was read widely by Buddhists as well as non-Buddhists in China.

By the sixth century CE, there had been significant cultural exchange alongside trade between India and China. A large number of Indan Buddhist monks, like Bodhidharma of Kanchipuram, travelled to China to impart Buddhist teachings and help with the translation of Buddhist texts. Many artisans and painters too, went to work in Buddhist monasteries, making statues and paintings. The Indian style of Buddhist cave temples spread to the Xinjiang and Gansu provinces in western China (the cave temples of Mogao, Kizil, Kumtura, and Maijishan) from the third century CE onwards and subsequently reached further inland to the cave temples of Yungang and Longmen.

Faxian's account motivated many other Chinese Buddhists to undertake long and hazardous but spiritually fulfilling journeys to India. The most remarkable of those future travellers was Xuanzang, who left China in 629 CE at the age of twenty-seven. Travelling through a path north of the Taklamakan Desert towards Central Asia, and escaping robbers along the way, Xuanzang stopped in several towns before reaching Samarkand. There he noticed caravans from India loaded with gems, spices, and cotton, converging with Chinese caravans carrying silks, before heading to Persia and beyond that to Rome.

Author Sally Hovey Wriggins writes in *The Silk Road Journey with Xuanzang*:

> The Buddhist monk was not simply travelling over thousands of miles of dangerous deserts and mountains as if he were a Chinese Marco Polo; he was on a pilgrimage of the soul. His was both an inward and outward journey, and therefore, it carried an aura of special value.

In Balkh, Xuanzang studied the Theravada (a more conservative form of Buddhism that claims to maintain Buddha's original vision and teachings) scriptures at the Nawbahar monastery with 3,000 monks. When he entered India and reached Peshawar, he could see the fading glory of Buddhism, though Kanishka's stupa still existed. He saw hundreds of other monasteries in places like Udyana and

Taxila where he studied Mahayana (an umbrella body of Buddhist traditions and texts that incorporated new doctrines in addition to Buddha's core teachings) texts. In the Gangetic plains, he visited Mathura and Kannauj, the capital of King Harshavardhana of the Pushyabhuti dynasty. Xuanzang and Harshavardhana were both very impressed with each other and became friends.

As Xuanzang travelled through northern and eastern India, he found many monasteries to be either dilapidated or deserted, with few exceptions like the ancient university of Nalanda, which was still going strong, thanks to the patronage of the Pala kings. Nalanda had around 10,000 students of various nationalities besides those from the Indian subcontinent. Xuanzang spent two years at Nalanda studying logic, grammar, Sanskrit, and the Yogachara (one of the main traditions of Mahayana Buddhism).

The intrepid traveller's return journey was no less challenging. While trying to cross the Indus River, a storm sprang up where Xuanzang lost many boxes containing his collection of precious manuscripts and relics, while in Kashgar, his caravan was chased by robbers. Finally, he reached home in 645 CE after sixteen long years and was welcomed by cheering crowds. Emperor Taizong received him and was impressed by his tales of the foreign lands he had visited. On the emperor's request, Xuanzang wrote a detailed twelve-volume travel account called *The Great Tang Dynasty Record of the Western Regions*, describing the geography, customs, legends, commerce, and politics of the regions he had travelled through during his sixteen-year-long journey.

Xuanzang's travels were fictionalised in a sixteenth-century novel called *Journey to the West.* The enduringly popular tale is one of the four great classical novels of Chinese literature. The central character of the story, the monkey king named Sun Wukong, who protects Xuanzang during his journey to India, seems uncannily similar to Hanuman, the monkey hero of the Indian epic Ramayana.

A variant of Buddhism known as Chan Buddhism (which traces its roots to the Indian practice of *dhyana* or meditation), originated in China during the reign of the Tang dynasty (618 CE–907 CE). It spread further from China to Vietnam, Korea, and Japan where it became Thien, Seon, and Zen Buddhism respectively.

Besides the transmission of Buddhist texts, the Indo-Chinese interaction had also promoted the diffusion of knowledge in a variety of other disciplines such as mathematics, astronomy, architecture, medicine, music, linguistics, painting, and temple architecture. The envoys of the Tang Empire, Wang Xuance and Yi Libiao, were welcomed by King Harshavardhana, who sent similar diplomatic missions to China. During the bilateral exchange, the method of manufacturing sugar was transported from India to China. The sugar refining technique was further perfected by the Chinese and later returned to India, which explains the Hindi word for Chinese as well as sugar: *chini*.

There was also a belief in China, especially among the ruling elites, that Indian doctors knew the secrets of extending life. Several Indian doctors were therefore brought to China to concoct life-enhancing drugs and elixirs for various emperors.

ROMANISATION, SINICISATION, AND INDIANISATION

The Roman Empire became a vast melting pot covering an area of 5 million square kilometres stretching from North Africa to Syria to Britain, with a shared identity, culture, language, architectural traditions, and legal and political institutions.

Contemporaneously, China's influence was spreading in Asia. Its contact with Japan went back to around 200 CE, and with Korea, it predated even that as Chinese lands were contiguous to the Korean peninsula, with no geographical barriers in between. The Chinese passed on to Japan and Korea a whole host of things, like a Confucian philosophical worldview, Taoism, Buddhism, the ancient Han writing system, centralised government models, methods of rice cultivation, temple architecture styles, art, literature, and cuisine. In Southeast Asia, the Chinese came as merchants looking for maritime routes as an alternative to the overland path to Rome that was blocked by nomadic tribes in Central Asia.

The Indianisation of Southeast Asia was a slower process that began with visits by Hindu and Buddhist traders, priests, and occasionally princes to the Southeast Asian states. As settlements of Indian traders sprang up in Malaya, Indonesia, southern Vietnam, and Cambodia, their influence gained momentum. They brought Pali, Sanskrit, and Tamil languages, religious thought, and literature along with trade goods. The Kalinga region was an important source of cotton textiles, and the term *kling* was used in the Indonesian archipelago to describe both clothes and Indian people.

Buddhism had reached Sri Lanka and Thailand in the third century BCE when King Ashoka sent Buddhist monks to propagate Buddhism. From Sri Lanka, as well as directly from India, Buddhism spread to Cambodia, Sumatra, Java, and Burma. Sanskrit inscriptions from the fourth century CE found in Borneo confirm the performance of Vedic ceremonies by Brahmins for local chiefs. The dominant form of Hinduism reaching Southeast Asia was Shaivism, followed by Vaishnavism while Garuda (the flagship airline of Indonesia carries the same name), the eagle mount of Vishnu, gained a mass following in Indonesia.

Around the seventh century CE , the *Ramayana* and *Mahabharata,* the great Hindu epics, reached the islands of Java and Bali, the latter being a name derived from the *Ramayana.* Similarly, Cambodia was derived from *Kambujas,* an early tribe from north India, or *Kamboja,* a region adjoining Gandhara in northwest India. Madura in Indonesia (and Madurai in Tamil Nadu) was derived from Mathura in North India[14], and Sumatra comes from the Sanskrit word *samudra,* meaning sea. The Hinduised kingdom of Champa in south-central Vietnam was founded in the late second century CE, and its four key states were named after four regions in India—Quang Nam (Amaravati), Binh Dinh (Vijaya), Nha Trang (Kauthara), and Phan Rang (Panduranga).

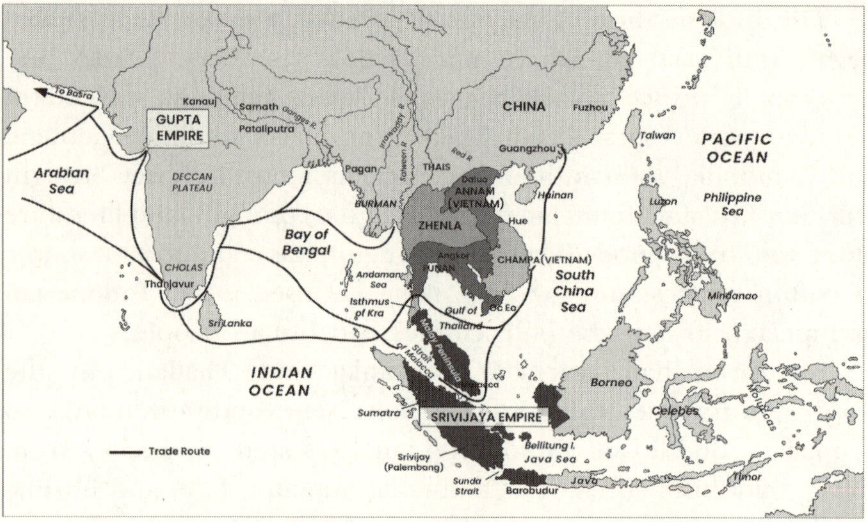

Hindu and Buddhist kingdoms in Southeast Asia

Intertwined with the historical evidence are many legends and fables about Indian presence from the region, like the one about a Brahmin merchant from India named Kaundinya, who defeated a local princess from the Mekong delta in a battle and then married her, thus starting the Funan kingdom in Cambodia and introducing Indian culture in the region. A popular South Korean book of fables, *Samguk Yusa* (*Memorabilia of the Three Kingdoms*), describes a legend, according to which an Indian princess of the Ayuta (believed to be Ayodhya) kingdom, named Suriratna and also known as Heo Hwang-ok, went to Korea in 48 CE. There she married a local king and started the Karak dynasty.

Indian literature of the time refers to trading expeditions to a place identified as Suvarnadvipa (island of gold) or Suvarnabhumi (land of gold) or Suvarnanagara (city of gold). The geographical details of the region are not clear, and it may have been Burma, Thailand, Sumatra or some other part of Southeast Asia. In these stories, the journeys to Suvarnadvipa were highly treacherous—one Buddhist story talked about *yakshis* (female goblins) who seduced shipwrecked sailors and then devoured them. Many sailors lost their lives, though the brave and fortunate ones who survived the journey stood to gain immense wealth.

ROME AND PATALIPUTRA

In the early fourth century CE, there arose in India a ruler named Chandra Gupta I who grew his minor kingdom in Magadha (present-day Bihar) into a prominent regional power. His successors, Samudra Gupta, who ruled from 335 to 375 CE, and Chandra Gupta II, the most renowned of all Gupta emperors who ruled from 375 to 415 CE, took the Gupta Empire to its apogee, spreading all over northern and central India. The Guptas restored the glory and splendour of the erstwhile Mauryan Empire, and Pataliputra once again became the seat of power in India. In his travel account, Faxian had attested to the prosperity of the people, the benevolence of the administration, and the low levels of crime in the empire, although he also wrote about the severe discrimination against the untouchables by upper-caste individuals.

The Gupta Empire flourished through the fourth and fifth centuries CE, and this period, called the Golden Age of India, was marked by great achievements in art, literature, mathematics, astronomy, medicine, religion, and philosophy.

Aryabhata, the greatest mathematician and astronomer that India ever produced, lived near Pataliputra in the fifth century CE. Known for treatises like *Aryabhatiya* and the now lost *Aryabhatasiddhanta*, known through the writings of his contemporary Varahamihira, Aryabhata propounded ideas that are foundational to modern astronomy and mathematics. He was the first in India to postulate that the earth is a sphere that rotates on its axis and revolves around the sun. Aryabhata calculated the circumference of the earth and the length of the solar year with far more accuracy than any other scholar from any other civilisation of his time. He is also believed to have envisioned the concept of zero.

Kalidasa, the Sanskrit poet and dramatist, who lived in the fifth century CE in the city of Ujjain, is considered the most celebrated

Indian writer of all ages. His works were defined by spellbinding imagery, evocative landscapes, and aesthetic sensitivity while capturing the essence of the sophisticated aristocracy and culture of the Gupta period.

Kalidasa's best-known work is *Abhijnanashakuntala* (*The Recognition of Shakuntala*), often referred to as *Shakuntala*. An epic narrative, the work tells of the seduction of the hermit-girl Shakuntala by King Dushyanta while he is on a hunting expedition, his subsequent rejection of Shakuntala when she comes to his court, pregnant with his child, and their final reunion. It was *Shakuntala* that first introduced Indian literature to Europe in modern times, enthralling men like Goethe, the famed German writer and statesman.

Varahamihira (505–587 CE) was an astronomer, astrologer, and mathematician from Ujjain. With the Indo-Roman interaction ensuring a steady stream of schorlarly works flowing into India, he had acquired a deep understanding of Roman and Greek astronomy. He wrote a book on astronomy called the *Pancha-siddhantika* (*Five Doctrines or Studies*); two of these studies—the *Romaka Siddhanta* (*The Roman Tradition*) and the *Paulisa Siddhanta* (*The Paulus Tradition*)—reflected a sound understanding of Roman astronomy.[15]

The Fall of Rome and the Guptas

There was no single reason behind the fall of the Roman Empire, more specifically, the Western Roman Empire. Some have reasoned that the empire covered too vast an area to be controlled by a central administration while others have attributed the fall to the import-heavy trade with Asia that drained its wealth. Then there was the crippling effect of the Antonine Plague that tore through the empire and killed an estimated quarter to a third of the entire population in the second and third centuries CE.

The one factor that would ultimately be instrumental in bringing down Rome arose thousands of kilometres to the east—the marauding bands of short-statured horse-riding people called the

Huns. The exact origins of the Huns are not clear. They were most likely a branch of the Xiongnu nomadic people who had started to move westwards in the fourth century CE after being uprooted by the Han Empire. Unlike the Mongols who stopped at Hungary in the thirteenth century CE, the Huns had charged right into the heart of Europe. Attila the Hun, also known as the 'scourge of God', was one of the most fearsome enemies the Romans ever faced. Under his rule from 434 to 453 CE, the Huns became the most powerful and ruthless military force in Europe.

The brutal Hun invasions uprooted tribes like the Alans, the Goths, and the Vandals, which, in turn, triggered mass migrations into the Roman territories. Rome had been troubled by the Germanic tribes, or the barbarians as the Romans called them, for centuries, but it had never faced disruption at this scale. Uprisings and attacks became a common feature in the empire, and Rome was sacked on multiple occasions.

Already in a state of long-term decline, the Western Roman Empire suffered the final deathblow in 476 CE when the Germanic leader Odoacer staged a rebellion and ousted the Emperor Romulus Augustulus. Over time, Rome's population, which had peaked at a million, dropped to around 60,000, and its glorious monuments turned to decrepit ruins. It was the end of one of the greatest powers in world history and the beginning of what has been called the Dark Ages, although modern historians now agree that the subsequent centuries were not as dark as believed earlier.

Meanwhile, following the earlier pattern of Saka and Kushan invasions from Central Asia, a branch of the Huns began raiding India around 470 CE. Initially, they were held back by the Gupta king Skandagupta, but a few decades later, the Hun leader Toramana consolidated his power in Punjab and made Sialkot his base. His son Mihirakula, who was known for his brutality, succeeded him in 515 CE and was particularly savage towards the Buddhists.[16] The Huns destroyed many Buddhist monasteries and centres of learning like Taxila, contributing to the demise of Buddhism in India. The constant attacks by the Huns also led to the crumbling of the Gupta

Empire by 550 CE, a development which facilitated the emergence of a number of smaller kingdoms.

The Caste System

The origins of the infamous caste system of India are obscure and may go back to 1,000 BCE or even earlier. Ironically, the Gupta period, which was the pinnacle of intellectual achievements in India, also saw the hardening of the pyramidal caste system. With the fall of Rome, India's trade with the West declined sharply, further impacting other sections of the economy. It has been suggested that a fiscal crisis led to the devaluation of high-value Gupta coins. Urban centres got depopulated, and villages became the nucleus of socio-economic life in India, surviving on barter and sustenance basis. The rigid rules of the caste system were imposed stringently, dividing village communities and assigning them fixed occupations and hierarchical roles. Historian Abraham Eraly writes in *The First Spring*,

> Buddhism, which had provided the value system essential for a progressive and humane civilisation, virtually disappeared from India at this time, and its place was taken by Puranic Hinduism which emphasised fatalism and passivity. And, worst of all, the deadening grip of the caste system now straitjacketed Indian society, thwarting progress, denying even the possibility of progress.

The debilitating effect of the caste system on the social fabric of India has continued to hold back the country's potential well into the modern times. The social reformer and national leader B.R. Ambedkar lamented, 'There cannot be a more degrading system of social organisation than the caste system. It is the system that deadens, paralyses and cripples the people from helpful activity.'[17]

The modern Western civilisation is a legacy of the Roman Empire, though its origins can ultimately be traced to ancient Greece. The term 'Europe' is also seen as being synonymous with the West. But did the Greeks see themselves as Europeans or Westerners?

In Greek mythology, Europa was the daughter of Agenor, a Phoenician king of Tyre, which is in Lebanon. In art, architecture, and astronomy, the Greeks owed much to the ancient Egyptians and Babylonians from the East. When the Greek civilisation was at its peak, western and northern Europe had no empires, cities, or coinage. Historian Peter Frankopan points out in *The Silk Roads*:

> In truth, France, Germany, Austria, Spain, Portugal and England had nothing to do with Athens and the world of ancient Greeks, and were largely peripheral in the history of Rome from its earliest days to its demise.

Therefore, what they experienced in the fourteenth and the fifteenth centuries was a Naissance (birth) rather than a Renaissance.[18]

The Greeks, instead, had far greater interaction with the East (Persians and Indians besides the Phoenicians, Babylonians, and Egyptians). What was that exchange like?

9

THE GREEK CONNECTION

550 BCE–100 BCE

The Greeks came and saw, but India conquered.

—A.K. Narain, historian and author of *The Indo-Greeks*

Ancient Greeks had nothing more than a fantastical imagination of India, and had most likely never heard of China. Aristotle, who has been called 'the man who knew everything',[1] had speculated that one could see the end of the earth from the top of the Hindu Kush mountains. In the year 327 BCE, his student, Alexander the Great, stood on that very spot.

The following year, Alexander's mighty army charged down the steep mountain passes into the Indian subcontinent and defeated the valiant king Porus's forces on the banks of the Jhelum River (known to the Greeks as Hydaspes) in the Punjab region. An iconic dialogue took place between Alexander and Porus, as is widely believed in India, and popularised by blockbuster movies like *Sikandar* (1941) and *Sikandar E Azam* (1965). When Alexander asked Porus how he wished to be treated, the latter famously replied: 'As befits a king'. Impressed by the courageous defender's noble bearing, Alexander restored his kingdom to him.[2]

Alexander's decade-long conquest was one of the most significant events in the history of the world, which brought together the West and the East. For over 2,000 years, he would remain a celebrated figure throughout the regions he conquered, emulated by many a commander, king, emperor, and sultan.

The Indo-Greek connection, however, goes back two centuries before Alexander reached India and survived for another two after he left.

PERSIA, THE MEETING GROUND

The earliest direct contact between the Greeks and the Indians occurred in the Persian Empire that was founded in 550 BCE by Cyrus the Great of the Achaemenid dynasty. Stretching from the shores of the Aegean Sea to the Himalayas, it was the world's first true empire that had assimilated diverse and far-flung communities and principalities under one umbrella.

It was during the reign of Darius the Great (550–486 BCE) that the Persian empire reached its peak. Darius strengthened the military and sponsored spectacular construction projects in Persepolis (near modern Shiraz in southern Iran), their magnificent capital, and other cities like Babylon (south of Baghdad in Iraq), Pasargadae (near Persepolis), and Susa (near modern Shush in southwestern Iran). Without fail, the rulers of the conquered kingdoms made an annual journey to Persepolis, also called the 'Palace of all Nations', carrying expensive gifts and tributes for the shahenshah, the title given to the Persian emperor. The empire became a cosmopolitan hub, drawing craftsmen, engineers, sailors, and administrators hailing from Greece to India. The Persian court also provided refuge to many statesmen who had escaped from the ravages of the warring Greek city-states. Persian cities were sufficiently polyglot for the Greeks and Indians to communicate with each other.

To explore the possibility of sea trade between India and Persia, Darius ordered an expedition to assess whether the Indus region was worth securing for the empire or not. A Greek navigator named Scylax was commissioned to sail down the Indus River and through the Arabian Sea to the Persian coast. Commanding a fleet carrying Greek and Phoenician sailors and Persian troops for security, Scylax began the voyage into the uncharted waters around 517 BCE. Exploring the course of the Indus River, they reached the Indus Delta, where they built a naval station called Pattala and prepared for the subsequent westward sea voyage. But, being unfamiliar with the monsoon winds, it took them several months in the waters to reach the Persian coast, from where they continued their exploration and reached Egypt almost two years after having left India.

Scylax wrote an account of his voyage covering his observations along the Indus River. His work is lost now, but it was used by the Greek author Hecataeus, the 'father of geography', in his work *Periodos Ges* (*Tour Round the World*). A generation later, Herodotus (484–425 BCE), the 'father of history', drew much of his information about India from Scylax's account and wrote a text that was later studied by Aristotle.

Encouraged by Scylax's findings and taking advantage of the political disunity on the north-west frontier of India, Darius annexed the region west of the Indus River around 515 BCE. The new satrapy (province in ancient Persia) was called Hindush, named after Sindhu (the Sanskrit name of the Indus River), which became 'Hindu' in the Persian language. In Greek, the Persian 'Hindu' became 'Indos' and later 'Indus' in Latin. And the surrounding country came to be called India.[3]

As per Herodotus, Hindush was the most populous and fertile satrapy that yielded the highest revenue in the Achaemenid Empire. Now more and more Indians served as mercenaries in the Persian Empire, and a colony of Indians came up near the old Sumerian city of Nippur. Texts from this time bear testimony to Indians engaged in various trades in Persia, like the woman named Busasa who maintained a tavern in the town of Kish.[4] Similarly, the bas-reliefs of ancient Persepolis show people of Hindush bringing gifts, particularly cotton.

Darius built a canal connecting the Mediterranean with the Red

Sea—a precursor to the modern Suez Canal and a gateway for the Indo-Greek trade. He then turned his attention to the western end of his empire and brought Ionia (the central region of the western coast of modern Turkey), Thrace (now a part of Bulgaria, Greece, and Turkey), and Macedonia (modern-day Greek province of Macedonia, Republic of Northern Macedonia, and part of Bulgaria) under his control by 512 BCE. When Ionia rebelled against the Persian rule, it was supported by Athens and Eretria (in southern Greece), drawing the ire of Darius. A Persian force suppressed the rebellion and destroyed Eretria, but they were defeated by the Athenians at Marathon in 490 BCE. This embarrassing blow prompted Darius to plan for a punitive expedition, but it never came to fruition as he died in 486 BCE.

The Persians had exiled many rebelling Greeks to the far eastern parts of their empire in Bactria (modern Afghanistan, Uzbekistan, and Tajikistan). They had also settled other Greeks in the same eastern regions as a reward for their assistance in suppressing the Ionian rebellion. Among these newly arrived Greeks, the most prominent were the Ionians, called *Yauna* by the Persians and Yavana by the Indians.

Driven to complete the mission of punishing the Greeks for their support of the Ionians, Darius's son Xerxes gathered a massive invading army in 480 BCE and marched on the Dardanelles, the narrow strait dividing Asia and Europe. Xerxes's army included Indian infantrymen and cavalrymen, who, as claimed by Herodotus, were fighting so far out in the west for the first time. Given the dire situation and determined not to go down without a fight, the Athenians and the Spartans buried their differences and joined hands. The entire population of Athens was transported to the island of Salamis before the Persians stormed into the deserted city, burning down the Acropolis and desecrating its holiest temples. However, in a dramatic turn of events, Xerxes's large fleet was enticed into a narrow strait and then ambushed by Greek ships commanded by the great Athenian general Themistocles, turning the invasion into a catastrophic defeat. The stunning Greek victory ended Xerxes's ambitions in Greece, but it wasn't the end of the Persian Empire as it lasted for another 150 years, though in a state of progressive decline. The Greek city-states, meanwhile, formed an alliance, the Delian League, to fend off any future invasions.

Persia continued to be a stage for Indo-Greek contact. Around 400 BCE, Ctesias, a Greek physician who served in the Persian court for seventeen years, wrote a substantial book on the history of India titled *Indica*. Based on the stories of Persian travellers, Indian merchants, and envoys that he had gathered over the years, the account was mostly an intermixture of myths and fables. One of the earliest attempts at orientalising India, portraying it as an exotic land of wonders, the account became popular in Greece and would influence the Greek perception of India for centuries.

THE CRADLE OF WESTERN CIVILISATION

Nearly 2,500 years ago, no one would have expected the tiny city-state of Athens, surrounded as it was by enemies, to become the birthplace of the western civilisation and change the world. The other Greek city-states had better credentials—Sparta was more powerful, Corinth was wealthier, and Syracuse was larger. Was it sheer luck or did Athens, named after Athena, the goddess of wisdom and knowledge, create its own destiny? This question has stumped historians for ages, and there is still no consensus.

In 507 BCE, the Athenian statesman Cleisthenes reformed the political structure of Athens and introduced a new system of public participation in politics that he called *demokratia* (meaning 'rule by the people'). Debate and participation in public affairs became a way of life, though Athenian democracy did not translate to equality by any means as it excluded women, slaves, and the poor. Nevertheless, democracy became one of ancient Greece's most enduring contributions to the modern world and earned Cleisthenes the title of 'Father of Democracy'.

Located at the centre of a vast trading network in the Mediterranean, Athens grew into a wealthy hub and was able to offer a quality of life to its residents that no other state could. As expert shipbuilders and sailors, Athenians travelled to cities along the Mediterranean coast, bringing back new ideas and skills. With democracy at its heart, and openness to foreign people and ideas an important part of its ethos, Athens became a magnet for thinkers, called sophists, who migrated to the city from other parts of the Hellenic (classical Greek) world. Herodotus was one such great mind who moved from Greek Anatolia to Athens.

After the victory over the Persians in 480 BCE, the Athenians returned to their city and started rebuilding it. The tributes that Athens received as a leader of the Delian League from other member states helped fund these lavish construction projects. As a symbol of Athenian power, the Acropolis was entirely rebuilt over a period of forty years with the magnificent Parthenon, a temple dedicated to Athen's patron goddess Athena, at its centre. By the time peace with Persia was officially established in 449 BCE, Athens had stepped into a golden age.

Unlike the Spartans, who concentrated their energies on perfecting their war machine, the Athenians were a contented lot who derived joy from intellectual pursuits. An integral part of Greek culture was the symposium, which was essentially a party hosted by a wealthy individual where men gathered to drink together and discuss politics, poetry, and daily events. The practice bears resemblance to the seventeenth-century culture of coffee houses and salons in Britain and France that preceded the Age of Enlightenment or the Bengali *adda* (informal social gathering where a variety of topics are discussed) culture in Calcutta and Dhaka, which is said to have contributed to the Bengal Renaissance in the late eighteenth and early nineteenth centuries.

Greek theatre became popular in the fifth century BCE with two types of plays—tragedies and comedies—being performed that encouraged new thinking and public discussions. The first plays were performed at the Theatre of Dionysus in Athens and these proved to be so popular that new theatres sprang up all over Greece.

Another Athenian forum for exchanging ideas was the agora,

a designated open space where people would routinely gather to hear public announcements or discuss politics or any other subjects under the sun. Socrates, the eccentric genius and founder of Western philosophy, spent his days in the agora, asking questions of those who would speak with him. It was in the agora that Socrates met a young poet named Aristocles, who later became the great philosopher known as Plato. Aristotle, the third of the 'Big Three of Greek Philosophy', was Plato's student for some twenty years.

Athen's golden age ended in 431 BCE with the start of the Peloponnesian Wars (431–404 BCE) against Sparta. The long-drawn conflict was damaging to both the sides, but Sparta eventually prevailed, thanks to the assistance provided by Persia, which found an opportunity to avenge its earlier defeat.

THE WORLD CONQUEROR

Though the Greeks had made peace with the Persians, they never forgave Xerxes for his act of sacrilege. In the fourth century BCE, an anti-Persian crusade came to the fore that was led by a rather unexpected group—the peripheral kingdom of the Macedonians, who were generally dismissed as barbarians by the other Greek city-states.

The Macedonians had been the real beneficiaries of the Peloponnesian wars as they found an opportunity to invade and dominate the weakened Greek city-states. King Philip of Macedon introduced a new kind of infantry, known as the Macedonian phalanx, whose tight formation was considered nearly impenetrable. Philip was keen to have his teenage son Alexander groomed as a refined future leader and hired none other than Aristotle as his private tutor. Alexander's education under Aristotle infused him with a life-long love for knowledge, philosophy, and culture.

By 338 BCE, Philip had established his control over all of Greece through war and diplomacy. Unfortunately, his dream of conquering the Persian Empire was cut short as he was assassinated in 336 BCE.

Yearning to fulfil his father's dream, the charismatic Alexander became the king of Macedonia at the ripe age of twenty. A congress of the Greek city-states was held at Corinth where they agreed to join forces for an invasion of Persia commanded by the young ruler. An army was assembled in northern Greece with more than 43,000 infantry men and 5,500 cavalry men, one of the toughest and most professional fighting forces of its time. In 334 BCE, Alexander embarked on his epic march towards the East where glory, fame, and fortune awaited him. History was about to be created.

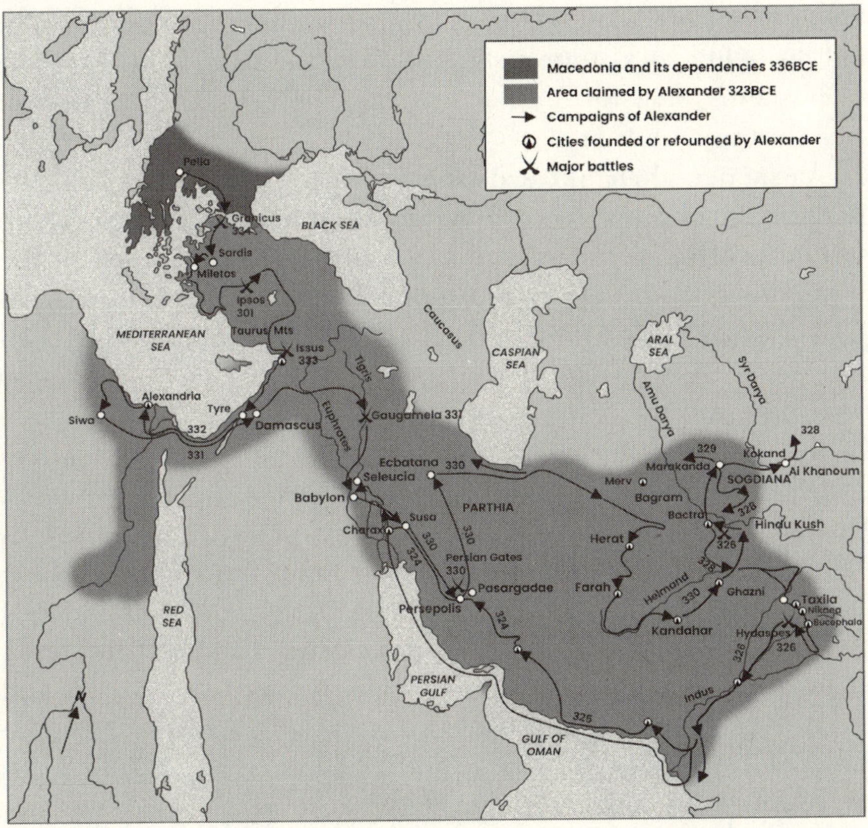

Alexander's world conquest

The Persian king Darius III had a massive army of 6,00,000 soldiers who were drawn from every corner of the empire, including the Indus Valley. Oddly enough, the Persian army also had thousands of Greek mercenaries. Unperturbed by the Greek intrusion, Darius made no serious effort to counter Alexander, gravely underestimating his Macedonian opponent who was about to become the Persian Empire's nemesis.

Alexander defeated a Persian army contingent at the Granicus River near the Dardanelles. By the following year, he had conquered most of Asia Minor prior to marching eastwards. Darius finally met him at the Battle of Issus (near the border of Syria and Turkey) in 333 BCE, but overwhelmed by Alexander's unique army formation and his bold attack strategy, he fled from the battlefield. Issus was a devastating blow for the Persians, and the news reverberated all over Greece and Anatolia.

Alexander then pressed south, taking over cities on the Mediterranean coast, and conquered Egypt in early 331 BCE, where he founded the city of Alexandria. Later that year, in one of the most consequential battles in history, Alexander met Darius again at Gaugamela (near Mosul in Iraq) where Darius, after having been decisively defeated, managed to escape to Ecbatana (modern-day Hamadan in Iran).

In 330 BCE, Alexander reached Persepolis where his forces brutally ravaged and burnt the ancient capital of the Achaemenids. The Greeks' jaws dropped when the city's vaults were opened, as the gold and treasures inside were 300 times the annual revenue of the entire Athenian Empire.[5] Chasing Darius, Alexander headed north to Ecbatana, only to find out that Darius had been murdered by his own lieutenants. The epic rivalry between the Greeks and the Persians thus ended, and the 220-year-old Achaemenid Empire was over. Twenty-six-year-old Alexander had avenged Xerxes's deeds and fulfilled his father's dream, but his desire for glory was not yet satiated.

Beyond Persia

The Greek army continued advancing into what is now Afghanistan. A string of towns were founded and named after Alexander—Alexandria on the Oxus (Ai Khanoum), Alexandria in Aria (Herat), Alexandria in Arachosia (Kandahar), Alexandria ad Caucasum (Bagram). Maracanda (Samarkand) became Alexander's base in Central Asia for a year and a half.

Throughout his campaign, Alexander had encountered Greek mercenary soldiers and communities of people who claimed to be descendants of Greeks. An extraordinary incident took place, we are told, somewhere near the Afghanistan–Pakistan border when the Greek army was about to attack a small town called Nysa. The residents of the town came out pleading protection on unusual grounds. They claimed to be descendants of the followers of the Greek god Dionysus who had stayed at Nysa (hence the name) on his epic journey to India in mythical times. The Greeks, who were ruthless, yet also possessed by legends of gods and demons, believed the story and Nysa was spared.

Another group of Greek people called the Branchidae, who lived in a town between Balkh and Samarkand and claimed descent from Branchos, the mythical founder of the temple of Apollo in Ionia, were not so fortunate. They had fled from Ionia over a hundred years earlier fearing for their lives after they had yielded the temple's treasures to the invading army of Xerxes. The Branchidae tried their best, but they could not win Alexander's mercy. The entire town was razed, and the whole population brutally massacred.[6]

The End of the Known World

The Greek thrust into India began with Alexander's army general and 'dearest of all his friends'[7] Hephaestion leading the main army and marching over the direct route into India via the Khyber Pass. Alexander took an alternate route further north where he fought some of the fiercest battles against obscure hill tribes before descending to the plains of India.

Hephaestion besieged the capital city of the Gandhara kingdom called Peucelaotis or Pushkalavati (located outside the modern town of Charsadda, northeast of Peshawar). After a month-long siege, the capital was stormed and its king Astis was killed. Hephaestion then moved on to the Indus River where his army built a bridge of boats over the mighty river. It was here that Hephaestion was joined by Alexander.

After crossing the Indus, Alexander met King Ambhi of Takshashila (around 30 kilometres from Islamabad, Pakistan), or Taxila as the Greeks called it, another capital of the Gandhara kingdom, who surrendered without a fight. Ambhi entertained Alexander royally and presented lavish gifts to him besides allowing the Greek army to fell wood for boats and bridges. Ambassadors from other kings and chieftains in the region paid visits to Alexander and duly offered their submission. One king, however, refused to bow down—Porus, the ruler of the realm between the Hydaspes (Jhelum) and the Acesines (Chenab) rivers, and an enemy of Ambhi.

In the late spring of 326 BCE, with the rivers of Punjab rising rapidly once it started raining and about to become impassable, Alexander decided to not waste any time and cut short his stay at Taxila, moving forward for the next battle with the defiant king. Porus sent his son with 2,000 troops and 50 chariots to prevent Alexander from crossing the Jhelum River. But Alexander's seasoned force quickly overpowered the young prince, whose chariots had been rendered immobilised due to the rain-soaked muddy grounds.

Porus subsequently met Alexander on the banks of the Jhelum River with as large a force as he could muster, including 200 war elephants. The elephants posed an initial challenge, but the Greeks had faced them earlier at Gaugamela and knew how to get around them. Forcing their infantry close to the elephant legion, the Greeks shot down the mahouts and wounded the giant pachyderms, who went berserk, attacking and trampling their own soldiers. After a desperate fight, Porus's army was outflanked and routed by

Alexander's fearsome cavalry and mounted archers, leaving up to 20,000 dead. Surprisingly, there is no mention of either Alexander's conquest or even Porus in any of the ancient Indian texts. Whatever we know today is through the Greek accounts.

Alexander founded a town called Nikaea (meaning victory) at the site of the battle. Although the town itself has not been located to date, the ancient settlement of Mong or Mung, located in Pakistan, is believed by many to be Nikaea. He founded another city called Alexandria Bucephalous or Bucephala in honour of his beloved horse Bucephalus who died in the battle. The town of Jalalpur in the Jhelum district of Pakistan is said to be the same place.

By now, the Greek soldiers were thousands of kilometres away from home and had not seen their loved ones for eight years. The incessant battles, the harsh landscapes, the heat and humidity of the monsoon season in India, and the constant threat of falling victim to snake bites and diseases like malaria and dysentery had challenged the will of the hardiest of the warriors. Many of them had started grumbling, and disillusionment was clearly visible in the Greek camp. That continuing the campaign would be a poor strategy had become obvious when the battle with Porus, a relatively minor king, turned into a rough encounter, while further inland lay much larger kingdoms with massive armies. In his speech, Alexander tried to push his weary troops to continue beyond the Beas River, but he was greeted with a dissenting silence. When Coenus, one of the senior commanders, stood up in defiance, Alexander was furious, even though he could sense the mood of his men. Not left with many choices, he gave in, and his men started preparing for the return journey.

A portion of the army returned through the same overland route via the mountain passes that they had taken into India. The rest of the force boarded ships that were assembled on the banks of the Jhelum River. The enormous fleet of ships carrying strange foreigners sailing down the Jhelum, and then the Indus, was an astonishing, never-before-seen spectacle for the people living along the river banks. By no means was the voyage a smooth one as the

Greek army had to fight native kings and chieftains along the way, with one of the encounters with a tribe called Malloi or Malava nearly costing Alexander his life.

After reaching the Indus delta, the army was further split into two. A fleet carrying 20,000 troops headed by Alexander's friend and mentor, General Nearchus, sailed further down the Indus into the sea, heading towards the Persian Gulf. Nearchus was tasked with the exploration of the coast and the search for harbours.

Alexander decided to lead the rest of his force westwards through the Makran desert that lies between Pakistan and southern Iran. It is not clear why he chose to slog through one of the most inhospitable regions on earth where his army faced such extreme hardships that the trials and troubles they had experienced during their war campaigns earlier all paled in comparison. Many soldiers perished as they ran out of water and food while the burning sun became intolerable, adding to their mounting miseries.

After sixty days of torturous trekking, Alexander and his men finally emerged from the hellish desert and reached southern Persia in early 324 BCE, nearly two years after the battle with Porus. They were joined by Nearchus's fleet that had arrived there safely. Week-long celebrations and revelry followed. In Susa (modern-day Shush in Iran), a mass marriage ceremony was held where nearly 10,000 troops took Persian wives. Alexander and Hephaestion married the daughters of King Darius.

In the following months, as they continued westwards, Alexander took to heavy drinking and turned highly insecure and irascible; in a state of paranoia and intoxication, he ended up killing his trusted general Parmenion as well as his close friend Cleitus who had once saved his life in a battle. Henceforth, the atmosphere in his camp became increasingly volatile and mutinous. In his last days in Babylon, Alexander developed a raging fever and died in 323 BCE.

With there being no clear successor to Alexander's seat, his military generals got embroiled in wars of succession that lasted for three decades. In the end, the empire was divided between three generals—Antigonid, who took control of Macedonia, Ptolemy, who became the king of Egypt, an ancient land even in the fourth century BCE, and who started a dynasty that lasted for three centuries until Cleopatra, and Seleucus, who established an empire that endured for over two centuries and covered virtually the entire Asian realm of the Persian empire.

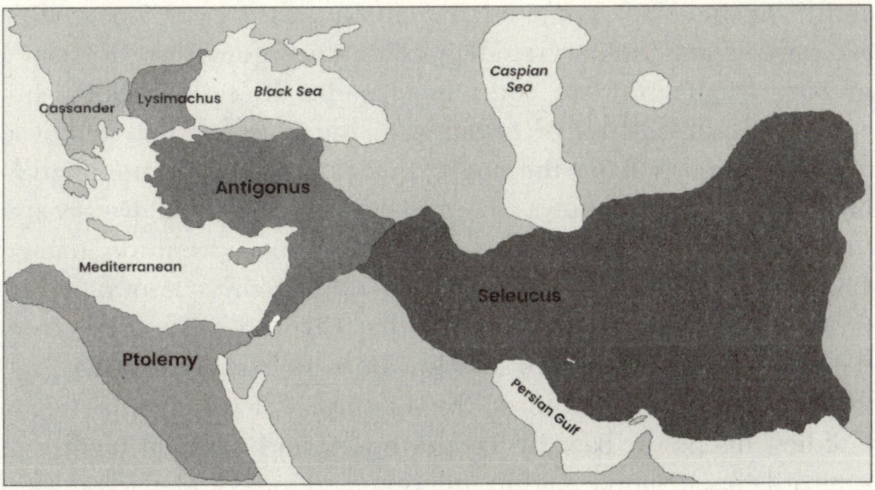

Empires of Alexander's successors

Greek generals and scholars, like Nearchus, Onesikritos, Aristobulus, and Callisthenes, who had accompanied Alexander's army, left vivid memoirs and accounts of India. A blend of fact and fable, these accounts give intriguing descriptions of a variety of things: the cotton plant as a tree that 'bore wool instead of fruit', the sugarcane plant that had 'honey as its sap', and crystallised sugar that was called 'stones the colour of frankincense, sweeter than figs or honey'. These works did not survive for more than a few centuries, but their content was captured partly by later Greco-Roman writers like Strabo, Pliny, and Arrian.

THE FIRST INDIAN EMPIRE

In the early years of his empire, Seleucus was occupied in fighting incessant wars of succession, and in the process lost focus on the eastern frontier where he had satrapies in the Indus region. In the meantime in India, there emerged a mysterious figure, a Brahmin named Kautilya (also known as Chanakya), who is said to be the author of the *Arthashastra*, an ancient Sanskrit treatise on politics, economics, and military strategy. The story goes that he served in King Dhana Nanda's court in Magadha in eastern India, but at some point fell out of favour with the king and was removed unceremoniously from the court. Infuriated over the humiliation meted out to him, Kautilya vowed to destroy the Nanda dynasty and fled from the city. He then met with a young adventurer named Chandragupta Maurya, about whom not much is known either. From certain accounts, it appears that Chandragupta came from the eastern Gangetic valley and was born to humble origins.

Groomed and mentored by Kautilya, Chandragupta began building his power base in the north-west and directed his troops against Dhana Nanda, raiding the outer regions of Magadha. After a few failed attempts, Chandragupta captured Magadha's capital, Pataliputra, in 321 BCE, thereby laying the foundation of the first and the greatest empire of ancient India.

By 305 BCE, Seleucus had secured the rest of his empire and turned his attention to India where he was confronted by Chandragupta, who had built a massive army by now. We don't know the exact nature of the interaction that took place between the two, but Chandragupta probably had the upper hand. A Seleucid princess was married to Chandragupta, who also got control over the lands from Herat to Indus. In return, Chandragupta presented Seleucus with 500 war elephants. The peace settlement and the agreed frontier between the two empires allowed Chandragupta to focus on rapidly expanding his realm across India. With a colossal army of over 6,00,000 men, he brought most of the subcontinent under his control. Besides Pataliputra as his primary capital, Taxila in the north-west and Ujjain in central India became the subsidiary capitals of the Mauryan empire.

Chandragupta's glorious reign lasted for twenty-four years, after which he renounced the throne and became a pious Jain monk, spending his final years in the holy town of Shravanabelagola (150 kilometres west of Bangalore).

Meanwhile in Ptolemy's Egypt, Alexandria became the capital of culture and scholarship and a thriving centre of trade. The Library of Alexandria was the greatest library of the ancient era, while the 330-feet tall Lighthouse of Alexandria was the biggest lighthouse in the known world and is said to have inspired Arab minaret architecture. Mauryan India had extensive relations with Egypt and several settlements of Indian merchants in Egypt, and conversely, Egyptian colonies in India have been reported. There are records of an ambassador from Ptolemaic Egypt arriving in Pataliputra, presumably to counter the Seleucid diplomatic relations with India.

Indica by Megasthenes

Seleucus and Chandragupta maintained peaceful relations for years. Seleucus sent an ambassador named Megasthenes to India around 300 BCE, who wrote a book called *Indica.* The original account has been lost and what remains is a partial reconstruction by later historians such as Strabo, Pliny, Diodorus, and Arrian.

Megasthenes lived mostly in Pataliputra and described it as the most important city of India, located at the confluence of Ganga and another river which was 80 stadia (ancient unit of length where one stade is equal to 180 metres) in length and 15 in breadth. The city had 570 towers, 64 gates, and a deep ditch in front for defence. About India, he wrote,

> India, which is in shape quadrilateral, has its eastern as well as its western side bounded by the great sea, but on the northern side it is divided by Mount Hemodos from that part of Scythia which is inhabited by those Scythians who are called the Sakai, while the fourth or western side is bounded by the river called

> the Indus, which is perhaps the largest of all rivers in the world after the Nile.

On occasions, Megasthenes was overly imaginative in describing his experience:

> On a mountain called Nulo there live men whose feet are turned backwards, and who have eight toes on each foot; while on many of the mountains there lives a race of men having heads like those of dogs, who are clothed with the skins of wild beasts, whose speech is barking, and who, being armed with claws, live by hunting and fowling.

Nevertheless, the *Indica* was a groundbreaking work of ethnography and provided the most comprehensive account of India to the classical world. In modern times, it turned out to be a valuable source for the scholars working on the reconstruction of India's ancient past.

Bindusara (320–272 BCE)

Chandragupta's son Bindusara continued to maintain friendly relations with the Greek kingdoms of Asia and Egypt, that referred to him as 'Amitrochates' (from the Sanskrit *Amitraghata*, meaning destroyer of foes). Greek accounts describe an incident where Bindusara requested Antiochus I (son of Seleucus) to send him dried figs, sweet wine, and a sophist. Antiochus replied: 'We shall send you figs and wine, but Greek laws forbid a sophist from being sold'. A Seleucid ambassador named Deimachus spent time in Bindusara's court at Pataliputra and wrote an account, which, like many others from the time, is lost to us.

Ashoka the Great (304–232 BCE)

One of Bindusara's sixteen wives was Subhadrangi who gave birth to two sons—Ashoka and Vitashoka. There's a possibility that Bindusara and Ashoka had Greek ancestry since Chandragupta Maurya was married to a Seleucid princess. Ashoka stood out from an early age, and Bindusara made him the viceroy of Ujjain when he was only eighteen and later sent him to Taxila to suppress a rebellion. Following Bindusara's death, a fierce struggle for succession ensued among his sons, which Ashoka won after ruthlessly killing his brother and step brothers.

During the early years of his reign, Ashoka ruled with an iron fist, maintaining an extensive espionage network, prisons, and torture chambers. Embarking upon an aggressive campaign of imperial expansion, he conquered the mighty kingdom of Kalinga (present-day Orissa) around 261 BCE in what turned out to be an overwhelmingly brutal and bloody war. Kalinga was ravaged—1,00,000 people were reportedly slaughtered and over 1,50,000 surviving men, women, and children were uprooted from their homes. The savagery unleashed by his army over the innocent people of Kalinga filled Ashoka with remorse, turning the war into a life-changing event. He embraced Buddhism and became a lifelong advocate of non-violence, although some commentators have suggested it may have been the ambitious emperor's propaganda. Ashoka banned the practice of animal sacrifice, something that Buddhism had long opposed, and restricted the slaughter of animals for meat. His philosophy had a deep-seated impact on Indian culture and society, which has lasted to date.

The way Constantine brought Christianity to prominence in the Roman Empire, Ashoka's support transformed Buddhism from a local cult to a state religion. He commissioned the construction of many stupas like the Great Stupa of Sanchi and the Dhamek Stupa at Sarnath, and dispatched his son Mahinda and daughter Sanghamitta to Sri Lanka to spread the message.

After the Kalinga war, Ashoka stopped further military campaigns and began to issue edicts that were carved on rocks and placed throughout the empire. Through these edicts, Ashoka promoted his moral policy of dhamma that advocated non-violence and religious tolerance, instructed his officials to help the poor and the elderly, and announced the establishment of medical facilities for humans and animals. The edicts were carved in the vernacular Prakrit languages, except in the north-western corner of the empire where they were set in Greek and Aramaic. Attesting to his non-violent spiritual conquests, Ashoka's thirteenth edict mentions that he carried the *punnyateja* (meaning holy flame) westwards to the Greek kingdoms of Turameya (Ptolemy of Egypt), Antakini (Antigonus of Macedonia), Maka (Magas of Cyrenia in North Africa), Antiyoka (Antiochus of Syria), and Alikasundara (Alexander of Epirus in Greece).

Later during his reign, Ashoka erected commemorative pillars with similar inscriptions. Beautifully proportioned and crowned with exquisitely sculpted animal figures, the finely polished sandstone pillars are massive—12 to 15 metres in height and around 50 tonnes in weight—and it must have required great engineering effort in getting them transported across the empire. The animal capitals of these pillars bear resemblance to those at Persepolis while the idea of Ashokan decrees and rock edicts seems to have been inspired by those of the Persian Achaemenian emperors, particularly Darius. It is worth noting that there were hardly any stone carvings in India before Ashoka, and then all of a sudden appeared this highly sophisticated and mature art form. Ananda Coomaraswamy, a historian of Indian art, observed: 'India, in the centuries and perhaps millennium BCE was an integral part of an "Ancient East" that extended from the Mediterranean to the Ganges valley'.

Discovery of the Forgotten Mauryan Past

The Mauryan past is a matter of pride for Indians. After Independence, the Lion Capital (the four lions that originally graced the top of the Ashokan pillar at Sarnath) was chosen as the national emblem of India, and the Ashoka Chakra became part of India's national flag. Today, major roads, universities, and even luxury hotels take their names from that glorious era. What is less known, however, is that Mauryan history was completely forgotten in India, and that Chandragupta and Ashoka were unknown figures until a few talented and curious Westerners toiled away for years and meticulously reconstructed the Mauryan past. It bears digressing to briefly narrate the interesting story of their discoveries.

The French Orientalist Joseph de Guignes was probably the first person to suggest in 1776 that the 'Sandracottos' mentioned in Greek accounts was Chandragupta Maurya. When the British Orientalist and jurist Sir William Jones arrived in India in 1784, he identified traits in Indian gods that were common with those ascribed to their classical Greek counterparts. One of the first papers he wrote on India was 'The Gods of Greece, Italy and India'. The Asiatic Society he founded started accumulating ancient Indian texts that talked about many kings and places. But there was a problem—there were no dates or chronological records that could be called historical writing.

Megasthenes had described the Mauryan capital of Palibothra that was located at the confluence of the Ganga and the Erranaboas River. Now, it wasn't clear which Indian river was Megasthenes's Erranaboas referring to. One geographer conjectured that Erranaboas must be the Jumna (Yamuna) River, which pointed to the city of Allahabad as Palibothra. Another candidate was the city of Kannauj, although Patna, whose older name was Pataliputra, seemed the closest bet. The only problem was that no river joined Ganga at Patna. Geographer James Rennell revealed in his *Memoir and Map of Hindoostan*, published in 1788, that at an earlier point in time, the Son River might have joined the Ganga at Patna. When Jones stumbled upon a reference to the Son River as the *Hiranyabahu* (meaning golden-armed), a word that was phonetically similar to the Greek Erranaboas, he confirmed that Pataliputra was Palibothra.[8]

The great Indian emperor Sandracottos mentioned in the Greek accounts, had no corresponding references in Sanskrit texts until Jones discovered an obscure political drama where a usurper named Chandragupta made Pataliputra his capital and received foreign ambassadors there. Sandracottos, he concluded, was none other than Chandragupta. Validated against the dates in Greek accounts, the chronology of ancient India was thus established.

The discovery of Ashoka took even more considerable effort. The Asiatic Society had been receiving reports from British soldiers and officials posted all over India about coins, rock edicts, and pillars with inscriptions on them. However, no one could read these inscriptions as they were written in scripts that remained unknown and indecipherable until an assiduous, scientifically inclined scholar named James Prinsep got involved with the Society around 1830. Prinsep meticulously catalogued the ancient coins that had been discovered and toiled for four years before he could decipher what were the Brahmi and Kharoshthi scripts. He announced his first translation that mentioned a king called 'Devanampiya (meaning dear to the gods) Piyadasi (meaning good looking)' who had authorised the religious edicts to be published.[9]

But who was Piyadasi? The identity of this mysterious king was established when a British scholar of Buddhism in Sri Lanka discovered that Piyadasi was an epithet for Ashoka. The dots were now connected. As more and more Ashokan inscriptions were translated, a reasonably comprehensive portrait of Ashoka was crystallised.

FROM TAXILA TO HARVARD

Taxila's existence as a noted centre of Vedic learning dates back to the sixth or the seventh century BCE. Described as a wealthy and well-governed city in Greek accounts, Taxila underwent a fusion with Hellenic culture after Alexander's campaign. It is also said to be the hometown of Kautilya, the learned visionary behind the Mauryan Empire.

In a long and somewhat haphazard yet intriguing chain of events spread over 2,000 years and multiple continents, one can roughly trace a continuity of educational traditions from the ancient city of Taxila all the way to the Harvard University.

As Buddhism began to flourish during Ashoka's reign, dwelling places called *viharas* (from where the Indian state of Bihar got its name) were built as shelters for wandering monks. Increasingly, as donations and support from prosperous merchants and devotees poured in, viharas began to grow along trading routes. From the first century CE onwards, they evolved into institutions of Buddhist education; Taxila transformed into a great Buddhist centre of learning, arguably the earliest university in the world. Some of the viharas grew into large monastic complexes called *mahaviharas* (meaning great viharas), such as Nagarjunakonda in Andhra Pradesh, founded in the third century CE, and Nalanda, the renowned university founded in the fifth century CE that had thousands of students.

Through the mountain passes of north-west India, Buddhist viharas spread to places like Balkh (Afghanistan), where the Nava Vihara (New Monastery) was established, and further into Central Asia, where the Uzbek city of Bukhara derives its name from the word vihara. Historian Christopher Beckwith points to a fascinating connection between the Islamic and Buddhist education systems in his book *Empires of the Silk Roads*:

> Central Asian scholars also developed an Islamic system of higher education modelled on the Central Asian system of the Buddhist *vihara*, or monastic college .... The *vihara* seems to have been Islamicised as the madrasa in Central Asia in the eighth and ninth centuries.[10]

The following centuries were a period of great scholarly achievements in the Islamic world as we saw earlier, that facilitated a diffusion of knowledge from Central Asia and Persia to North Africa and southern Europe. With the passage of a few more centuries, as the Islamic world was getting past its peak and Christian Europe was awakening, the translation movement gathered momentum and European scholars like Adelard of Bath and Gerard of Cremona had access to the libraries and the vast body of knowledge in Muslim Spain and the Near East. Universities sprung up in Bologna, Salamanca, Paris, Oxford, and Cambridge from the late eleventh to the early thirteenth centuries. Beckwith unravels another link, stating:

> The college (College des Dix-huit, the founding unit of University of Paris) retained most of the essential characteristics of its direct ancestors, the madrasa and vihara, including the pious foundation that supported the student residents and a professor, and perhaps the architectural form as well. The transmission of Islamic knowledge, techniques, and institutions to the West thus fuelled the intellectual revolution of the High Middle Ages.

Islamic influence over European universities continued and Latin translations of works by Muslim scholars like Avicenna and Averroes were formally incorporated into their curriculum.[11] When the English scholar Daniel of Morley, who had lived in Toledo, returned to England, he was disappointed with the state of liberal arts, philosophy, and science there. In his work *Philosophia,* which he dedicated to the 'precious multitude of books' that he had brought with him from Toledo, he introduced Arabic mathematical theory to western Europe and is believed to have contributed to the intellectual atmosphere of the University of Oxford in its early days.

A few centuries later, English Puritans, who were graduates of Oxford and Cambridge, emigrated to America and founded Harvard College in 1636. In the subsequent centuries, as America rapidly expanded westward, the Harvard template was replicated across the vast nation.

THE BACTRIAN-GREEKS AND THE INDO-GREEKS

Seleucus was faced with the perpetual challenge of controlling his eastern frontier in Bactria and had made his son Antiochus I a joint king for the volatile region. For the next several decades, there was a constant struggle for power between the Seleucid descendants (Antiochus I and Antiochus II) and the Seleucid satraps (Diodotos and Diodotos II). Around 230 BCE, Euthydemos, probably another descendant of the Seleucids, rose to power, initiating a new Bactrian-Greek kingdom that saw several dynasties rule Bactria over the next century.

With the Mauryan dynasty of India in decline after Ashoka's death, the Bactrian-Greek kings started eyeing Indian territories. By 180 BCE, some of these Bactrian-Greek kings came to rule the Indian region exclusively and have been called the first Indo-Greek kings. In ancient Indian literature, they have been referred to as Yavanas. Over time, these entities became a true mix of Greek and Indian culture, many of them devoutly committed to Indian deities and beliefs.

Somewhere during the Indo-Greek association, several Greek words entered Indian vocabulary—*kendra* (centre), *kona* (angle), *suranga* (tunnel), *kalama* (pen).[12] Even astrology, an extremely popular pastime in India to date, is not referenced in ancient Vedic or Buddhist texts and seems to have developed under the Greek influence.

The influx of the Parthians and the Scythian tribes in what is now Central Asia and eastern Iran, distanced the Seleucids from the Bactrian-Greeks, pushing the latter group further into India. Simultaneously, the Seleucids were estranged from their Greek homeland as the Romans emerged as a rising power on their western front. Due to these political divisions and siloed domains, the Indo-Greek kings are absent from Greek imagination and historical accounts.

Menander

The most prominent name among the Indo-Greek rulers was Menander or Milinda, as he is called in the Buddhist tradition, who ruled from somewhere around 160 BCE to 135 BCE. With his capital at Sakala (Sialkot, Pakistan), he ruled over much of Afghanistan, Pakistan, and the Indo-Gangetic plains till Mathura. Indo-Greek power and commerce was at its peak during Menander's reign, as reflected in the variety and spread of coins issued by him and from an inscription referring to him that was discovered in north-west Pakistan.

Menander's decision to convert to Buddhism is attributed to his lengthy intellectual exchange with the Buddhist elder Nagasena, as recorded in the *Milindapanha* (*Questions of King Menander*), possibly modelled on *The Dialogues of Plato*, where Plato adopted the Socratic method of presenting philosophical arguments in a question-and-answer form. When Menander died, many cities are said to have mourned his death, and his ashes were divided among them to erect monuments on the relics, a typical Buddhist custom.[13]

Other than Menander, the only other Indo-Greek king mentioned in ancient Indian sources is Antialcidas, who ruled from Taxila around 115 BCE. He had sent an ambassador named Heliodorus to the court of Kasiputra Bhagabhadra, a king of the Shunga dynasty, in central India in 110 BCE, and a pillar was erected in what is now Besnagar (near the town of Vidisha in Central India) to commemorate the diplomatic visit. The pillar survived, but its story was forgotten until it was rediscovered in the nineteenth century and the inscription on it, written in the Brahmi script, was deciphered. Historians were astonished to find out that Heliodorus was a devotee of Lord Vishnu. Today, the locals have converted the pillar into a deity in itself known as the Khambh (pillar) Baba.[14]

One unique feature of the Indo-Greek rule was the large number of coins issued by them. They introduced innovations such as die-striking and were the first rulers in India to issue coins that were ascribed to particular kings, deities (Indian and Hellenistic), and even legends. It appears that there were at least forty different Indo-Greek kings and two queens who ruled at different times. When a major hoard of coins spanning over 400 years was unearthed in Afghanistan in the nineteenth century, James Prinsep and archaeologist Alexander Cunningham studied them carefully and charted the rise and fall of the Indo-Greek dynasties.

After 120 BCE, a number of small Indo-Greek kingdoms survived for several decades, though they were often embroiled in fighting each other. Gradually, they merged with the communities around them and became an inseparable part of India. Not many traces of that era have survived, other than a community of light-skinned people called the Kalash who live in the remote Chitral district of north-western Pakistan, and continue to maintain their distinct way of life, beliefs, and language. One popular hypothesis is that they are Greeks and descendants of Alexander the Great's soldiers.

The Greek historian Aristobulus, who accompanied Alexander, described in his account of the Indus region 'a thousand ruined and deserted cities'.[15] Which cities was he referring to?

And in the late eighteenth century, when Sir William Jones arrived in India and started studying Sanskrit texts, he noticed that the Sanskrit grammar and vocabulary bore a striking resemblance to Persian, Greek, and Latin, in which Jones was an expert. Was there an even older connection between India and Greece?

10

THE PAST GETS HAZIER

3,000 BCE–500 BCE

A language is a more ancient and inevitable thing than any state.

—Joseph Brodsky, Nobel Prize-winning poet and essayist

The story of India from 3,000 BCE to 500 BCE is full of intriguing mysteries and unsolved puzzles that have left historians in a quandary, drawn academics into endless debates, tempted commentators into propagating unsubstantiated theories, and provided fodder to political propagandists.

Many curious minds from around the world have taken up the challenges and spent their entire careers trying to unravel these mysteries and reconstruct the long-lost past. Their work has involved deciphering unknown scripts and analysing unearthed towns, material finds, ancient burial sites, linguistic clues, and geological evidence. Despite several path-breaking discoveries, however, much remains obscure and unresolved.

INDIA GETS OLDER BY 2,000 YEARS

In 1827, James Lewis, an English soldier of the East India Company's Bengal Artillery, deserted his regiment and escaped to the Punjab region, which was beyond British control at the time. Using

Charles Masson as his alias, he wandered around in the area and stumbled upon an ancient ruin at a village called Harappa (200 kilometres south of Lahore). He described it in his travelogue as 'a ruinous brick castle having remarkable high walls and towers'.[1] What Masson saw was similar to the deserted cities that Aristobulus had reported seeing in the fourth century BCE. For some reason, however, Masson's findings did not invite any further investigation.

Three decades later, the British annexed Punjab and began laying down railway lines through the region. Struggling to find ballast to stabilise the track in the rockless alluvial plains, the engineers working on the Lahore–Multan line found an alternative in the ruins of the nearby village of Harappa, which had a bountiful supply of bricks. They soon began plundering the ruins, entirely unaware of their antiquity.

The pillaging by the railway engineers left archaeologist Alexander Cunningham a distraught man. He had earlier excavated ancient sites like Sarnath and Sanchi, and was aware of Harappa as a site with possible archaeological importance. Cunningham rushed to the ruins where he found several artefacts. He concluded that the site belonged to the Mauryan age and dated it back to around 300 BCE, the oldest period then for Indian archaeology. Among the Harappan artefacts was a black stone seal marked with the image of a bull and strange characters, which he assumed to be an archaic script going back to the Magadhan era, around 500 BCE. There would be no further exploration in Harappa and no follow-up for another six decades.

In 1902, scholar and archaeologist John Marshall, who had worked on excavations in Crete (Greece), arrived in India as the director-general of the Archaeological Survey of India (ASI) at the age of twenty-five. Marshall brought with him a new energy and an enthusiasm for conserving the ancient monuments in India that had long been neglected.

In 1917, Marshall asked the archaeologist Daya Ram Sahni to study Harappa. After four years of excavations, Sahni unearthed ancient pottery, brick structures, bangles, terracotta toys, and inscribed seals. What was remarkable was the standardised 1:2:4 proportion of the bricks' height, width, and length, which is the ideal ratio for structural stability. Marshall was pleased with the findings and pushed for further excavations. Two years later, archaeologist R.D. Banerjee excavated another site called Mohenjo-daro (meaning 'mound of the dead') in Sindh. He found pottery, bricks, and seals identical to those from Harappa. The uniformity between the two sites was puzzling as they were over 600 kilometres apart. The nondescript villages of Harappa and Mohenjo-daro were about to become world famous.[2]

Marshall announced the discovery in the *Illustrated London News* on 24 September 1924:

> Not often has it been to archaeologists, as it was given to Schliemann at Tiryns and Mycenae, or to Stein in the deserts of Turkestan, to light upon the remains of a long-forgotten civilisation. It looks, however, at this moment, as if we were on the threshold of such a discovery in the plains of the Indus.[3]

All of a sudden, Indian history had taken a giant leap into the past. From a 3,000-year-old civilisation, India had become over 5,000 years old, a contemporary of the ancient civilisations of Egypt and Mesopotamia. Curiously, all the three civilisations had developed along large rivers passing through deserts or arid regions and were located at a similar latitude—around the Tropic of Cancer.

The Indus Valley Civilisation

The Harappa and Mohenjo-daro excavations were followed by the discovery of several other sites in the subsequent years. The ancient civilisation was called the Harappan Civilisation or the Indus Valley Civilisation, although further discoveries confirmed that it was not limited to the Indus region. By 1947, around 40 sites had been discovered, and most of them ended up in Pakistan, prompting India to search for archaeological remains in its territory. In the following years, the number of sites multiplied, reaching 100 by 1960 and 800 by 1979.[4] The latest count is around 3,700 sites, spread over 8,00,000 square kilometres from Afghanistan to Gujarat and Haryana. Besides Mohenjo-daro and Harappa, prominent sites of the ancient civilisation include Rakhigarhi (near Delhi), Kalibangan (in Rajasthan), and Dholavira and Lothal (in Gujarat).

Radiocarbon dating has shown that the first Indus Valley cities came up around 2,600 BCE, and that by 1,900 BCE the civilisation had largely disintegrated. The Indus cities were surprisingly well-planned, and there was a remarkable degree of consistency in town planning over such a vast area. Mohenjo-daro, with an area of up to 300 hectares, is the largest city, not only in the Indus Valley Civilisation but also in the entire ancient world. Its population was estimated to be around 50,000. Mohenjo-daro had a great bath where people could congregate for ritual ablutions, a huge granary, and wide streets laid out in a grid pattern.

In Egypt and Mesopotamia, vast resources were spent on building lavish ziggurats (temples), pyramids, palaces, and tombs of the ruling class, while the commoners were relegated to humbler forms of housing. The Indus cities, on the other hand, had a spartan plan with no such grand monuments. The burial rituals followed in the Indus Valley Civilisation were much more austere as compared to the elaborate funerals that were held for members of the royal families of the Egyptian and Mesopotamian civilisations, which raises the possibility of the Indus society being far more egalitarian.

Europe had no semblance of civilisation for nearly 3,000 years while Egypt, Mesopotamia, and the Indus Valley had built cities, imposing structures, and complex societies, and also invented writing, customs, and rituals. The Indus cities, for instance, had a sophisticated sanitation system that allowed sewage from houses to be emptied into drains that flowed into brick-lined sewers running below the major streets. It would take another 2,000 years before a comparable sanitation system was built by the Romans. One can only imagine the shock and bewilderment that the Europeans would have experienced had they managed to reach the bustling cities of Egypt, Mesopotamia or Indus Valley.

The Indus people built boats and were capable of navigating the rivers in the Indus region as well as into the sea. Sailing from ports like Lothal in Gujarat, they followed a route hugging the Makran Coast to the ancient commercial centres and trans-shipment points of Dilmun (Bahrain) and Magan or Makan (Oman). Mesopotamian records refer to trade relations with Meluha, which was the ancient name given to the Indus region, or possibly the city of Mohenjo-daro. The Indus Valley people were exporting cotton, sugarcane, sesame, timber, copper, carnelian beads, pearls, ivory, and even animals like elephants, rhinoceroses, monkeys, and peacocks to Mesopotamia.

The Unsolved Riddles

One of the most enduring mysteries of the ancient world is the Indus script, which has remained undeciphered to date. Over 4,000 inscriptions, most of them on seals, tablets, pottery or ornaments, have been discovered. The script contains about 400 signs, of which only 200 are used more than five times. Scholars debate whether the script is a writing system or merely a set of non-linguistic symbols, many believing that it is a combination of words and phonetic signs.

Over the last century, more than a hundred decipherments have been proposed by experts, though none has been credibly accepted. One scholar has even gone so far as to suggest a similarity between the Indus script and Rongorongo, an undeciphered writing system of glyphs native to the Easter Island, located in the middle of the South Pacific Ocean. Others believe that the reconstruction of the Indus script is impossible. This constraint has prevented us from understanding the story of an entire civilisation.

Several questions remain unanswered: Was the Indus Civilisation an empire? Were there any political or religious leaders? Did the Indus people have a military set-up? There are no royal or imperial monuments in the Indus cities, and no weapons or evidence of armed conflict has been unearthed. So how did the civilisation enforce order and the rule of law over such a vast region with thousands of settlements? Who controlled the trade with Mesopotamia and within the Indus cities? Strangely, no objects of Mesopotamian origin have been found in the Indus cities, other than one Dilmun-type seal discovered at Lothal. What explains this one-sided exchange?

The sites in Rajasthan and Haryana are way east of the Indus Valley. Were they on the banks of a river that has dried up? Was it the mythical Sarasvati River? Is the intermittent Ghaggar-Hakra River a remnant of the Sarasvati River?

We also do not know why this advanced civilisation collapsed around 1,900 BCE and its cities abandoned after some seven or eight centuries of habitation. Several theories have been put forth—an earthquake or a tectonic uplift resulted in the damming of the lower course of the Indus or perhaps it was the flooding caused by excessive deforestation brought about by the burgeoning population.

What happened to the people after they abandoned the Indus cities? Did they spread out to the east and the south in the subcontinent? Are the Dravidian languages (a family of some seventy languages of which Tamil, Telugu, Kannada, and Malayalam are the most commonly spoken) linked to the language of the Indus Civilisation? Interestingly, a language called Brahui, which is spoken by around 2 million people in Balochistan (Pakistan), is related to the Dravidian family of languages. How did Brahui get isolated from the other Dravidian languages? Was it the intrusion of some foreign tribes that pushed Dravidian speakers apart, creating isolated enclaves? Is Brahui a remnant of an ancient Dravidian migration into India from the West? Some linguists believe that the Dravidian languages are related to the Finno-Ugrian family of languages of Eastern Europe, while others have linked the Dravidian languages to the Elamite language spoken in ancient Iran and Iraq. The Proto-Dravidian language may have separated from the proto-languages in Iran and Iraq as early as 7,000 BCE.

What kind of religious beliefs did the Indus Valley people have? Did they worship any deities? An excavated seal had shown a three-faced human-like figure, seated on a throne and surrounded by animals. Marshall had identified it as proto-Shiva, thereby establishing a connection with early Hinduism, although modern scholars remain sceptical. Then who were the people who composed the Vedas in Sanskrit starting from 1,500 BCE? The Aryans or the Indo-Aryans?

The term 'Aryan' was first used in the 1850s by the French diplomat, writer, and ethnologist Arthur de Gobineau, known for his racist theories, to describe the white races or the Germanic peoples, who were purported to be superior to all races. When the German archaeologist Heinrich Schliemann famously discovered the lost city of Troy on the Aegean coast of Turkey in 1871, he uncovered around 1,800 variations of the swastika. The advocates of the Aryan master race theory were quick to interpret and co-opt the swastika as a 'purely Aryan symbol' and a proof of the Indo-European origins of the race. In the twentieth century, Germany's Nazi Party, who adopted the swastika as their official symbol, latched on to the imaginary tale of a superhuman Aryan race that originated at Thule, the northernmost mythical island believed to be somewhere near Scandinavia.

According to the Aryan invasion hypothesis, light-skinned Aryans invaded India from the north-west (Central Asia and eastern Iran via modern Afghanistan), and caused the collapse of the Indus Valley Civilisation. Furthermore, it suggests that the Vedic religion emerged from the Aryan culture and brought new literary traditions into India. This theory helped the British imperialists justify their own rule over the Indians as a continuation of the natural order of outsiders dominating the natives. Scholars have, however, discredited the Aryan invasion theory as no supporting evidence of any massacres or destruction have been found in the Indus Valley sites. They have also rejected the term Aryan as a racial designation since it was used in ancient Indian and Iranian literature in a linguistic sense. Rather than a violent invasion, a gradual diffusion of new populations into India seems to be a more plausible explanation.

The topic has since become increasingly controversial, marked by conjecture and fierce debates in popular media. The research and investigation have moved beyond archaeology and linguistics to genetic analysis, yet the arguments continue.

THE INDO-EUROPEAN ENIGMA

It was in the 1580s in Goa that two individuals—a Florentine merchant named Filippo Sassetti and Jesuit Thomas Stephens, the first Englishman in India—reported noticing a similarity between Sanskrit and the European languages. Two centuries later, a French Jesuit named Gaston-Laurent Coeurdoux wrote a letter to the French Orientalist Anquetil-Duperron, describing a commonality he noticed between Sanskrit, Greek, and Latin. Sir William Jones noticed the same when he announced to the Asiatic Society in February 1786:

> The Sanskrit language, whatever be its antiquity, is of a wonderful structure; more perfect than the Greek, more copious than the Latin, and more exquisitely refined than either; yet bearing to both of them a stronger affinity, both in the roots of verbs and the forms of grammar, than can possibly have been produced by accident; so strong, indeed, that no philologer could examine them all without believing them to have sprung from some common source, which perhaps no longer exists.

His assertion rocked the communities of scholars and colonialists in Europe, opening new lines of investigation. As defined by the Europeans, the colonisers' languages had stood at the top of the philological hierarchy, while those of the conquered peoples were relegated to the bottom.[5] But Jones's discovery had brought Sanskrit to the same level as the language of the colonial masters, or even higher since the Vedas were much older than any other European text. Many European scholars, Germans in particular, now started looking at India as the ultimate origin of civilisation. German scholar and critic August Wilhelm von Schlegel wrote in a letter in 1803: 'Everything, yes, everything without exception has its origin in India'.[6]

A new field of comparative philology was born and it became a rage in Europe. The newly discovered family of languages came to be known as the Indo-European languages (a term coined by the British polymath Thomas Young in 1813), currently spoken by around 40 per cent of the world's population with Hindi, Bengali, English, Spanish, French, Russian, German, and Iranian as the most common variants. Thereafter began the search for a common, lost parent—the Proto-Indo-European (PIE) language. Was there a unique culture associated with the parent Indo-European language? If yes, where did that culture originate?

Locating the Indo-European Homeland

Many speculations abound about the original homeland of the Indo-Europeans, and many have also questioned the very idea of pursuing a land-of-origin theory. The commonly agreed-upon homeland appears to be in the steppe region north of the Black and Caspian seas—the Pontic-Caspian steppe—in what is the southern part of modern Ukraine and Russia, which was first identified in the 1950s by the Lithuanian-American archaeologist Marija Gimbutas, who called it the *Urheimat* (meaning homeland).

Around 4,000 BCE, as the climate became warmer, the Pontic-Caspian steppe became a far more comfortable place for pastoralists to live. Herds became larger, and migrations over longer distances became the norm. That is when we also see the earliest evidence of the domestication of horses in the region, conceivably as a source of meat. The idea of humans riding a horse probably came later, although whenever it happened it must have been a radical innovation as it facilitated transportation across long stretches of grassland. Alongside the growing pastoralism emerged an archaic form of the Proto-Indo-European language. Integrating archaeological data with linguistic studies, Marija Gimbutas introduced the Kurgan hypothesis in 1956 which proposes that the people of a Kurgan (Slavic term for distinctive burial mounds) culture in the Pontic-Caspian steppe were the most likely speakers of the Proto-Indo-European language.

The other major invention was the wheel, although it's not clear when or where it took place. The subsequent conception of the axle meant that the first wagons were ready between 3,400 and 3,000 BCE. The word 'wagon' originates from the Proto-Indo-European root word *weg*, which is also the root of the Sanskrit word *vahana*.

Horses and wagons meant that the vast steppes could now be traversed and that they were not a geographic barrier anymore. The Yamnaya, the nomadic pastoralist people who lived around southern Ukraine and Russia and were associated with the practice of building kurgans, could now cover much longer distances, carrying long-term supplies, with their cattle and sheep in tow. Unlike the sedentary agrarian civilisations where rising populations resulted in larger, denser settlements, for the nomadic pastoralists, it led to ever wider dispersal. The Proto-Indo-European language travelled along with the caravans as they migrated westwards into Central Europe around 3,000 BCE. Over the next 1,000 years, some of the descendants of the Yamnaya people are said to have migrated southwards into Central Asia towards Iran and India.

By 3,000 BCE, the early Proto-Indo-European language began to branch out, starting with the Anatolian and Tocharian (a group of extinct Indo-European languages that were spoken in northwest China) offshoots, followed by the Celtic and the Germanic ones. By 2,500 BCE, it further split into the Slavic, Baltic, and Greek languages. Between 2,500 and 2,200 BCE, an early form of the Indo-Iranian language had developed, while the parent Proto language disappeared.

Around 2,000 BCE, a new culture, known as the Sintashta, emerged in the Urals. They were known for building chariots, breeding and training horses, and producing sophisticated new weapons. The Sintashta archaeological site, located in Chelyabinsk Oblast in southern Russia, close to the border with Kazakhstan, is a fortified, circular settlement, 140 metres in diameter.[7] The earliest known chariots have been discovered there, and the burial sacrifices show striking parallels to the rituals mentioned in the *Rigveda.* The Sintashta culture is regarded as the origin of the Indo-Iranian culture, which included similar practices involving horses and chariots, burial rituals, and consuming *soma* (a stimulant drug).

The spread of the Indo-European languages

Further south is the Bactria–Margiana Archaeological Complex (BMAC), which has been dated from around 2,000 to 1,500 BCE.[8] It covered large parts of Afghanistan, Uzbekistan, and Turkmenistan and inherited from Sintashta the practice of domesticating horses and the skill of making chariots. Being close to the Indus Valley Civilisation, the BMAC had trading relations with them. The northernmost settlement of the Indus Valley Civilisation was a trading post in northern Afghanistan called Shortugai, which was located near the lapis lazuli mines found in the region. The expansion of the BMAC to the borders of the Indus Valley and the Iranian plateau likely introduced the Indo-Iranian language and culture to Iran and north-west India. By 1,500 BCE, the towns of BMAC in Central Asia and eastern Iran were abandoned. Around the same time, the Vedic culture took root in India, which suggests the migration of people from the BMAC regions and the transmission of ideas and concepts into India.

The Indo-European Culture and Traditions

As the Proto-Indo-European language and culture spread deep into Europe and Asia, they merged with local non-Indo-European languages and customs, spawning new languages and dialects. However, certain elements of the Indo-European culture remained common among the descendant cultures.

The most distinctive Indo-European trait was cattle raising; cows were highly valued as they provided more milk than any other herd animal. They were even deemed sacred in Proto-Indo-European mythology and rituals. Community events involved feasts, gift exchanges, the performance of praise poetry and rituals including animal sacrifice, and the distribution of meat and mead.[9] More productive pastoral economies brought wealth and power, turning many of the cultures militaristic. Horses remained a symbol of strength and power while chariots became the favoured weapons of war from Asia to Europe, as attested by ancient texts. There are several parallels in social divisions based on professions between ancient India, Iran, Greece, Rome, and Gaul.

The Proto-Indo-European vocabulary retained some of the cardinal words despite the migrations across vast distances over centuries or even millennia. The word for horse—*asva* in Sanskrit, *aspa* in Avestan, *equus* in Latin—remained similar. For father, it was *pitr* in Sanskrit, *pater* in Greek, and *piter* in Latin. The modern English 'mead' comes from the same root as the Sanskrit *madhu*, Greek *methy*, and Slavonic *medu*. Likewise, many words for family members, counting numbers, terms associated with agriculture, cattle raising, horses, and mythology continued to have common roots.

THE VEDIC ERA

The Indus Valley Civilisation had started to decline around 1,900 BCE and disappeared by 1,700 BCE. The Indo-Aryan speakers are believed to have begun trickling in from the BMAC region in

Afghanistan and southern Iran well before the collapse of the Indus Valley Civilisation. If that migration indeed took place, how was the interaction between the Indus Valley people and the newly arrived Indo-Aryans?

The terracotta seals recovered from the Indus Valley sites depict many animals, but the horse is not one of them.[10] However, after 1,500 BCE, horses became prominent in the seals alongside cattle, which were seen as a form of wealth. The cattle-rearing community of the Indus Valley cities came to be dominated by a horse-and-chariot-based class.

While the Indus Valley Civilisation was highly urbanised, the early Indo-Aryan society was rural and pastoral. For a thousand years, from 1,500 to 500 BCE, no cities or urban settlements were built. Consequently, they did not have a political hierarchy, and their basic social unit was the *jana* (tribe), made up of several *gramas* (family clusters). Overlapping the social divisions of *varna* (any of the four main Hindu castes; Brahmins, Kshatriyas, Vaishyas, or Shudras) and *jati* (a community or a sub-caste), the various clans were divided into *gotras* (literally, a cow-pen) as a lineage group. This social structure presumably evolved into the caste system over the following centuries, spreading to villages across the vast landscape and becoming a permanent defining feature of the subcontinent.

Strangely, there are no physical structures, art or sculpture from that age. Neither are there any inscriptions since the Indo-Aryans had no script. Nevertheless, this utter lack of material evidence is well compensated for by the extensive body of Vedic literature that has no parallel in any other ancient civilisation. In praise of the Vedas, Henry David Thoreau wrote:

> Whenever I have read any part of the Vedas, I've felt that some unearthly and unknown light illuminated me. In the great teaching of the Vedas, there is no touch of sectarianism. It is of all ages, climes and nationalities and is the royal road for the attainment of the Great Knowledge. When I'm at it, I feel that I'm under the spangled heavens of a summer night.

The word 'veda' is derived from the Sanskirt root *vid,* meaning knowledge or sacred knowledge such as priestly hymns, chants, and rituals. The Vedic corpus consists primarily of the four Vedas—*Rigveda, Samveda, Yajurveda* and *Atharvaveda*; the Brahmanas are detailed commentaries on the hymns of the four Vedas. The *Rigveda* is held to be the first Veda and was composed between 1,500 and 1,000 BCE. The *Yajurveda* and *Samveda* were compiled in the succeeding centuries, and the *Atharvaveda* was the last of the Vedas.

The Vedas were committed to memory by priests and then transmitted orally to their successors. It is possible that this oral transmission was intended to keep the Vedic knowledge restricted to an elite minority. Although Vedic literature does not have any chronological records, it still provides reasonably good evidence of the conditions during the period as they have been preserved close to their original form.

The Rigveda

The *Rigveda* is a compendium of 1,028 hymns with nearly 1,54,000 words. The hymns are addressed to gods like Indra (the god of war and thunder, and the subject of a quarter of the *Rigveda*), Agni (the god of fire), and Varuna (the ruler of the sky), whom they praise and pray to for victory in battle, long life, and cattle. As the Indo-Aryans were a patriarchal society, they prayed to the gods for sons, while no desire for daughters has been expressed in the *Rigveda.* This trait has sadly carried on well into the modern times, as reflected in the female foeticide statistics in India. There are frequent references to *gavishti,* meaning raids or fights for cattle. The horse is mentioned 215 times, and there are descriptions of the ritual of *vajapeya* (horse sacrifice), chariot-racing, and soma. Around thirty Aryan clans are mentioned along with their dark-skinned enemies—the *dasas* or *dasyus*—who have also been described as *anasa* or noseless. The geographical references in the *Rigveda* place it in the north-west and Punjab with frequent mentions of the Sindhu (Indus) River and the Sarasvati (possibly Ghaggar-Hakra)

River. The later Vedas have references to the Ganga River, indicating an eastward shift of the civilisation after 1,000 BCE.

Connections with Texts from Outside India

The earliest written evidence for an Indo-Aryan language comes from far away in northern Syria. That is where the kingdom of Mitanni came up between 1,500 and 1,300 BCE. The Mitanni people seem to have been an early part of the migration of the Indo-Iranian peoples into Central Asia, Iran, and northwest India.

The Mitanni people spoke a dialect of the Old Indic Sanskrit and all their rulers had Indo-Aryan names, like Tus'ratta I (Sanskrit *tvesa-ratha*, meaning 'having an attacking chariot'). Famed as great charioteers, the Mitanni prayed to Indo-Aryan gods (Indra, Varuna, Mithra, and Nasatyas) and their capital city was Wassukanni (Sanskrit *vasu-khani*, meaning 'wealth-mine'). Around 1,500 BCE, a manual was written on horsemanship and chariotry by a man named Kikkuli, who describes his profession as *assussanni* (*asvasani*, meaning 'procuring horses'). The text is full of Indo-Aryan terminology, and the numbers of laps covered by the chariots are described in Indic numerals—*aikauartanna*, *teravartanna*, *panzavartanna*, and *shauaoartanna* for one, three, five, and seven laps of the race.[11]

The *Rigveda* has striking similarities in terms of language and thought with the great body of early Iranian religious literature called Avesta, which was composed as early as 1,400 BCE in Avestan, the oldest Iranian language. The Avesta is also a compendium of hymns that were produced in a similar rural setting where cattle raising was held in esteem together with agriculture. The Avesta and the Rigveda have identical references to horses, chariots, rituals, fire worship, soma (*haoma* in Avestan), and names of deities, although the Indic gods were reversed as demons in the Avesta. The word for 'oblation' or 'worship' is *yasna* in Avestan and *yajna* in Vedic Sanskrit, while 'prayer chant' is *manthra* in Avestan and *mantra* in Vedic Sanskrit. Speakers of Avestan called themselves *Arya*, from which is derived *Aryanam* (meaning country of the Aryas), which became Iran. Some have even speculated that Eire (the old name of Ireland) is a cognate of the word 'Aryan'.[12]

Parallels have been found in ancient Greek mythological texts as well. Homer's *Odyssey* refers to horses, horse-drawn chariots, and a social life similar to that described in ancient Indian texts. The Greek god Ouranos and the Vedic god Varuna have similar-sounding names besides other related traits.[13] The Vedic people were particular about the spoken word and one who could not pronounce Sanskrit words was called *barbar* (meaning stammerer). The Greek word *barbaroi* had the same meaning.[14]

THE AXIAL AGE

In 1949, a German philosopher named Karl Jaspers introduced in his book *The Origin and Goal of History,* a term called the 'Axial Age', referring to the period from the eighth century BCE to the third century BCE. Jaspers posited that this age was unique and pivotal in human history, unleashing a fundamental spiritual change across the world. In a parallel development, new ways of thinking appeared in India, Persia, China, and the Greco-Roman world, even though there was no visible direct cultural contact between them.

Jaspers pointed out the emergence of Confucius and Lao-Tse in China; Gautam Buddha, Mahavira (the founder of Jainism), and Gosala (the founder of the Ajivika sect) in India; Zoroaster in Persia; and Homer, Socrates, Plato, and other philosophers in Greece around the same time or within a few centuries of each other. These thinkers displayed great originality, and yet their beliefs were marked by a surprising similarity in terms of reason, rationality, ethics, and the ideal path for humanity. Rather than being focused on local issues, their thinking was universal and could apply to humankind as a whole. Jaspers reasoned that there was some profound element intrinsic to humanity that was behind this parallel spiritual development.

What else could explain this phenomenon? Possibly, a common factor among the various civilisations was the vigorous commercial activity and the rise of prosperous kingdoms that provided a stable and secure environment in which learning could flourish.

The sixth century BCE saw sixteen Mahajanapadas ('great kingdoms') come up, stretching from Afghanistan and north-west India to Bihar and Bengal. They had evolved from semi-nomadic tribal units to highly organised political structures with agrarian economies and vast trade networks. In that progressive era, a new way of thinking developed in defiance of the authority of the Brahmins, caste stratification, and the Vedic rituals. A multitude of thinkers of the time proposed new ideas, and soon over sixty different philosophical or religious schools flourished in India.[15] Many of them were characterised by rationalism and not faith. Of these, only three religious reform movements endured for a long time—Ajivikas, Buddhism, and Jainism, and only the last two have survived to date.

Similarly, the theology of Zoroaster, who composed the oldest parts of the Avesta, the *Gathas,* was partly a reaction against the remnant Indo-Aryan population in Iran. Zoroaster was against the glorification of war and animal sacrifice in Indo-Aryan poetry. It was probably the success of Zoroastrianism that split the Indo-Aryan culture between India and the Mitanni kingdom of Syria. That may also explain why the Iranian word *daeva,* a cognate of the Indic word *deva* (for god), came to mean 'demon'[16], and why the Indo-Aryan gods Varuna and Indra were downgraded to the role of demons.

FURTHER INTO THE PAST

We have covered a long period of 5,000 years in this book. However, readers must note that it is only a tiny fraction of the 2,00,000 years of human existence. It is not that the human story beyond 5,000 to 6,000 years is any less exciting, but uncovering it gets ever trickier due to the absence of written records. Historians have, therefore, drawn the boundary of history at that juncture, labelling the period before that as 'proto-history' or 'pre-history'. Not everyone agrees with such a demarcation though, like Daniel Lord Smail, Professor of History at Harvard University, and the author of *On Deep History and the Brain,* who says that 'historians need to develop the habit of looking backward.'

Despite the scanty evidence, one thing remains clear—the human past was interconnected all along. It was around 12,000 years ago when our hunter-gatherer forefathers living in the Middle East stumbled upon the idea that food could be grown. They began experimenting with farming and managed to grow wild varieties of wheat, barley, lentils, and peas, and also herd wild animals like goats and wild oxen. The first settled agricultural communities originated in a region called the Fertile Crescent, spread over modern-day Iraq, Syria, Lebanon, Jordan, Israel, and Egypt. Over a period, farming spread to Europe and Asia, reaching Mehrgarh at the foot of the Bolan Pass in Balochistan around 9,000 years ago, where wheat and barley were grown. Agricultural settlements gradually evolved into societies that invented new tools, trades, rituals, customs, hierarchical structures, and writing systems. The progress of humanity suddenly switched over to a superfast track that had no precedent in the past.

But why Eurasia and why not Africa or the Americas? Geographer and historian Jared Diamond has argued that Eurasia was better suited for the spread of farming techniques due to its east–west orientation. It was easier for innovations like farming and herding to succeed across Eurasia as the environments on the same latitudes were mostly similar. In contrast, the human communities in Africa or the Americas were at a disadvantage due to their north–south orientation, where the habitats could change drastically.

The human story remains connected as we travel further back in time—to around 60,000 years ago—when small bands of anatomically modern humans ventured out of Africa. They reached India about 50,000 years ago, and from there they spread further into Southeast Asia, which was one land mass back then named Sundaland, exposed due to much lower sea levels, and subsequently into Australia. Supposedly, 30,000 years ago, they reached Europe, and around 15,000 years ago, they crossed Beringia, the land bridge between Siberia and Alaska, and entered the Americas.

The long-lasting human journey to all the corners of our planet must have entailed countless stories of courage, fear, adventure, ingenuity, discovery, triumph, failure, camaraderie, and survival that will forever remain largely unknown. But we do have clues at our disposal, such as tools, weapons, and objects made of rock and bone, burial sites, and DNA samples that help us to partially reconstruct the past. There are also prehistoric rock and cave paintings discovered in places as far afield as Lascaux (France), Bhimbetka (India), Kakadu National Park (Australia), and Serra da Capivara National Park (Brazil) that are remarkably similar, as if humans are predisposed to draw in a certain way.

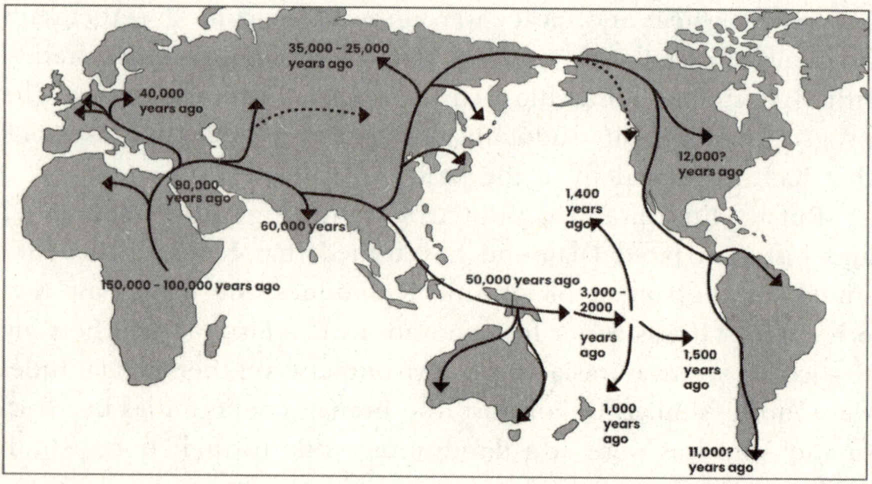

Modern humans embark on their global journey

Owing to environmental variation and natural selection, the various branches of human populations evolved a range of skin tones, colours of hair and eyes, blood types, and few other adaptations, but these differences are superficial at best. The seven billion of us are, in fact, 99.9 per cent identical in our genetic makeup. According to mitochondrial DNA studies, the entire humanity shares a common ancestor—one woman, referred to as the 'Mitochondrial Eve' or the 'mother of all humans', who lived between 1,00,000 and 2,00,000 years ago in southern Africa. The ancient Sanskrit phrase *Vasudhaiva Kutumbakam*, meaning 'the world is one family', could not be more true.

SOURCES OF MAPS

Chapter 1

First, Second and Third World countries

Link: https://www.coolgeography.co.uk/GCSE/AQA/Development_Gap/Mapping_dev/Mapping_Development.htm

Chapter 2

Distance saved by the Suez Canal

Link: https://www.yumpu.com/en/document/view/17792836/suez-and-panama-canals

The British Empire in 1914

Link: https://www.superprof.co.uk/blog/british-empire-history/

Chapter 4

European settlements in India

Link: https://commons.wikimedia.org/wiki/File:European_settlements_in_India_1501-1739.png

Chapter 5

Columbus's landmark voyage

Link: https://crossingtheoceansea.com/OceanSeaPages/OS-63-Columbus1stVoyage.html

The demarcation line of the Treaty of Tordesillas

Link: http://www.xochitl.net/hum2461/maps/tordesillasmap.htm

Vasco da Gama's route to Asia

Cunliffe, Barry. *By Steppe, Desert, and Ocean: The Birth of Eurasia.* Oxford: Oxford University Press, 2015. p. 471.

The Gunpowder Empires

Link: https://www.commackschools.org/Downloads/IB-AP-_Unit_10_Gunpowder_Empires2.pdf

Chapter 6

The Mongol Empire after Genghis Khan

Link: https://causseywhap.weebly.com/the-mongol-empire—tyler-briscoe.html

Travel routes of the early Western travellers to Asia

Cunliffe, Barry. *By Steppe, Desert, and Ocean: The Birth of Eurasia.* Oxford: Oxford University Press, 2015. p. 444.

Chapter 7

Early spread of Islam

Link: https://www.studentsofhistory.com/the-growth-pread-of-islam

The spread of Hindu and Buddhist Cultures to Southeast Asia

Link: https://slideplayer.com/slide/13072055/

Chapter 8

The Roman Empire in 117 CE

Link: https://www.biblestudy.org/maps/roman-empire.html

Indo-Roman trade route

McLaughlin, Raoul. *The Roman Empire and the Indian Ocean. The Ancient World Economy & the Kingdoms of Africa, Arabia & India.* South Yorkshire: Pen & Sword Books, 2014. p. 18.

Faxian's pilgrimage to India

Cunliffe, Barry. *By Steppe, Desert, and Ocean: The Birth of Eurasia.* Oxford: Oxford University Press, 2015. p. 314.

Hindu and Buddhist kingdoms in Southeast Asia

Link: https://slideplayer.com/slide/14563160/

Chapter 9

Alexander's world conquest

Cunliffe, Barry. *By Steppe, Desert, and Ocean: The Birth of Eurasia.* Oxford: Oxford University Press, 2015. p. 217.

Empires of Alexander's successors

Link: https://www.globalsecurity.org/military/world/europe/gr-history-hellenistic-antigonus.htm

Chapter 10

The spread of the Indo-European languages

Anthony, David W. *The Horse, the Wheel, and Language: How Bronze-Age Riders from the Eurasian Steppes Shaped the Modern World.* Princeton: Princeton University Press, 2007. Chapter 1, Figure 1.2.

Modern humans embark on a global journey

Link: https://commons.wikimedia.org/wiki/File:Human_migration_out_of_Africa.png

ACKNOWLEDGEMENTS

My profound gratitude to the travellers, writers, and professors whose travel accounts and insightful books left me with a lifelong curiosity about our global past. Their names are listed in the bibliography section. I want to thank the helpful staff members of the Central City Library in Auckland, the British Library in London, the National Library of Scotland in Edinburgh, and many other public libraries in the United States, the United Kingdom, and New Zealand, where I spent time looking for answers and connections.

A warm thanks to my friends, particularly Nagarajan Srinivasan and Aditya Kulkarni, and my nephew, Sahil Singh, who read the early drafts and provided incisive comments and advice. To editor Tara Khandelwal for her careful review of the manuscript during the initial stages, and her valuable feedback.

My special thanks to the organisers of the Bangalore Literature Festival where my book idea was shortlisted in 2018, and I got an opportunity to pitch it to a panel comprising several commissioning editors and publishers. Among the panel members was Rashmi Menon, Managing Editor, Amaryllis, whose welcoming attitude and openness to ideas gave me the confidence to complete writing the book. Two years later when I shared the manuscript, it was a sheer delight to hear from Rashmi about Amaryllis's decision to publish my book. Ever since, she has been a source of encouragement and advice.

I am grateful to the following talented individuals assigned on this project by Rashmi: editors Archana Ramachandran and Gayatri Goswami for their meticulous review, corrections, insightful comments, and suggestions. Illustrator Wasim Helal who drew the maps that should help readers get a geographical perspective, and Ankita Menghwani who assisted with the cover design.

Above all, this book would not have been written without the support of my wife, co-driver and co-traveller, Monica, who patiently listened to my ideas over the years, read and critiqued every draft diligently, and kept me motivated all along.

NOTES

Introduction

1. Michael Pearson, *The Indian Ocean.* London: Routledge, 2003. p. 3.
2. Lakshmi Subramanian, *Medieval Seafarers of India.* New Delhi: The Lotus Collection, Roli Books, 1999. pp. 10–11.
3. Professor Sanjay Subrahmanyam's talk at the 'Worlds Meet: A Historians' Look at Global Processes,' Macro History Symposium 2019, Israel. https://www.youtube.com/watch?v=a0bUy1614Es.

Chapter 1

1. According to Angus Maddison, in 1931 there were 1,68,000 Britons in India, out of which 60,000 were in the army and police and 4,000 in civil government, the remaining forming the private sector and family dependents. Angus Maddison, 'The Interaction between Asia and the West' in *Contours of World Economy 1–2030 AD: Essays in Macro-Economic History.* Oxford: Oxford University Press, 2007.
2. Peter Frankopan, *The Silk Roads: A New History of the World.* London: Bloomsbury, 2015. p. 369.
3. John Steele Gordon, *An Empire of Wealth: The Epic History of American Economic Power.* New York: HarperCollins, 2004. pp. 289–293.
4. With roots in nineteenth-century Europe, the American eugenics movement became a popular social movement that peaked in the 1920s and 1930s, advocating controlled selective breeding of human populations to remove 'undesirable' genetic traits. Laws were enacted that legalised forced sterilisations and prohibited individuals with mental or physical defects and mixed-race couples from marrying.
5. Srinath Raghavan, 'Rumour and Revolt', in *India's War: The Making of Modern South Asia 1939–1945.* London: Penguin Random House, 2016.

6. Alex von Tunzlemann, *Indian Summer: The Secret History of the End of an Empire.* London: Simon & Schuster, 2012. pp. 128–129.
7. Display at the National Maritime Museum, Greenwich, London.
8. Pankaj Mishra, 'Exit Wounds', in *The New Yorker,* 6 August 2007, https://www.newyorker.com/magazine/2007/08/13/exit-wounds.
9. Jon Wilson, *India Conquered: Britain's Raj and the Chaos of Empire.* London: Simon & Schuster, 2016. Chapter 14.
10. Yasmin Khan, *The Raj at War.* New Delhi: Penguin Books, 2015. pp. 155–156.
11. Gerhard Weinberg wrote in the introduction of his popular book *A World at Arms: A Global History of World War II,* 'Both by comparison with that terrible event, and when set against all other wars of which we have any knowledge, the second world-wide conflagration of this century surely deserves to be called "The Greatest War".'
12. Nisid Hajari, *Midnight's Furies: The Deadly Legacy of India's Partition.* New Delhi: Viking, 2015. p. 7.
13. Khan, *The Raj at War.* Prologue, p. x.
14. Dominique Lapierre and Larry Collins, *Freedom at Midnight.* London: Simon & Schuster, 1975. p. 263.
15. Stanley Wolpert, *Shameful Flight: The Last Years of the British Empire in India.* New York: Oxford University Press, 2006. p. 2.
16. Speech by Churchill called 'Our Duty in India': https://winstonchurchill.org/resources/speeches/1930-1938-the-wilderness/our-duty-in-india/
17. Ramachandra Guha, *India After Gandhi: The History of the World's Largest Democracy.* London: Picador, 2008. p. 155.
18. Ross Bassett, *The Technological Indian.* Cambridge, Massachusetts: Harvard University Press, 2016. p. 195.
19. Gurcharan Das, *India Unbound: From Independence to the Global Information Age.* New Delhi: Penguin Books, 2000. pp. 92–93, 158, 168.
20. Bertil Lintner, *China's India War: Collision Course on the Roof of the World.* Oxford: Oxford University Press, 2018. Introduction and Acknowledgements section.
21. Srinath Raghavan, *1971: A Global History of the Creation of Bangladesh.* Cambridge, Massachusetts: Harvard University Press, 2013. p. 206.

Chapter 2

1. Christian Classics Ethereal Library https://ccel.org/ccel/spurgeon/sermons03/sermons03. Last accessed on 6 May 2022.
2. Damodar Singhal, *India and World Civilisation.* Michigan: Michigan State University Press, 1969. Part 2, Chapter 6.
3. Dan Jones and Marina Amaral, *The Colour of Time: A New History of the*

World 1850–1950. London: Head of Zeus Ltd., 2019. p. 40.
4. Anatol Lieven, *Pakistan: A Hard Country.* London: Penguin Books, 2011. p. 50.
5. Michael Axworthy, *Iran: Empire of the Mind: A History from Zoroaster to the Present Day.* London: Penguin Books, 2008. Chapter 6.
6. Niall Ferguson, *Empire: The Rise and Demise of British World Order and the Lessons for Global Power.* New York: Basic Books, 2004. p. xix.
7. Lawrence James, *The Rise and Fall of the British Empire.* New York: St. Martin's Griffin, 1997. p. 217.
8. Thomas Sowell, *Migrations and Cultures: A World View.* New York: Basic Books, 1996. pp. 73–82.
9. Richard Overy, *Complete History of the World.* London: HarperCollins, 1978. p. 242.
10. Tansen Sen, *India, China, and the World: A Connected History.* Maryland: Rowman & Littlefield, 2017. p. 297.
11. Overy, *Complete History of the World.* p. 234.
12. Ian Morris, *Why the West Rules—For Now: The Patterns of History and What They Reveal about the Future.* London: Profile Books, 2011. p. 510.
13. Sowell, *Migrations and Cultures.* p. 54.
14. Bassett, *The Technological Indian.* p. 2.
15. Das, *India Unbound.* p. 29.
16. Bassett, *The Technological Indian.* p. 70.
17. Michael Silvestri, *Ireland and India: Nationalism, Empire and Memory.* New York: Palgrave Macmillan, 2009. pp. 2–3.
18. James, *The Rise and Fall of the British Empire.* p. 359.

Chapter 3

1. Maya Jasanoff, *Edge of Empire: Lives, Culture and Conquest in the East 1750–1850.* New York: Knopf, 2005. pp. 73–80.
2. Peter Hopkirk, *The Great Game: On Secret Service in High Asia.* London: John Murray, 1990. Chapter 2.
3. Prasenjit K. Basu, *Asia Reborn: A Continent Rises from the Ravages of Colonialism and War to a New Dynamism.* New Delhi: Aleph Book Company, 2017. Chapter 1.
4. Jasanoff, *Edge of Empire.* p. 34.
5. Roger Jeffrey, *India in Edinburgh: 1750s to the Present.* New Delhi: Social Science Press, 2019. pp. 30–45.
6. Jasanoff, *Edge of Empire.* pp. 149–156.
7. Colleen Taylor Sen, *Feasts and Fasts: A History of Food in India.* New Delhi: Speaking Tiger, 2015. p. 220.
8. Jasanoff, *Edge of Empire.* p. 47.

9. Jyoti Mohan, *Claiming India: French Scholars and the Preoccupation with India in the Nineteenth Century*. New Delhi: Sage Publications, 2018. Chapter 3.
10. Robert Irwin, *For Lust of Knowing: The Orientalists and their Enemies*. London: Allen Lane, 2006. p. 122.
11. Jasanoff, *Edge of Empire*. p. 124.
12. Susan S. Bean, *Yankee India: American Commercial and Cultural Encounters with India in the Age of Sail 1784–1860*. Salem: Peabody Essex Museum, 2001. p. 17.
13. Bean, pp. 11–19.
14. Bean, p. 268.
15. Ben Macintyre, *Josiah the Great: The True Story of the Man who Would Be King*. London: Harper Press, 2004.
16. Sven Beckert, *Empire of Cotton: A Global History*. London: Allen Lane, 2014. p. 64.
17. Fernand Braudel, *A History of Civilizations*. London: Penguin Books, 1995. p. 382.
18. Robert V. Remini, *A Short History of the United States*. New York: HarperCollins, 2009. p. 76.
19. Beckert, *Empire of Cotton*. p. 45.

Chapter 4

1. John Keay, *The Honourable Company: A History of the English East India Company*. London: HarperCollins, 1991. p. 3.
2. Ian Mortimer, *The Time Traveller's Guide to Elizabethan England*. London: Vintage Books, 2013. Introduction.
3. Jerry Brotton, *The Sultan and the Queen: The Untold Story of Elizabeth and Islam*. New York: Viking, 2016. p. 42.
4. Brotton, *The Sultan and the Queen*. p. 50.
5. Jonathan Gill Harris, *The First Firangis*. New Delhi: Aleph Book Company, 2015. pp. 56–65.
6. William Foster, *Early Travels in India: 1583–1619*. London: Humphrey Milford, Oxford University Press, 1921. pp. 1–5.
7. Foster, *Early Travels in India*. p. 17.
8. Landes, *The Wealth and Poverty of Nations*. p. 140.
9. Michael Krondl, *The Taste of Conquest: The Rise and Fall of Three Great Cities of Spice*. New York: Ballantine Books, 2007. Part 3: Amsterdam.
10. John Steele Gordon, *An Empire of Wealth: The Epic History of American Economic Power*. New York: HarperCollins, 2004. pp. 11–15.
11. David S. Landes, *The Wealth and Poverty of Nations*. USA: W.W. Norton & Company, 1998. pp. 150–51.

12. Harris, *The First Firangis.* pp. 99–105.
13. Philip Mason, *The Men Who Ruled India.* New Delhi: Rupa Publications, 1985. p.8. First published by Jonathan Cape in two volumes as *The Founders* (1953) and *The Guardians* (1954).
14. S.A.A. Rizvi, *The Wonder that Was India Vol. II 1200–1700.* London: Sidgwick & Jackson, 1987. pp. 227–230.
15. John M. Hobson, *The Eastern Origins of Western Civilisation.* Cambridge: Cambridge University Press, 2004. Chapter 4.
16. M. Jacob Seth, *Armenians in India: From the Earliest Times to the Present Day.* Calcutta: Asian Educational Services, 1937. p. 242.
17. Pearson, *The Indian Ocean.* p. 165.
18. Maddison, *Contours of World Economy.* Chapter 2.
19. Toby E. Huff, *Intellectual Curiosity and the Scientific Revolution.* Cambridge: Cambridge University Press, 2011. pp. 115–125, 185–86.
20. Huff, *Intellectual Curiosity and the Scientific Revolution.* p. 155.

Chapter 5

1. Carter Vaughn Findley, *The Turks in World History.* Oxford: Oxford University Press, 2005. p. 14.
2. Krondl, *The Taste of Conquest.* 'First Taste: St Albans'.
3. Castlereagh, p. 23.
4. Castlereagh. p. 77.
5. Thomas Standage, *An Edible History of Humanity.* London: Atlantic Books, 2012. Chapter 6.
6. Jerry Brotton, *A History of the World in Twelve Maps.* Penguin Books. Kindle Edition. p. 189.
7. Standage, *An Edible History of Humanity.* Chapter 6.
8. Catherine B. Asher and Cynthia Talbot. *India before Europe.* Cambridge: Cambridge University Press, 2006. p. 57.
9. Wheeler M. Thackston, *The Baburnama: Memoirs of Babur, Prince and Emperor.* New York: Modern Library, 2002. pp. 352–53.
10. Asher and Talbot. *India before Europe.* pp. 158–60.
11. Subramanian, *Medieval Seafarers of India.* pp. 90–91.
12. Roy Moxhalm, *The Theft of India: The European Conquests of India, 1498–1765.* New Delhi: HarperCollins Publishers India, 2016. Chapter 6.
13. Pearson, *The Indian Ocean.* p. 166.

Chapter 6

1. Jack Weatherford, *Genghis Khan and the Making of the Modern World.* New York: Broadway Books, 2004. p. 14.

2. Weatherford, p. 165.
3. Findley, *The Turks in World History*. p. 82.
4. Barry Cunliffe, *By Steppe, Desert, and Ocean: The Birth of Eurasia*. Oxford: Oxford University Press, 2015. p. 451.
5. Charles Van Doren, *A History of Knowledge: Past, Present, Future*. New York: Ballantine Books, 1991. p. 152.
6. Harris, *The First Firangis*. p. 211.

Chapter 7

1. Robert G. Hoyland, *In God's Path: The Arab Conquests and the Creation of an Islamic Empire*. Oxford: Oxford University Press, 2015. Chapter 6.
2. Hoyland, Chapter 6.
3. Ligaya Mishan, 'A Bid to Maintain One of the World's Oldest Culinary Traditions', in *The New York Times*, 8 May 2019, https://www.nytimes.com/2019/05/08/t-magazine/parsi-food.html.
4. Hobson, *The Eastern Origins of Western Civilisation*. Chapter 5.
5. S. Frederick Starr, *Lost Enlightenment: Central Asia's Golden Age from the Arab Conquest to Tamerlane*. Princeton: Princeton University Press, 2013. Chapter 5.
6. Asher and Talbot, *India before Europe*. p. 19.
7. Edward Sachau, *Alberuni's India*. New Delhi: Indialog Publications, 2003. p. xxii.
8. Christopher Beckwith, *Empires of the Silk Road: A History of Central Eurasia from the Bronze Age to the Present*. Princeton: Princeton University Press, 2009. p. 153.
9. Sachau, p. 198.
10. Sen, *Feasts and Fasts*. pp. 134–36.
11. Beckwith, *Empires of the Silk Road*. p. 178.
12. Violet Moller, *The Map of Knowledge: How Classical Ideas were Lost and Found: A History in Seven Cities*. London: Picador, 2019. Chapter 5.
13. Moller, *The Map of Knowledge*. Chapter 5.
14. John Steele Gordon, *An Empire of Wealth: The Epic History of American Economic Power*. New York: HarperCollins, 2004. p. 8.
15. Diana Darke, *Stealing from the Saracens: How Islamic Architecture Shaped Europe*. London: Hurst, 2020.
16. 'Soltaniyeh', UNESCO. Accessed 13 April 2022. https://whc.unesco.org/en/list/1188/.
17. Beckwith, *Empires of the Silk Road*. p. 179.
18. Hermann Kulke, K. Kesavapany, and Vijay Sakhuja, *Nagapattinam to Suvarnadwipa: Reflections on the Chola Naval Expeditions to Southeast Asia*. Singapore: ISEAS Publishing, 2009. pp. 2–3.

19. Nile Green, *Sufism: A Global History.* West Sussex: Wiley-Blackwell, 2012. p. 99.
20. Thackston, *The Baburnama.* p. 327.
21. Asher and Talbot, *India before Europe.* pp. 85–87.
22. Green, *Sufism: A Global History.* p. 146, n. 67.

Chapter 8

1. Joseph Randolph Bowers, *Solitude Awakens: The Heart Forest Mountain Way.* Australia: Ability Therapy Specialists Pty Limited, 2019. p. 33.
2. Sheldon Pollock, *The Language of the Gods in the World of Men: Sanskrit, Culture, and Power in Premodern India.* California: University of California Press, 2009. Title of Part 1.
3. Philip A. Stadter, *Plutarch and his Roman Readers.* Oxford: Oxford University Press, 2014. p. 291.
4. Jeff Wallenfeldt, 'What Did Cleopatra Look Like?' Britannica. Accessed 13 April 2022. https://www.britannica.com/story/what-did-cleopatra-look-like.
5. Oxford Essential Quotations. Oxford Reference. Accessed 13 April 2022. https://www.oxfordreference.com/view/10.1093/acref/9780191826719.001.0001/q-oro-ed4-00006891.
6. 'Roman Britain'. BBC History. Accessed 13 April 2022 https://www.bbc.co.uk/history/british/timeline/romanbritain_timeline_noflash.shtml.
7. Raoul McLaughlin, *The Roman Empire and the Indian Ocean: The Ancient World Economy & the Kingdoms of Africa, Arabia & India.* South Yorkshire: Pen & Sword Books, 2014. Chapter 2.
8. Nicholas Ostler, *Empires of the Word: A Language History of the World.* London: HarperCollins, 2005. p. 192.
9. William Bernstein, *A Splendid Exchange: How Trade Shaped the World.* New York: Grove Press, 2008. p. 10.
10. McLaughlin, *The Roman Empire and the Indian Ocean.* Chapter 8.
11. McLaughlin. Chapter 7.
12. Romila Thapar, *The Penguin History of Early India: From the Origins to AD 1300.* New Delhi: Penguin Books India, 2003. p. 222.
13. Sen, *India, China, and the World.* p. 45.
14. K.A. Nilakanta Sastri, *A History of South India from Prehistoric Times to the Fall of Vijayanagar.* Chennai: Oxford University Press, 1976. p. 63.
15. McLaughlin, *The Roman Empire and the Indian Ocean.* Chapter 13.
16. A.L. Basham, *The Wonder that Was India.* London: Sidgwick & Jackson, 1954. p. 267.
17. B.R. Ambedkar, *Annihilation of Caste.* London: Verso, 2014. Originally self-published in 1936. Section 17.7.

18. Peter Frankopan, *The Silk Roads: A New History of the World.* London: Bloomsbury, 2015. p. 219

Chapter 9

1. Joshua J. Mark, 'Aristotle', World History Encyclopedia. Accessed 13 April 2022. https://www.worldhistory.org/aristotle/.
2. Michael Wood, *In the Footsteps of Alexander the Great.* London: BBC Books, 1997. p. 187.
3. Asko Parpola, *The Roots of Hinduism: The Early Aryans and the Indus Civilisation.* Oxford: Oxford University Press, 2015. p. 3.
4. A.K. Narain, *The Indo-Greeks.* New Delhi: B.R. Publishing, 1957. p. 249.
5. Wood, *In the Footsteps of Alexander the Great.* p. 109.
6. Narain, *The Indo-Greeks.* pp. 10–11.
7. Quintus Curtius Rufus, *The History of Alexander,* trans. John Yardley. London: Penguin Books, 1984. Book 3.
8. Keay, *India Discovered.* pp. 35–36.
9. Abraham Eraly, *Gem in the Lotus: The Seeding of Indian Civilisation.* New Delhi: Viking, 2000. p. 383.
10. Beckwith, *Empires of the Silk Road.* p. 154.
11. Axworthy, *Iran: Empire of the Mind.* Chapter 3.
12. Basham, *The Wonder that Was India.* p. 233.
13. Narain, *The Indo-Greeks.* pp. 265–70.
14. Sam Miller, *A Strange Kind of Paradise: India through Foreign Eyes.* New Delhi: Penguin Books India, 2014. pp. 26–27.
15. Eraly, *Gem in the Lotus.* p. 18.

Chapter 10

1. Eraly, *Gem in the Lotus.* p.18.
2. Michel Danino, *The Lost River: On the trail of the Sarasvati.* New Delhi: Penguin Books India, 2010. pp. 86–87.
3. Sudeshna Gupta, 'The Indus Civilization', *History Today.* Accessed 14 April 2022. https://www.historytoday.com/archive/indus-civilization.
4. Danino, *The Lost River,* p. 91.
5. Thomas McEvilley, *The Shape of Ancient Thought: Comparative Studies in Greek and Indian Philosophies.* New York: Allworth Press, 2001. p. xxii.
6. Irwin, *For Lust of Knowing.* p. 156.
7. David W. Anthony, *The Horse, the Wheel, and Language: How Bronze-Age Riders from the Eurasian Steppes Shaped the Modern World.* Princeton: Princeton University Press, 2007. Chapter 15.

8. R.S. Sharma, *India's Ancient Past.* New Delhi: Oxford University Press, 2005. Chapter 12.
9. Anthony, *The Horse, the Wheel, and Language.* Chapter 14.
10. Tony Joseph, *Early Indians: The Story of Our Ancestors and Where We Came From.* New Delhi: Juggernaut Books, 2018. Chapter 3.
11. Damodar Singhal, *India and World Civilisation Volumes 1 & 2.* Michigan: Michigan State University Press, 1969. Part 1 Chapter 1.
12. Basham, *The Wonder that Was India.* p. 29.
13. Anthony, *The Horse, the Wheel, and Language.* Chapter 2.
14. Singhal, *India and World Civilisation.* Part 1, Chapter 1.
15. Eraly, *Gem in the Lotus.* p. 212.
16. Irfan Habib and Vijay Kumar Thakur, *The Vedic Age.* New Delhi: Tulika Books, 2003. p. 21.

SELECT BIBLIOGRAPHY

Acemoglu, Daron and James A. Robinson. *Why Nations Fail: The Origins of Power, Prosperity and Poverty.* London: Profile Books, 2012.

Ahsan, Aitzaz. *The Indus Saga: From Pataliputra to Partition.* New Delhi: The Lotus Collection (Roli Books), 2005.

Albinia, Alice. *Empires of the Indus: The Story of a River.* London: John Murray, 2008.

Allen, Charles. *Plain Tales from the Raj: Images of British India in the Twentieth Century.* London: Abacus, 1975.

Charles, Allen. *Ashoka: The Search for India's Lost Emperor.* London: Little Brown Book Group, 2012.

Ambedkar, B.R. *Annihilation of Caste.* London: Verso, 2014. Originally self-published in 1936.

Ambedkar, B.R. *The Untouchables: Who were they and why they became Untouchables.* Originally published in 1946.

Ansary, Tamim. *Destiny Disrupted: A History of World through Islamic Eyes.* New York: Public Affairs, 2009.

Ansary, Tamim. *The Invention of Yesterday: A 50,000-Year History of Human Culture, Conflict, and Connection.* New York: PublicAffairs, 2019.

Anthony, David W. *The Horse, the Wheel, and Language: How Bronze-Age Riders from the Eurasian Steppes Shaped the Modern World.* Princeton: Princeton University Press, 2007.

Asher, Catherine B. and Cynthia Talbot. *India before Europe.* Cambridge: Cambridge University Press, 2006.

Auboyer, Jeanine. *Daily life in Ancient India: From Approximately 200 BC to AD 700.* London: Phoenix Press, 2002. First published in France in 1961.

Austin, Granville. *The Indian Constitution: Cornerstone of a Nation.* New Delhi: Oxford University Press, 1972.

Avari, Burjor. *India: The Ancient Past: A History of the Indian Subcontinent from 7000 BC to AD 1200.* London: Routledge, 2007.

Axworthy, Michael. *Iran: Empire of the Mind: A History from Zoroaster to the Present Day.* London: Penguin Books, 2008.

Bahn, Paul G. *The Atlas of World Archaeology.* Oxfordshire: Andromeda Oxford Limited, 2012.

Bandyopadhyay, Sekhar. *From Plassey to Partition and After: A History of Modern India.* Hyderabad: Orient Blackswan, 2004.

Barwise, J.M. and Nicholas White. *A Traveller's History of Southeast Asia.* Northampton, Massachusetts: Interlink Books, 2015.

Basham, A.L. *The Wonder that Was India.* London: Sidgwick & Jackson, 1954.

Bassett, Ross. *The Technological Indian.* Cambridge, Massachusetts: Harvard University Press, 2016.

Basu, Prasenjit K. *Asia Reborn: A Continent Rises from the Ravages of Colonialism and War to a New Dynamism.* New Delhi: Aleph Book Company, 2017.

Basu, Shrabani. *For King and Another Country: Indian Soldiers on the Western Front, 1914–18.* New Delhi: Bloomsbury Publishing, 2015.

Bauer, Susan Wise. *The History of the Medieval World.* New York: W.W. Norton & Co., 2010.

Bean, Susan S. *Yankee India: American Commercial and Cultural Encounters with India in the Age of Sail 1784–1860.* Salem: Peabody Essex Museum, 2001.

Beckert, Sven. *Empire of Cotton: A Global History.* London: Allen Lane, 2014.

Beckwith, Christopher. *Empires of the Silk Road: A History of Central Eurasia from the Bronze Age to the Present.* Princeton: Princeton University Press, 2009.

Bernstein, William. *A Splendid Exchange: How Trade Shaped the World.* New York: Grove Press, 2008.

Black, Jeremy. *World History Atlas.* London: Dorling Kindersley Limited, 1999.

Blainey, Geoffrey. *A Short History of the World.* Ringwood, Australia: Viking, 2000.

Boorstin, Daniel J. *The Discoverers: A History of Man's Search to Know His World and Himself.* New York: Vintage Books, 1985.

Braudel, Fernand. *A History of Civilizations.* London: Penguin Books, 1995.

Brook, Timothy. *Vermeer's Hat: Indra's Net and the Dawn of Globalisation.* London: Profile Books, 2008.

Brotton, Jerry. *The Sultan and the Queen: The Untold Story of Elizabeth and Islam.* New York: Viking, 2016.

Brotton, Jerry. *A History of the World in Twelve Maps.* London: Penguin Books, 2014.

Butman, John and Simon Targett. *New World, Inc.: The Story of the British Empire's Most Successful Start-up.* London: Atlantic Books, 2018.

Carr, Edward Hallet. *What Is History?* London: Vintage, 1967.

Castlereagh, Duncan. *The Great Age of Exploration.* London: Aldus Books, 1971.

Chakrabarty, Bidyut. *Communism in India: Events, Processes and Ideologies.* New York: Oxford University Press, 2014.

Chanda, Avik. *Dara Shukoh: The Man Who Would Be King.* New Delhi: HarperCollins, 2019.

Chandra, Bipan. *India Since Independence.* New Delhi: Penguin Books India, 2008.

Chaudhury, Nirad C. *Autobiography of an Unknown Indian.* Mumbai: Jaico Publishing House, 1964.

Crone, Patricia. *Pre-Industrial Societies: Anatomy of the Pre-Modern World.* London: Oneworld Publications, 2003.

Crowley, Roger. *City of Fortune: How Venice Won and Lost a Naval Empire.* London: Faber & Faber, 2011.

Cunliffe, Barry. *By Steppe, Desert, and Ocean: The Birth of Eurasia.* Oxford: Oxford University Press, 2015.

Dalrymple, William. *The Last Mughal: The Fall of a Dynasty, Delhi, 1857.* London: Bloomsbury, 2006.

Dalrymple, William. *The Anarchy: The Relentless Rise of the East India Company.* London: Bloomsbury Publishing, 2019.

Danino, Michel. *The Lost River: On the Trail of the Sarasvati.* New Delhi: Penguin Books India, 2010.

Das, Gurcharan. *India Unbound: From Independence to the Global Information Age.* New Delhi: Penguin Books, 2000.

Dasgupta, Subrata. *Awakening: The Story of the Bengal Renaissance.* New Delhi: Random House India, 2011.

Davids, Thomas William Rhys. *The Sacred Books of the East: The Questions of King Milinda.* Oxford: Clarendon Press, 1890.

Davies, Norman. *Europe: A History.* Oxford: Oxford University Press, 1994.

Davis, Richard H. *Global India Circa 100 CE: South Asia in Early World History.* Ann Arbor: Association for Asian Studies, 2009.

Diamond, Jared. *Guns, Germs, and Steel: A Short History of Everybody for the Last 13,000 Years.* London: Vintage, 1998.

Docherty, Paddy. *The Khyber Pass: A History of Empire and Invasion.* New York: Union Square Press, 2008.

Doniger, Wendy. *The Hindus: An Alternate History.* New York: The Penguin Press, 2009.

Dubois, Abbe J.A. *Hindu Manners, Customs and Ceremonies.* New Delhi: Rupa & Co., 1992.

Duncan, David Ewing. *The Calendar: Humanity's Epic Struggle to Determine a True and Accurate Year.* London: Fourth Estate, 1998.

Durant, Will. *The Case for India.* Originally published in 1930.

Durant, Will and Ariel Durant. *The Lessons of History.* New York: Simon & Schuster, 1968.

Eaton, Richard M. *India in the Persianate Age 1000–1765.* London: Allen Lane, 2019.

Eck, Diana L. *India: A Sacred Geography.* New York: Harmony, 2012.

Eck, Diana L. *Banaras: City of Light.* New York: Columbia University Press, 1998.

Edwardes, Michael. *Everyday Life in Early India.* Norwich: B.T. Batsford Ltd. And G.P. Putnam's Sons, 1969.

Eraly, Abraham. *The Age of Wrath: A History of the Delhi Sultanate.* New Delhi: Viking, 2014.

Eraly, Abraham. *The First Spring: Life in the Golden Age of India.* New Delhi: Viking, 2011.

Eraly, Abraham. *Gem in the Lotus: The Seeding of Indian Civilization.* New Delhi: Viking, 2000.

Ewans, Martin. *Afghanistan: A Short History of its People and Politics.* London: Curzon Press, 2001.

Ferguson, Niall. *Empire: The Rise and Demise of British World Order and the Lessons for Global Power.* New York: Basic Books, 2004.

Findley, Carter Vaughn. *The Turks in World History.* Oxford: Oxford University Press, 2005.

Foster, William. *Early Travels in India 1583–1619.* London: Humphrey Milford, Oxford University Press, 1921.

Frankopan, Peter. *The Silk Roads: A New History of the World.* London: Bloomsbury, 2015.

French, Patrick. *India: A Portrait.* New Delhi: Allen Lane, 2011.

Fukuzawa, Yukichi. *The Autobiography of Yukichi Fukuzawa.* New York: Columbia University Press, 1966. Originally published in Japanese in 1899.

Gandhi, Mohandas Karamchand. *The Story of My Experiments with Truth.* Ahmedabad: Navajivan Trust, 1927.

Gardner, Brian. *The East India Company.* New York: Barnes & Noble Books, 1971.

Gombrich, E.H. *A Little History of the World.* New Haven: Yale University Press, 2008. Originally published under the title *Weltgeschichte von der Urzeit bis zur Gegenwart* by Steyremuhl-Verlag, Vienna in 1936.

Gordon, John Steele. *An Empire of Wealth: The Epic History of American Economic Power.* New York: HarperCollins, 2004.

Gordon, Stewart. *When Asia Was the World.* Philadelphia: Da Capo Press, 2007.

Green, Peter. *A Concise History of Ancient Greece.* London: Thames and Hudson, 1973.

Green, Nile. *Sufism: A Global History.* West Sussex: Wiley-Blackwell, 2012.

Guha, Ramachandra. *India After Gandhi: The History of the World's Largest Democracy.* London: Picador, 2008.

Habib, Irfan, Iqbal Hussain, and Prabhat Patnaik. *Karl Marx on India.* New Delhi: Tulika Books, 2006.

Habib, Irfan and Vijay Kumar Thakur. *The Vedic Age.* New Delhi: Tulika Books, 2003.

Hajari, Nisid. *Midnight's Furies: The Deadly Legacy of India's Partition.* New Delhi: Viking, 2015.

Hansen, Valerie. *The Silk Road: A New History.* Oxford: Oxford University Press, 2015.

Harari, Yuval Noah. *Sapiens: A Brief History of Humankind.* London: Vintage, 2014.

Harris, Jonathan Gill. *The First Firangis.* New Delhi: Aleph Book Company, 2015.

Havell, E.B. *The Ancient and Medieval Architecture of India.* London: John Murray, 2015.

Hawes, James. *The Shortest History of Germany.* London: Old Street Publishing Ltd, 2017.

Hay, Stephen. *Sources of Indian Tradition, Vol 2.* New York: Columbia University Press, 1958.

Herman, Arthur. *How the Scots Invented the Modern World.* New York: Broadway Books, 2001.

Hibbert, Christopher. *London: The Biography of a City.* London: Allen Lane, 1977.

Hingley, Ronald. *A Concise History of Russia.* London: Thames and Hudson Ltd, 1972.

Hobsbawm, Eric. *The Age of Extremes: A History of the World, 1914–1991.* New York: Vintage, 1994.

Hobson, John M. *The Eastern Origins of Western Civilization.* Cambridge: Cambridge University Press, 2004.

Holdich, Thomas. *The Gates of India.* London: Macmillan and Co., 1910.

Hopkirk, Peter. *The Great Game: On Secret Service in High Asia.* London: John Murray, 1990.

Hosking, Geoffrey. *Russian History: A Very Short Introduction.* Oxford: Oxford University Press, 2012.

Hourani, Albert. *A History of the Arab Peoples.* London: Faber and Faber Ltd., 1991.

Hoyland, Robert G. *In God's Path: The Arab Conquests and the Creation of an Islamic Empire.* Oxford: Oxford University Press, 2015.

Huff, Toby E. *Intellectual Curiosity and the Scientific Revolution.* Cambridge: Cambridge University Press, 2011.

Huff, Toby E. *The Rise of Early Modern Science: Islam, China, and the West.* Cambridge: Cambridge University Press, 2017.

Irwin, Robert. *For Lust of Knowing: The Orientalists and Their Enemies.* London: Allen Lane, 2006.

I'tesamuddin, Mirza Sheikh. *The Wonders of Vilayet.* Leeds: Peepal Tree Press, 2001. Originally published in Persian in 1765.

James, Lawrence. *Raj: The Making and Unmaking of British India.* New York: St. Martin's Griffin, 2000.

James, Lawrence. *The Rise and Fall of the British Empire.* New York: St. Martin's Griffin, 1997.

Jasanoff, Maya. *Edge of Empire: Lives, Culture and Conquest in the East 1750–1850.* New York: Knopf, 2005.

Jeffrey, Roger. *India in Edinburgh: 1750s to the Present.* New Delhi: Social Science Press, 2019.

Jenkins, Simon. *A Short History of Europe: From Pericles to Putin.* London: Viking, 2018.

Jones, Dan and Marina Amaral. *The Colour of Time: A New History of the World 1850–1950.* London: Head of Zeus Ltd., 2019.

Jordanus, Friar. *Mirabilia Descripta: The Wonders of the East.* First published in 1863.

Joseph, Tony. *Early Indians: The Story of Our Ancestors and Where We Came From.* New Delhi: Juggernaut Books, 2018.

Kapoor, Pramod, J.P. Losty, et al. *Delhi: Red Fort to Raisina.* New Delhi: Roli Books, 2012.

Karashima, Noboru. *A Concise History of South India.* New Delhi: Oxford University Press, 2014.

Keay, John. *China: A History.* London: HarperPress, 2008.

Keay, John. *India: A History.* New York: Grove Press, 2000.

Keay, John. *India Discovered: The Recovery of a Lost Civilization.* London: HarperCollins, 2001.

Keay, John. *The Honourable Company: A History of the English East India Company.* London: HarperCollins, 1991.

Keegan, John. *The First World War.* London: Hutchinson, 1998.

Kershaw, Stephen. *Classical Civilization: From the Origins of Democracy to the Fall of the Roman Empire.* London: Robinson, 2010.

Khan, Yasmin. *The Great Partition: Making of India and Pakistan.* New Delhi: Viking, 2007.

Khan, Yasmin. *The Raj at War.* New Delhi: Penguin Books, 2015.

Khilnani, Sunil. *Incarnations: A History of India in Fifty Lives.* London: Penguin Random House, 2016.

Khilnani, Sunil. *The Idea of India.* New Delhi: Penguin Books, 1998.

Kosambi, Damodar Dharmanand. *An Introduction to the Study of Indian History.* New Delhi: Sage Publications, 2016. Originally published by Popular Prakashan in 1956.

Krondl, Michael. *The Taste of Conquest: The Rise and Fall of Three Great Cities of Spice.* New York: Ballantine Books, 2007.

Kulke, Hermann, K. Kesavapany, and Vijay Sakhuja. *Nagapattinam to Suvarnadwipa: Reflections on the Chola Naval Expeditions to Southeast Asia.* Singapore: Institute of Southeast Asian Studies (ISEAS) Publishing, 2009.

Kumar, Girja. *The Indus People: Saraiki Saga and Sufi-Sant Renaissance.* New Delhi: Vitasta Publishing, 2013.

Kumar, Anuradha. *Across the Seven Seas: Indian Travellers' Tales from the Past.* India: Hachette, 2015.

Kurlansky, Mark. *Salt: A World History.* London: Vintage, 2002.

Landes, David S. *The Wealth and Poverty of Nations.* USA: W.W. Norton & Company, 1998

Lang, John. *Wanderings in India and Other Sketches of Life in Hindostan.* New Delhi: Rupa Publications, 2015.

Lapierre, Dominique and Larry Collins. *Freedom at Midnight.* London: Simon & Schuster, 1975.

Lascelles, Christopher. *A Short History of the World.* UK: Crux Publishing, 2019.

Lau, Lisa and O. Trivedi. *Re-orientalism and Indian Writing in English.* London:

Palgrave Pivot, 2014.

Legge, James. *Record of Buddhistic Kingdoms: An Account by Fa-Hien.* New Delhi: Asian Educational Services, 1993. First published in Oxford in 1886.

Lieven, Anatol. *Pakistan: A Hard Country.* London: Penguin, 2011.

Lintner, Bertil. *China's India War: Collision Course on the Roof of the World.* Oxford: Oxford University Press, 2018.

Luce, Edward. *In Spite of the Gods: The Rise of Modern India.* New York: Anchor Books, 2008.

MacGregor, Neil. *A History of the World in 100 Objects.* London: Allen Lane, 2010.

Macintyre, Ben. *Josiah the Great: The True Story of the Man Who Would Be King.* London: Harper Press, 2004.

Macikintosh-Smith, Tim. *The Travels of Ibn Battutah.* London: Picador, 2002.

Maddison, Angus. *Contours of World Economy 1–2030 AD: Essays in Macro-Economic History.* Oxford: Oxford University Press, 2007.

Mahmood, Ali. *Muslims: The Real History.* New Delhi: Rupa Publications, 2018.

Major, R.H. *India in the Fifteenth Century.* Cambridge: Cambridge University Press, 2012. Originally published in 1857.

Mallory, J.P. *In Search of the Indo-Europeans: Language, Archaeology and Myth.* London: Thames and Hudson, 1989.

Man, John. *Attila the Hun: A Barbarian King and the Fall of Rome.* London: Bantam Press, 2005.

Marr, Andrew. *A History of the World.* London: Macmillan, 2012.

Marshall, Tim. *Prisoners of Geography: Ten Maps that Tell You Everything You Need to Know about Global Politics.* London: Elliott & Thompson, 2015.

Marshall, Bruce. *The Real World.* Boston: Houghton Mifflin Company, 1991.

Masani, Zareer. *Macaulay: Pioneer of India's Modernization.* New Delhi: Random House India, 2012.

Mason, Philip. *The Men Who Ruled India.* New Delhi: Rupa Publications, 1985. First published by Jonathan Cape in two volumes as *The Founders* (1953) and *The Guardians* (1954).

Mayo, Katherine. *Mother India.* Toronto: Aegitas, 2015. Originally published in 1927.

McCrindle, John W. *Ancient India as Described by Megasthenes and Arrian.* New Delhi: Munshiram Manoharlal Publishers, 2000. First published in 1877.

McCullough, David. *1776.* New York: Simon & Schuster, 2005.

McEvilley, Thomas. *The Shape of Ancient Thought: Comparative Studies in Greek and*

Indian Philosophies. New York: Allworth Press, 2001.

McLaughlin, Raoul. *The Roman Empire and the Indian Ocean. The Ancient World Economy & the Kingdoms of Africa, Arabia & India.* South Yorkshire: Pen & Sword Books, 2014.

Miller, Sam. *A Strange Kind of Paradise: India through Foreign Eyes.* New Delhi: Penguin Books, 2014.

Ministry of External Affairs, The Public Diplomacy Division. *Encyclopedia of India-China Cultural Contacts, Volumes 1 & 2.*

Mishra, Pankaj. *From the Ruins of Empire: The Revolt against the West and the Remaking of Asia.* London: Penguin Books, 2012.

Mohan, Jyoti. *Claiming India: French Scholars and the Preoccupation with India in the Nineteenth Century.* New Delhi: Sage Publications, 2018.

Moller, Violet. *The Map of Knowledge: How Classical Ideas Were Lost and Found: A History in Seven Cities.* London: Picador, 2019.

Morris, Ian. *Why the West Rules—For Now: The Patterns of History and What They Reveal about the Future.* London: Profile Books, 2011.

Mortimer, Ian. *The Time Traveller's Guide to Elizabethan England.* London: Vintage Books, 2013.

Moxhalm, Roy. *The Theft of India: The European Conquests of India 1498–1765.* New Delhi: HarperCollins Publishers India, 2016.

Mukerjee, Madhusree. *Churchill's Secret War: The British Empire and the Ravaging of India during World War II.* New Delhi: Penguin Random House India, 2010.

Mukhoty, Ira. *Akbar: The Great Mughal.* New Delhi: Aleph Book Company, 2020.

Müller, Max. *India: What Can It Teach Us?* Originally published in 1883.

Nanda, B.R. *Witness to Partition: A Memoir.* New Delhi: Rupa & Co., 2003.

Narain, A.K. *The Indo-Greeks.* New Delhi: B.R. Publishing, 1957.

Nehru, Jawahar Lal. *The Discovery of India.* Calcutta: The Signet Press, 1946.

Osterhammel, Jurgen and Sebastian Conrad. *An Emerging Modern World 1750–1870.* Cambridge, Massachusetts: The Belknap Press of the Harvard University Press, 2018.

Ostler, Nicholas. *Empires of the Word: A Language History of the World.* London: HarperCollins, 2005.

Overy, Richard. *Complete History of the World.* London: HarperCollins, 1978.

Parpola, Asko. *The Roots of Hinduism: The Early Aryans and the Indus Civilisation.* Oxford: Oxford University Press, 2015.

Parthasarthy, Prasannan. *Why Europe Grew Rich and Asia Did Not: Global Economic Divergence 1600–1850.* Cambridge: Cambridge University Press, 2011.

Paz, Octavio. *In Light of India.* London: The Harvill Press, 1997.

Pearson, Michael. *The Indian Ocean.* London: Routledge, 2003.

Peck, Lucy. *Lahore: The Architectural Heritage.* New Delhi: The Lotus Collection, Roli Books, 2017.

Pillai, Manu S. *The Ivory Throne: Chronicles of the House of Travancore.* New Delhi: HarperCollins Publishers India, 2015.

Plokhy, Serhii. *The Gates of Europe: A History of Ukraine.* London: Allen Lane, 2015.

Pollock, Sheldon and Benjamin Elman. *What China and India Once Were: The Pasts that May Shape the Global Future.* New York: Columbia University Press, 2018.

Polo, Marco. *The Travels of Marco Polo.* Edited by Morris Rossabi. New York: Fall River Press, 2012.

Puri, Samir. *The Great Imperial Hangover: How Empires Have Shaped the World.* London: Atlantic Books, 2020.

Raghavan, Srinath. *1971: A Global History of the Creation of Bangladesh.* Cambridge, Massachusetts: Harvard University Press, 2013.

Raghavan, Srinath. *India's War: The Making of Modern South Asia 1939–1945.* London: Penguin Random House, 2016.

Rai, Lala Lajpat. *The United States of America: A Hindu's Impression and a Study.* Calcutta: R. Chatterjee, 1916.

Remini, Robert V. *A Short History of the United States.* New York: HarperCollins, 2009.

Rizvi, S.A.A. *The Wonder that was India Vol. II 1200–1700.* London: Sidgwick & Jackson, 1987.

Robb, Graham. *The Discovery of France: A Historical Geography.* London: Picador Classic, 2007.

Ronald, Susan. *The Pirate Queen: Elizabeth I, Her Private Adventures and the Dawn of Empire.* Gloucestershire: Sutton Publishing, 2007.

Roy, Tirthankar. *India in the World Economy: From Antiquity to the Present.* Cambridge: Cambridge University Press, 2012.

Sachau, Edward. *Alberuni's India.* New Delhi: Indialog Publications, 2003.

Said, Edward. *Orientalism: Western Conceptions of the Orient.* London: Routledge & Kegan Paul, 1978.

Sanyal, Sanjeev. *Land of the Seven Rivers.* New Delhi: Viking, 2012.

Sanyal, Sanjeev. *Ocean of Churn: How the Indian Ocean Shaped Human History.* New

Delhi: Penguin Random House India, 2016.

Saran, Shyam. *How India Sees the World: Kautilya to the 21st Century.* New Delhi: Juggernaut Books, 2017.

Sastri, K.A. Nilakanta. *A History of South India from Prehistoric Times to the Fall of Vijayanagar.* Madras: Oxford University Press, 1976.

Schama, Simon. *A History of Britain: At the Edge of the World? 3000 BC–AD 1603.* London: BBC Worldwide Ltd, 2000.

Schuman, Michael. *The Miracle: The Epic Story of Asia's Quest for Wealth.* New York: HarperCollins, 2009.

Sen, Amartya. *The Argumentative Indian: Writings on Indian History, Culture and Identity.* London: Picador, 2006.

Sen, Colleen Taylor. *Feasts and Fasts: A History of Food in India.* New Delhi: Speaking Tiger, 2015.

Sen, Tansen. *India, China, and the World: A Connected History.* Maryland: Rowman & Littlefield, 2017.

Sengupta, Ranjana. *Delhi Metropolitan: The Making of an Unlikely City.* New Delhi: Penguin Books, 2008.

Service, Robert. *Comrades: Communism: A World History.* London: Macmillan, 2007.

Seth, M. Jacob. *Armenians in India: From the Earliest Times to the Present Day.* Calcutta: Asian Educational Services, 1937.

Sewell, Robert. *A Forgotten Empire: Vijayanagar.* New Delhi: Asian Educational Services, 1982.

Sharma, R.S. *India's Ancient Past.* New Delhi: Oxford University Press, 2005.

Shulman, David. *Tamil: A Biography.* Cambridge, Massachusetts: The Belknap Press of the Harvard University Press, 2016.

Silvestri, Michael. *Ireland and India: Nationalism, Empire and Memory.* New York: Palgrave Macmillan, 2009.

Singh, Upinder. *A History of Ancient and Early Medieval India: From the Stone Age to the 12th Century.* New Delhi: Dorling Kindersley, 2009.

Singh, Khushwant. *Train to Pakistan.* New Delhi: The Lotus Collection, Roli Books, 2006.

Singhal, Damodar. *India and World Civilization, Volumes 1 & 2.* Michigan: Michigan State University Press, 1969.

Sircar, D.C. *Studies in the Geography of Ancient and Medieval India.* Delhi: Motilal Banarsidass, 1971.

Sowell, Thomas. *Migrations and Cultures: A World View.* New York: Basic Books, 1996.

Standage, Thomas. *An Edible History of Humanity.* London: Atlantic Books, 2012.

Starr, S. Frederick. *Lost Enlightenment: Central Asia's Golden Age from the Arab Conquest to Tamerlane.* Princeton: Princeton University Press, 2013.

Subrahmanyam, Sanjay. *From Tagus to the Ganges: Explorations in Connected History.* New Delhi: Oxford University Press, 2005.

Subramanian, Lakshmi. *Medieval Seafarers of India.* New Delhi: The Lotus Collection, Roli Books, 1999.

Tadgell, Christopher. *The History of Architecture in India.* London: Architecture Design and Technology Press, 1990.

Thackston, Wheeler M. *The Baburnama: Memoirs of Babur, Prince and Emperor.* New York: Modern Library, 2002.

Thapar, Romila. *The Penguin History of Early India: From the Origins to AD 1300.* New Delhi: Penguin Books India, 2003.

Tharoor, Shashi. *An Era of Darkness: The British Empire in India.* New Delhi: Aleph Book Company, 2016.

Tuchman, Barbara. *The Guns of August.* London: Penguin Books, 2014.

Tunzleman, Alex von. *Indian Summer: The Secret History of the End of an Empire.* London: Simon & Schuster, 2012.

Twain, Mark. *Following the Equator.* Originally published in 1897.

Van Doren, Charles. *A History of Knowledge: Past, Present, Future.* New York: Ballantine Books, 1991.

Watson, Peter. *The German Genius: Europe's Third Renaissance, the Second Scientific Revolution and the Twentieth Century.* London: Simon & Schuster, 2010.

Weatherford, Jack. *Genghis Khan and the Making of the Modern World.* New York: Broadway Books, 2004.

Weinberg, Gerhard. *A World at Arms: A Global History of World War II.* Cambridge: Cambridge University Press, 1994, 2005.

Wells, H.G. *A Short History of the World.* London: Cassell & Co., 1922.

Wilson, Jon. *India Conquered: Britain's Raj and the Chaos of Empire.* London: Simon & Schuster, 2016.

Wolpert, Stanley. *Shameful Flight: The Last Years of the British Empire in India.* New York: Oxford University Press, 2006.

Wood, Michael. *The Story of India.* London: BBC Digital, 2015.

Wood, Michael *In the Footsteps of Alexander the Great.* London: BBC Books, 1997.

Wriggins, Salley Hovey. *The Silk Road Journey with Xuanzang.* Boulder: Westview Press, 2004.

Yule, Henry and A.C. Burnell. *Hobson Jobson: The Definitive Glossary of British India.* Oxford: Oxford University Press, 2013.

Zinn, Howard. *A People's History of the United States.* London: Bello, 2014.

INDEX